HOT ROD
&
CUSTOM
CHRONICLE

THOM TAYLOR
AND THE AUTO EDITORS OF CONSUMER GUIDE®

Publications International, Ltd.

Louis Weber, CEO
Publications International, Ltd.
7373 North Cicero Avenue
Lincolnwood, Illinois 60712

Permission is never granted for commercial purposes.

ISBN-13: 978-1-4127-1226-2
ISBN-10: 1-4127-1226-2

Manufactured in China.

8 7 6 5 4 3 2 1

CREDITS

Photography:
The editors would like to thank the following people and organizations for supplying the photography that made this book possible. They are listed below, along with the page number(s) of their photos:

Darrel Arment: 16, 17, 58, 59, 70, 71, 72, 73, 76, 77, 78, 79, 82, 83, 86, 87, 112, 113, 130, 131, 198, 199; Kirk Bell: 135, 261, 278, 279, 281; Bo Bertilsson: 1, 4, 5, 215, 231, 232, 233, 251, 252, 254, 255, 256, 257, 266, 267; Pete Borriello: 118, 119; Chan Bush: 125; Jack Calori: 15, 31; Curt Catallo: 122, 123; Mike Chase: 176, 177; Coachcraft Archives: 28; Herschel "Junior" Conway: 85; Steve Coonan: 110, 111, 202, 203, 230, 231; John D'Agostino: 180, 250; Ford Photographic: 54, 133; Pat Ganahl Collection: 12, 13, 15, 18, 19, 25, 27, 28, 29, 35, 41, 43, 50, 51, 55, 56, 57, 60, 61, 62, 63, 65, 80, 81, 89, 90, 91, 93, 108, 122, 125, 132, 133, 134, 135, 138, 139, 142, 146, 147, 156, 161, 163, 170, 171, 172, 173, 180, 181, 186, 187, 190, 191, 192, 204, 205, 211, 231, 260, 270, 271, 275, 282, 283; Robert Genat, Zone Five Photo: 14, 92, 168, 169, 246, 247, 248, 249; Thomas Glatch: 272, 273; Ray Goulart: 109, 131; JR Goodman, copyright Katoman.com 2005: 149; Gary Greene: 74, 75, 120, 121, 178, 179; Sam Griffith: 225; Mark S. Gustavson Collection: 87, 114, 115, 133; Don Heiny: 66, 67, 104, 105; Harry Kapsalis: 124, 226, 227; Don Keefe: 149; Scott Killeen (courtesy of Posies Rods and Customs): 6, 7, 258, 259, 276, 277; Ron Kimball Photography: 252, 253, 256; Nick Komic: 58, 59, 116, 117, 150, 151, 222, 223; Jerry Kugel: 265; Vince Manocchi: 20, 21, 22, 23, 34, 35, 64, 65, 92, 93, 144, 145, 148, 158, 159, 182, 183, 194, 195, 196, 197, 214, 216, 217, 224, 225, 240, 241, 262, 263, 264, 265, 280, 281; Bruce Meyer: 209; Doug Mitchel: 130, 131, 166, 167, 212, 213, 228, 229, 274, 275; David Newhardt: 140, 141; Neil Nissing: 8, 9, 24, 25, 26, 27, 42, 43, 48, 49, 106, 107, 136, 137, 234, 235, 236, 237, 238, 239, 242, 243, 244, 245; Laura Pfau: 46, 47, 152, 153, 162, 163, 164, 165; Pontiac Motor Division: 149; Posies Rods and Customs: 191; Jim Potter Collection: 102, 103; Rasputin Studios: 279; Jeff Rose: 36, 37, 68, 69; Greg Sharp, NHRA Motorsports Museum Collection: 10, 12, 13, 19, 23, 38, 39, 40, 43, 44, 45, 50, 51, 53, 57, 59, 60, 61, 62, 73, 79, 81, 83, 84, 85, 88, 89, 91, 94, 95, 96, 97, 100, 101, 102, 103, 109, 111, 129, 135, 139, 143, 155, 157, 174, 175; Thom Taylor: 221, 229; Tony Thacker: 185, 193, 202, 203; Phil Toy: 30, 31, 32, 33, 52, 53, 126, 127, 128, 129, 188, 189, 218, 219; W.C. Waymack: 46, 47, 152, 153, 162, 163, 164, 165; Scott Williamson/Photodesign Studios: 124, 160, 161, 200, 201, 206, 207, 208, 209, 210, 211, 220, 221, 268, 269; Paul Zazarine: 98, 99.

Front Cover: Ron Kimball Photography
Back Cover: Pat Ganahl Collection

Owners:
Special thanks to the owners of the cars featured in this book for their cooperation:

Mike Alexander; David Allen; Julian Alvarez; Gordon Apker; John Athan; John Babcock; Skip Barber; Nick Barron; Steve and Mary Barton; Gene Blackford; Bill and Elaine Booth; Dave Burk; Lou Calasibetta; Curt Catallo; Steve, Lana, and Dee Chrisman; John D'Agostino; Jimmy Falschlehner; Ken "Posies" Fenical; Jon Fisher; Rob Fortier; Cole Foster; Mike and Lin Geary; Billy F. Gibbons; Ted Gildred; Ken Gross; Verne Hammond; Ed Hegarty; Pat Hurley; Ed Iskenderian; Aaron Kahan; Bob and Sharon Kolmos; Joe MacPherson; Ralph Marano; Barry Mazza; Ken McBride; Kurt and Amy McCormick; Steve and Beverly McMullen; Bruce Meyer; Bud Millard; Darrell Miller; Justin Mozart; Donald B. Orosco; Petersen Automotive Museum; Lee Pratt; Roger Ritzow; Jack Rosen; Greg Sharp; Junichi Shimodaira; Jerry Slover, Pete and Jake's Hot Rod Parts; So-Cal Speed Shop; David Sydorick; Bob Tinsley; Sandy Wachs; Jack Walker; Keith Weesner; Deron Wright; Jorge Zaragoza; Richard Zocchi.

The editors would also like to extend special thanks to the following people for their contributions to this book:

Tom Appel; Jim Aust; Bo Bertilsson; Gene Blackford; Roy Brizio; Ron Brooks; Jack Calori; Curt Catallo; Steve Coonan; John D'Agostino; Dave Darby; Larry Erickson; Ken Fenical; Bill Ganahl; Pat Ganahl; Teresa Garay, Petersen Automotive Museum; Robert Genat; Ken Gross; Mark S. Gustavson; Roger Harney; David J. Hogan; Rik Hoving; Jerry Kugel; Frank Livingston; Barry Mazza; Kurt McCormick; Bruce Meyer; Geoff Miles; Don Montgomery; Yoshi Morishima; Rich and Penny Pichette; Don Prieto; Jeff Rose; Greg Sharp; Don Sikora II; Tony Thacker; Elden Titus; Jerry Titus; Jack Walker; Scott Williamson; Ken Yanez; Richard Zocchi.

CONTENTS

FOREWORD

Hot rodding and customizing is an American phenomenon that should never have survived its 1930s roots, or at least its demise and virtual extinction in the mid '60s. But Yankee ingenuity and the persistence of the youth generation that made it flourish just after World War II kept the hobby alive and sustained its march toward immortality.

Speed equipment, dragstrips, enthusiast magazines, car shows, and even certain language and clothing are among the tangible contributions of the hot rod and custom to American culture. It's amazing that hot rodding lasted past those days in the 1930s when only a few chose to trudge out to the dry lakes for a bit of fun. By the same token, customizing started as an expensive and rare pursuit, but in the late '40s a few dedicated shops made it affordable to more than just the elite. They had the expertise and interest in performing arcane custom modifications, and they were content to do it for an honest hourly wage.

Though the hot rod and custom aftermarket has grown to a two-billion-dollar-a-year industry, I doubt that Vic Edelbrock, Sr., Kong Jackson, or any of the other speed pioneers ever thought manufacturing speed parts would amount to more than a way to have fun while staying involved in their avocation.

As a basis of comparison, consider racing pioneer and mechanical genius Harry Miller. Miller lacked a formal engineering background, as did many of the hot rod pioneers. His cars and engines virtually dominated Indy car racing throughout the 1920s and '30s, yet he died penniless and in obscurity in 1943. Based on that example, what could come from Stu Hilborn playing around with fuel injection, or Clay Smith hand-grinding cams in his garage? As we know, these men and many more helped establish hot rodding, as well as lakes and drag racing.

The same can be said for custom car pioneers Gil and Al Ayala, George and Sam Barris, Jimmy Summers, and many others. Some were proprietors of nothing more than "bump and dent" shops, but they in fact paved the way for the proliferation of customizing cars—and their efforts are still being copied and revered today. Modern offshoots of customizing include the aero-effects body kits, spoilers, and wings seen on everything from Honda Civics to SUVs.

The 1950s were the heyday for hot rods and customs, but by the 1960s, hot rods were slowly being succeeded by factory muscle cars. Similarly, custom cars were being upstaged by the likes of Buick Rivieras, Dodge Chargers, Ford Mustangs, and other sporty and personal luxury cars that exhibited more custom touches than could ever be welded, cut, bent, or otherwise fabricated into a '50 Merc. It was the march of progress and the natural evolution of speed and style. Faster and slicker and don't look back.

By the 1970s, that original generation of hot rodders and custom car owners had begun sending their kids off to college and finding themselves with more time and money. They soon became inspired by a wave of nostalgia and started looking for those special high school dream cars that they never could have afforded or built back in 1955. So began the second coming of hot rods and customs. It started in the early '70s for hot rodders, but didn't catch on with custom car fans until the early '80s. Same dudes, different decade.

With the maturity of the owners and builders came more respect and acceptance. And with that came still more hot rodders and custom fans. Soon there were more shows, rod runs, and other activities. Rods and customs were even discovered by Detroit and television.

Though muscle car collecting has really come into its own in the last decade or so, the custom car and hot rod phenomenon has not abated. And why should it? Rods and customs are unique, fun, exciting, cool, and strictly American—the perfect combination for immortality. Long may they live!

Let freedom ring, and pass me the ½-inch wrench.

CHAPTER 1: THE 1940s
Hot Rod and Custom Roots

The timeline for hot rods and customs starts before World War II. Teens itching to tinker with cars and go fast were racing cheap Ford Model Ts on Southern California's dry lakes and street racing in Los Angeles even in the 1920s. The Harper, Muroc, and El Mirage dry lakes—all 50 or so miles north of Los Angeles—saw racing activity from the '20s up to World War II. Racing at El Mirage continues today.

Speed junkies could jump in their hopped-up, chopped-down Model Ts and be at one of the dry lakes in less than three hours. Or, if the need was urgent, they could find a deserted back road or open field. At the lakes, the cars were timed with handheld stopwatches and placed in a class determined by the resultant time.

The vast majority of the cars being run were four-cylinder Ford Model Ts or their successor, the four-cylinder Model A. The cars were cheap, plentiful, lightweight, and easy to work on. They responded to simple "hop ups" like higher compression, ignition and timing adjustments, additional carburetors, and more radical cam grinds.

The drill was fairly simple: Buy the nicest roadster you could find (because roadsters were the lightest); strip off everything not needed to go fast, like the fenders, headlights, hood, and top; find some cheap used tires to replace your bald ones or to mount over your existing tires for a little extra tread; and go racing.

Paul Chappel's Speed Shop on San Fernando Road in Los Angeles and Bell Auto Supply in neighboring Bell were the first stores in the country devoted exclusively to supplying speed parts for those who wanted to run with the fast pack. Performance parts included high-compression heads, exotic overhead-cam conversions, and radical cams (also called "sticks").

The Ford flathead V-8 was born in 1932 and with it a new opportunity to go fast. Though slow to be accepted by hot rodders, more 65- and 85-horsepower flathead V-8s found their way into junkyards as the '30s progressed and thus began the transformation from four-bangers to flatheads. Also released in 1932 were the lightweight

'32 Ford or "Deuce" frame and roadster body. The combination was unbeatable in terms of performance potential and looks. To this day, a flathead-powered Deuce roadster is the quintessential hot rod. That engine and frame combination would also provide an excellent foundation for many types of bodies, or sometimes hardly any body at all.

As interest in racing grew, kids began to try out their "gow jobs" more often on public streets. What was mostly good, clean fun could get ugly—and it often did. "Speed contests," as the police called them, were occurring with greater frequency and more-dire consequences. Casualties were described in detail in local newspapers, branding the hot rodder as a social menace requiring increasing control or, better yet, elimination.

More hot rodders were finding the dry lakes a safer, less public alternative to racing on the streets. But this "detour" was having its own problems. Multiple casualties were reportedly occurring during the middle of the night on the dark racing courses of the dry lakes. Hot rodders ran unmonitored, without thinking that a like-minded racer could be coming from the other direction. The result was sometimes catastrophic.

Help was on the way, though. In 1937, the Southern California Timing Association was formed. The SCTA formalized classes, developed more sophisticated timing systems, and made racing safer and more organized. Then, in 1941, a monthly publication called *Throttle Magazine* was created to track racing results, feature some of the better cars, and report on new safety and

speed issues. The scene was starting to gel, but after Pearl Harbor was bombed on December 7, 1941, and the U.S. became involved World War II, hot rodding would have to wait.

The custom car craze also began before WWII. In fact, its roots go back even further—to before World War I. Individualizing or "customizing" cars was popular with the well-heeled in the U.S. and Europe as far back as the development of the automobile. The most expensive cars of the 1920s, like Duesenbergs and Rolls-Royces, could be purchased as chassis only, to be custom-bodied by the shop or "coachbuilder" of the owner's choice. Coachbuilders had actually been established in the late 1800s to build custom bodies for horse-drawn carriages. With the development of the automobile, shops such as Brewster, Hibbard and Darrin, and LeBaron (Dietrich) in New York; and Bohman & Schwartz, Coachcraft, Earl Automobile Works, and Don Lee Cadillac in Southern California, were building bodies for high-end cars.

Some rather flamboyant automobiles were created from those stock Duesenbergs, Hispano-Suizas, Packards, and Pierce-Arrows for Hollywood actors such as Fatty Arbuckle, Charlie Chaplin, and Clark Gable. With their long, low proportions and ostentatious styling, these customs went beyond the coachbuilders' typical stately and elegant offerings. They demanded attention wherever they rolled.

The desire to have a standout automobile among the moneyed Hollywood elite filtered down to lesser actors and others who were not as wealthy but had just as much desire to drive unique cars. As dictated by income, their customs of choice tended to be less-expensive production cars like Fords, Mercurys, DeSotos, and Studebakers. With chrome emblems removed, fake pipes leading from the hood sides to the fenders, padded convertible tops, and "flipper" hubcaps, these relatively common cars took on a unique, expensive, custom look.

As the 1940s began, the fad continued to trickle down to car enthusiasts throughout the Los Angeles area. Now it involved older used cars that were transformed into "mystery cars" through sometimes minor, sometimes major body modifications. But it remained a relatively small and localized fad before many of the participants in this trend were called into service in WWII.

Southern California wasn't the only place you could get custom work done. As early as the late 1930s, Harry Westergard was customizing '36 Ford cabriolets and coupes out of his home garage in the Northern California city of Sacramento. Westergard chopped tops, incorporated grilles from more-expensive cars like Packards and LaSalles, formed custom hoods, and lowered suspensions. He also shaved door handles, then added Buick solenoids to open the doors.

Westergard would forever perpetuate the art of customizing through his influence on locals Dick Bertolucci and especially George and Sam Barris—all of whom started performing custom bodywork in the 1940s. George Barris worked for Westergard for a while, but then moved to SoCal and opened his own shop in '44. Sam Barris joined his brother in '46, and together they built what would become the most famous custom shop of all time. Meanwhile, Bertolucci started out of his father's garage in '48.

While the Barris brothers had both NorCal and SoCal ties, Los Angeles had other customizers of its own. Jimmy Summers had been doing pioneering custom work on more pedestrian production cars out of his Melrose Avenue shop since the 1930s, as had Roy Hagy from his Hagy's Streamline Shop on Vermont. Also on Vermont was none other than the Carson Top Shop, which

created the iconic padded Carson top in 1935. Link Paola was doing typical custom work just east of Los Angeles in the Montrose/Glendale area, as were the Bistagne Brothers.

By the end of the decade, Gil and Al Ayala were doing custom body work and paint from their East Los Angeles shop on Olympic Boulevard, and Bill Gaylord was customizing bodies and upholstery from his Lynwood shop. Even racing legend Frank Kurtis did custom work in L.A. between his racing activities.

Though any car was fodder for the customizer's torch, the popular choices were Fords and Mercurys from 1935 through the current models. Typical modifications involved trim removal; lowering the body by cutting or heating the springs; adding glass-pack mufflers to get that "burble" sound; frenching headlights; rounding the corners of the doors, hood, and trunk; chopping the top; and sectioning the body. Customs were usually finished with white tuck and roll interiors, deep dark lacquer paint jobs, and a choice of wheelcovers that included aftermarket "spinners" or production-car items like Cadillac "sombreros."

Customs from this era, ranging to about 1955, are considered to be the really classic examples of the genre. As customizing grew in popularity in the mid '50s, the cars started to receive baroque modifications with the introduction of dual and/or canted headlights, complicated trim, and scoops and vents anywhere from the quarter panels to the hood. Customizing of the late 1940s and early '50s was about integrating the separate fenders and tops into the body, eliminating the little trim pieces like badges and head- and taillight surrounds, and giving a car a simple, singular look as opposed to the stock appearance that could look like a bunch of different components bolted together.

Two things happened to spread the gospel of hot rods and customs during World War II. First, many servicemen were filtered through California on their journey to the Pacific. There, they witnessed firsthand America's car-culture capital, with its unique customs and

stripped down hot rods ripping through the streets. It must have left quite an impression on many.

Second, many GIs from Southern California spread information and pictures of hot cars to any soldier with time to spare. The racing and cruising activities must have seemed cool and exciting to any young soldier. Simple exposure must have been enough to spark the interest of young soldiers.

So once the seed was planted, it had to be nurtured, and for that we can thank Robert "Pete" Petersen and *Hot Rod* magazine, which came on to the scene in 1948.

After the war, the economy boomed. Young veterans had a bulletproof attitude after facing the horrors of combat, and they now found themselves with excesses of time and money, along with mechanical skills learned in the service. The postwar energy helped hot rodding and customizing grow more than it ever had in Southern California, and *Hot Rod* spread the word nationwide.

Hot Rod picked up where *Throttle* left off, the latter never returning after its one-year run in 1941. The fledgling magazine touched on all aspects of the car-enthusiast arena, covering hot rods, customs, drag racing, and even circle-track racing. *Hot Rod* also informed readers about the latest speed equipment, and taught them how to perform engine and body modifications. *Hot Rod* was in a good position to promote safety, and to help organize early drag racing and car shows, all of which helped promote and organize hot rodding itself. Speed-parts manufacturers and custom and performance shops had a place to advertise. It was a win-win situation for all involved.

As the end of the 1940s approached, hot rods and customs were poised to become not just a trend but a lifestyle. Postwar adolescents were discovering the freedom and social significance of driving a unique automobile on the streets of Downtown, USA. As we will see, many of the styles and innovations born in the '40s and refined in the '50s would forever change the way automotive enthusiasts spend their free time and present themselves to the outside world.

Early Hot Rods

In the 1920s, there were two common ways to make a car go faster—strip it of all nonessential components and hop up the four-cylinder engine with fancy parts like Cragar or Riley overhead-cam conversions or Winfield heads and carburetors. This was the era of the Great Depression, so most people had little discretionary income. Cars were still a luxury. Fast cars were an even greater luxury.

Kids fortunate enough to acquire a used Ford Model T or Model A usually started their pursuit of speed by removing the fenders and running boards. Flathead-equipped Model As and Ts became common a few years after the flathead was introduced in 1932, but four-cylinder cars remained competitive until the late '30s.

Aftermarket V-8 speed equipment came along in the mid 1930s. External parts were limited to homemade manifolds that held two or three carbs, milled heads, and custom-bent headers. Internal speed secrets were reground camshafts, rear-end gear changes, Auburn clutches, and hotter homemade ignitions. It was a simpler time when ingenuity properly applied brought the greatest results. Off-the-shelf horsepower was a long way off.

In addition to street use, some "hop ups" or "gow jobs" did double duty as circle-track and dry-lakes racers. Prior to the war, running 100 mph at the dry lakes was a big deal.

Hot rodding gradually gained in popularity throughout the 1930s, but by '42 the U.S. had entered World War II, so all leisure-time activities were put on hold. The seeds were planted, though, and rodding really took off when young men returned from the war with money, bravado, and technical skills.

Outlaw Image

Just after World War II, returning vets, having just risked their lives, sought excitement. Hot rods and motorcycles were the most readily available means to get their kicks.

To regular citizens, hot rodders were viewed as outlaws. Rodders lived up to that reputation by gathering at drive-ins and pairing off for impromptu drag races on the long, straight streets that crisscrossed the Los Angeles basin. Chapman Avenue, San Fernando Road, and Sepulveda Boulevard were among the favorite venues for kids to hold "speed contests," as the police called them.

The police often stopped hot rodders to cite them for violations and made big busts to shut down the racing. The arrests made headlines in the L.A. papers, furthering rodding's outlaw image.

The advent of *Hot Rod* magazine in 1948 marked the beginning of the turnaround. Efforts by conscientious hot rod car clubs with the help of the cooperative and insightful police chief Ralph Parker helped change the image of hot rodders over time.

The tide didn't turn overnight, and by 1950 the movie industry was making films that played on the nation's fears. "Exploitation" films with names like *Delinquent Daughters*, *Hot Rod Gang*, and *Dragstrip Riot* kept the outlaw image alive in the '50s.

Meanwhile, Wally Parks, as editor of *Hot Rod* and head of the NHRA, continued to improve hot rodding's reputation by working with the police and hot rod clubs.

Many of the clubs recognized the problem and encouraged their members to behave responsibly and assist fellow motorists. Gradually, the outlaw image began to fade.

Early Dry-Lakes Racing

Historians can't pinpoint who actually started dry-lakes racing. It just happened. During the late 1920s and early '30s, young men went to Southern California's vast isolated dry alkaline lake beds to experience the thrill of speed. There they could go as fast as they wished without worrying about the police or endangering anyone but themselves.

As this activity grew more popular, competition started between friends and rivals. Soon, so many cars were going in so many directions that it became very dangerous. The lakes were in serious need of organization. The formation of the Southern California Timing Association (SCTA) in 1937 brought sanity to an otherwise helter-skelter activity.

The largest of the Southern California dry lakes is Muroc, followed in size by El Mirage, Rosamond, and Harper. As part of the SCTA's effort to organize lakes racing, J. Otto Crocker set up the timing and scoring for the association. Now, drivers could get a record of their speed on something other than the speedometer. This gave the SCTA instant credibility. One problem did surface before long: The SCTA allowed only roadsters, bellytankers, and streamliners to run. Coupes and sedans were excluded.

Not to be left out, the coupe and sedan owners formed their own organization called the Russetta Timing Association, which even let roadsters run. While the two organizations brought rules, regulations, and classifications to the racing, there was still the prospect of crashes. Many times cars on solo runs would spin out and roll over at speeds in excess of

120 mph, usually with tragic results. Coupes, like the Pierson Brothers' chopped '34 (number 2D), were somewhat safer and often faster, even when racers swapped in the same Ford flathead V-8 engines.

Soon after the war, many racers became more serious about racing at the lakes. Cars modified with sleeker, lower bodies began to dominate, and soon street roadsters weren't competitive. Some racers even built "bellytankers" from P-38 aircraft fuel tanks.

By 1949, the SCTA had invited all types of cars to run. However, as drag racing and Bonneville took hold in the early '50s, only the hardcore still raced at the dry lakes and Russetta faded away. The SCTA survives to this day, and racers who don't mind the hot, dusty conditions still run a few meets at El Mirage.

Westergard Mercury

Although he is known as the grandfather of customizing, Harry Westergard's cars never received that much attention from the automotive media. The reason is simple. Westergard's career spanned from the late 1930s to the late '40s, and the hot rod and custom magazines like *Hot Rod*, *Motor Trend*, and *Hop Up* didn't exist until at least 1948.

One of Westergard's creations is the 1940 Mercury featured here. A man named Butler Rugard brought the car to Westergard's Sacramento shop shortly after he bought it new. There is no definitive documentation on the car, but it is believed that Butler initially just wanted a set of fadeaway fenders and that the customizing happened on and off over the next couple of years.

Fadeaway fenders were cutting edge for the day. The 1938 Buick Y Job show car predicted them with pontoon fenders that extended into the doors, but full fadeaways didn't make their debut until 1942 when they appeared on the Buick Super and Roadmaster models. So, for Butler Rugard to want them in 1940 and for Harry Westergard to create them from metal represents forward thinking.

By the time the car was done, it had much more than just fadeaways. Westergard was known for using Packard or LaSalle grilles, but in this instance, he installed a 1942 Buick grille flanked by Packard headlights. Using the Buick grille necessitated reworking the lower front portion of the hood to fit. It was the top of the hood, however, that received the most drastic changes. Westergard peaked the hood, and ran the upper beltline around the hood's perimeter. Along the way, he eliminated the flared humps of the Mercury hood, and gave the nose a stepped prowlike protrusion, much like a period "sharknose" Graham. Rippled '37 DeSoto bumpers were originally installed, but they were later replaced with '41 Packard units.

Other modifications were made as well. Westergard chopped the windshield about three inches and added a Carson-style top made from parts of the original convertible top. This also required cutting the side vent windows at the top and giving them new moldings. Teardrop fender skirts, a rolled and pleated interior, '41 Chevy taillights, Appleton spots, and stock wheels with Packard hubcaps completed Rugard's unique custom.

The car was shown at the first Autorama in Sacramento in 1950, and appeared in magazine coverage of the event. From there it faded into history until custom collector Jack Walker found the car in 2002 and teamed up with Ed Guffey to purchase it. The pair had the car restored to the way it appeared at the Autorama. Dave Dolman of Berdon, Nebraska, reworked the body; Bob Sipes of Pleasant Hill, Missouri, did the interior; Uncommon Engineering of Indianapolis built the Ford flathead V-8; and Sonny Rogers of Independence, Missouri, did all the mechanical work. The process took about a year and a half.

After its completion, the Westergard Merc was an honored participant at the first gathering of historic customs at the Pebble Beach Concours in 2005.

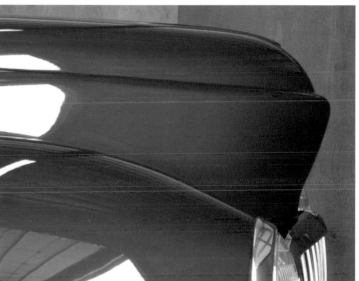

Circle-Track Roadsters

Circle-track historian Don Radbruch traces the roots of "roadster racing" to 1924 when three Model Ts lined up to have a go at each other on the one-mile dirt oval in Culver City, California. Before long, this form of competition spread nationwide. Radbruch reports that "… by 1938, more than 90 circle tracks were operating in the U.S."

After World War II, returning GIs picked up where they left off. Prewar four-cylinder, V-8, and Chevy-six-powered Model A and T roadsters were dusted off for action at local tracks. Winning drivers could expect a kiss from the trophy girl and, on a good night, as much as $65 in prize money.

On the track, street-driven roadsters faced everything from jalopies to purpose-built race cars that would become known as sprinters and midgets. The rules weren't set. The dirt and board tracks, mostly ovals, ranged in length from a quarter-mile to two miles. Up to 40 or 50 cars might run at a time in six-to-10-lap heats to qualify for 25-to-50-lap features.

The first use of the term "hot rod" isn't adequately documented, but it came into heavy use by the promoters of roadster racing. This is when street-driven roadster racers began applying the term to their cars. Local car clubs often frequented the tracks, too, either to compete with a club-built car, solicit new members, or merely to cheer on their favorite drivers.

After the races, many circle-track fans gathered at local drive-ins, and, inevitably, chose off for a bit of street racing.

The excitement of racing drew many new converts to the developing hot rod culture. Famous racers who got their start rodding include Manuel Ayulo, Jack McGrath, and Troy Ruttman.

Roadster racing reached its peak in the late 1940s and early '50s. By 1956, though, it had run its course, replaced by purpose-built midgets and sprinters. The term hot rod endured, however, now applied to the stripped-down street roadsters that were taking to the new drag strips. Like drag racing soon would, circle-track racing claimed many a hot rodder who became a serious racer.

The Elvis Car

Due to their frame design, Model A Fords don't look right as highboys. The time-honored solution to this problem is to mount a Model A body atop '32 Ford rails. One of the first cars to employ this trick was John Athan's '29 roadster.

As a teenager in 1937, John bought the body for $7 and the Deuce frame for $5.50. He began building the car, but didn't finish it until after he returned home from military duty during World War II.

While Deuce rails would come into common use, John's roadster featured numerous touches that made it one of a kind. The windshield glass is the rear window from a 1939 Chrysler, and the surround and posts were cast and machined by John in his machine shop. He also cast the carburetor stacks, as well as the triangular receivers that connect the wishbone ends to the frame on each side. "I sold a lot of those pieces to Ed Almquist back then," explained John, "He included them in his catalog. We made a few bucks."

Other unique items include the handmade engine-turned dash, the 1940 Mercury trunk-handle/license-plate light, and the custom-bent headers. Cutting and fitting the headers was tedious, but they gave the car a unique look that was far ahead of its time.

The roadster gained its greatest fame as Elvis Presley's ride in the 1957 film *Loving You*. After playing that role, it forever became known as "The Elvis Car," even though it found its way into other movies and television shows.

John lived the hot rod lifestyle in his car, cruising with friend Ed Iskenderian, flouting the law, and making speed runs at the dry lakes. He drove the car for 40 years until he put it into storage in 1978. Tom Leonardo, Jr., convinced John to let him restore it in '90. After the restoration, John had the car placed in the NHRA museum, where it served as a beautiful reminder of hot rodding's vibrant past.

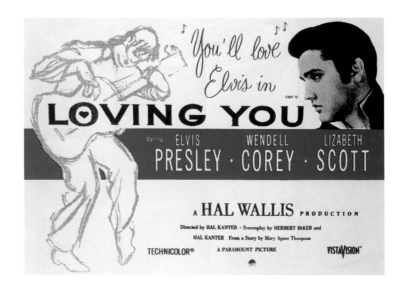

Isky T

One of the most famous speed-equipment manufacturers of all time is the legendary Ed "Isky" Iskenderian. But before he became a noted cam grinder, Ed was a teenager interested in fast cars. Ed built this 1924 Ford Model T roadster as a high school senior in 1940, and drove it to a speed of 120 mph at the El Mirage dry lake in '42.

Iskenderian's T is one of the oldest surviving unrestored hot rods known to exist and maybe the only untouched and original example of the prewar breed. Fortunately, Ed is pack rat—he has literally not thrown anything away since 1943, which is probably why this car remains a gem from hot rodding's roots.

Ed used a variety of engine configurations before settling on the setup shown. The car is powered by a venerable flathead Ford V-8 equipped with Maxi overhead-exhaust-valve cylinder heads and a Thickstun three-carb manifold. He made the valve covers and engraved his name into them.

The car's unusual stance can be attributed to the rear end, which is mounted behind the spring instead of directly below or in front of it. This adds six inches of wheelbase. The front axle is from a '32 Ford hung on a set of stock '37 Ford wishbones.

The unique grille shell is made from the tops of two 1933 Pontiac surrounds welded together with vertical bars added. Ed made the hood ornament in a high school shop class. The firewall has an engine-turned finish, a common touch on hot rods of this era. A pair of lakes pipes start at the exhaust ports and sweep gracefully past the driver's compartment.

Red Kelsey-Hayes wire wheels and matching naugahyde

upholstery were popular in prewar hot rods, as were Auburn dash panels. Ed mounted the tach on the steering-column support to provide a line of sight through the large "banjo" steering wheel.

The interior features a pair of dash plaques that are true gems from hot rodding's past. The one on the left is from the Western Timing Association (a short-lived rival to the SCTA) signifying that this car went 120 mph at El Mirage. Isky added the other tag later. It is an official Isky timing tag showing the lift and duration of the camshaft. Every cam Isky sells comes with one of these.

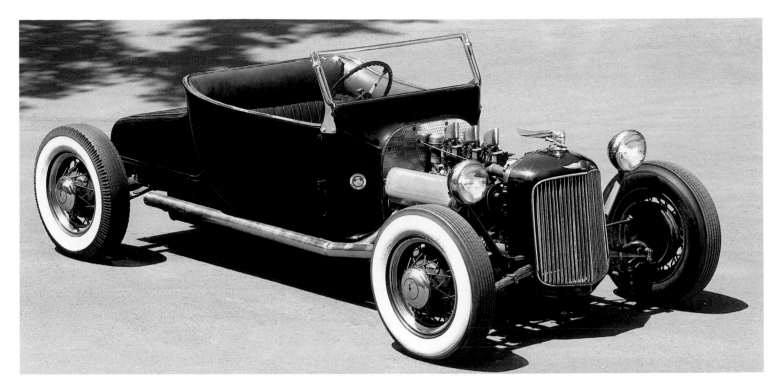

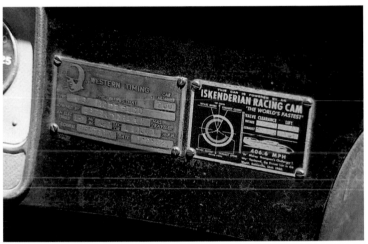

Doane Spencer Deuce

In the early 1940s, Doane Spencer and Jack Dorn were classmates at Hollywood High. In '41, Dorn bought a maroon '32 Ford roadster that he painted black and modified by filling the grille shell, installing a stock '37 Ford flathead V-8, and adding a DuVall windshield (compliments of Spencer). Spencer acquired the car in '44 for $500 and turned it into one of the most significant hot rods ever built.

A self-taught mechanical genius, Spencer lived on the edge of hot rod trends and technology. He removed the fenders and installed a 258-cid 1946 Mercury flathead V-8 with Ord heads and an Ord twin-carb log manifold. With details like the engine-turned dash, hand-rolled gas-tank cover, and fold-down armrest, the car won the Best Appearing Roadster award at the Pasadena Roadster Club's 1947 Reliability Run and was invited to be displayed at the first SCTA Hot Rod Show in '48.

Although beautiful, the Deuce was driven hard. Spencer raced his highboy at the El Mirage dry lake and drove it extensively, taking it through 42 states. At El Mirage, it ran 112.35 mph in 1947 with the 258-cid flathead. Spencer destroked the engine to 243 cubes in '49, and ran 126.76 mph—impressive for a street-driven roadster.

In the early 1950s, Spencer began to rebuild the roadster so he could run it in Mexico's *Carrera Panamericana*. He beefed up the suspension, ran the exhaust through the frame rails, and installed a Halibrand quick-change rear end, Halibrand magnesium wheels, and a new Lincoln overhead-valve V-8. Unfortunately, the Mexican road race was canceled before he could run it, so Spencer sold the car to *Rod & Custom* staffer Lynn Wineland.

Wineland modified the car further with a Ford Thunderbird V-8, a 1937 Ford tube axle, and rear radius rods. Spencer, in fact, performed some of the work. Wineland never completed the car, however, and sold it to fellow *R&C* staffer Neal East in 1968. East put the car back on the road with the flathead V-8 and a '48 Lincoln overdrive transmission.

East had the chassis and body freshened in 1985, and owned it until '95 when he sold it to collector Bruce Meyer, who had Pete Chapouris and his crew restore the car to show condition back to its most famous form.

In 1997, the legendary Doane Spencer Deuce was invited to appear in the first ever Hot Rod class at the Pebble Beach Concours d'Elegance. Like it had so many times before, it won first place.

Since then, Bruce has included the Deuce with a handful of other historic hot rods in the ongoing Bruce Meyer Hot Rod Gallery at the Petersen Automotive Museum in Los Angeles.

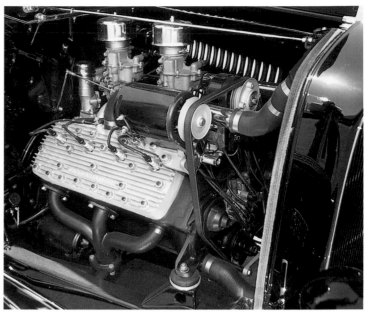

McGee/Scritchfield Deuce

Bob McGee returned home from the military in 1946 to discover that the hot rod he had left with his friend Bob Binyon for safe keeping had been totaled. Binyon fell asleep at the wheel and wrecked McGee's car in an orange grove, but endeavored to make it up to McGee by collecting the parts to create a replacement. McGee used those parts to create one of the most important cars in hot rod history.

Few hot rods have remained in the limelight as long as the McGee/Scritchfield roadster. While McGee was attending USC on a football scholarship, it became the first Deuce highboy to grace the cover of *Hot Rod* magazine, appearing on the October 1948 issue. On Sept. 19 of that year, it was the first hot rod to receive a "green cross for safety" window sticker when the SCTA was formally accepted into the National Safety Council.

McGee sold the Deuce in 1955 to Dick Hirschberg who installed a Corvette motor and painted it yellow. In '56, Hirschberg traded it straight up to Dick Scritchfield, a founding member of the L.A. Roadsters club and NHRA employee, for a 1948 Lincoln Continental.

In Scritchfield's hands, the car made many movie and television appearances, and inspired the L.A. Roadsters club logo. In the early '60s, Scritchfield had Bill Kaegle apply one of the first metalflake paint jobs for an article in *Hot Rod* magazine. In 1971, with a tunnel-ram-equipped 350-cid small-block Chevy and a T-10 four-speed transmission, the car ran 167.212 mph at Bonneville, setting a C/Roadster record that would stand until '79.

Scritchfield owned the car until 1989. The Deuce briefly passed through two more owners before collector Bruce Meyer acquired it and had the So-Cal Speed Shop restore it to the original Bob McGee configuration. This meant installing a flathead equipped with Federal-Mogul copper heads. The roadster's first public appearance after the restoration was at the 50th Grand National Roadster Show in 1999. It was also a prize winner at that year's Pebble Beach Concours d'Elegance, a testament to the quality of the So-Cal Speed Shop's work and McGee's cutting-edge look.

Though continually upgraded and modified over the years, the McGee/Scritchfield roadster has always been identifiable by its distinctive stance, extended decklid, hidden door hinges, and shortened front frame horns with molded and V'd spreader bar. McGee performed many of these modifications himself. They were unique for their day, and are often imitated by rodders more than 50 years later.

Circa 1958-59

Circa 1965-66

Pre-'49 Customs

Though the scene was still in its infancy, the custom car aesthetic had pretty much been established by 1940. Long and low was the way to go. Conventions such as shaved noses, decks, and door handles; chopped tops; and lowered stances were already well-established. Carson tops and DuVall windshields had been developed in the mid '30s. While 1936 Fords were early customizing favorites, '38-40 Fords and Mercs, and early '40s Chevys proved popular, too.

Coachbuilders such as Coachcraft, Bob Lee Cadillac, and Bohman & Schwarz were performing high-end work on expensive cars, but it was the smaller outfits run by the likes of Jimmy Summers and Roy Hagy in Los Angeles and Harry Westergard in Sacramento that performed the kind of work that the custom community would embrace. Early custom fans emerged from the rebellious young hot rod crowd. They didn't have the money to buy Buicks, Cadillacs, Lincolns, and Packards—or to pay expensive coachbuilders—but they wanted their cars to share the look of coachbuilt cars or high-dollar stock automobiles.

Westergard is widely recognized as the father of the early custom look, which usually involved a 1936 Ford coupe with a chopped top, upright LaSalle grille, solid hood sides, a recessed license plate, rear fender skirts, and Chevy headlights molded into the fenders. Westergard is also often credited with originating pushbutton doors that utilized solenoids to open electrically and allow for the removal of the door handles.

A car crazy kid in Sacramento named George Barris worked for Westergard in the late 1930s, then moved to Southern California in the early '40s and brought with him many of Westergard's tricks. Barris opened his own shop during the war, performing custom work. His brother Sam joined him after the war, and together the two took off, inventing new techniques, perfecting old ones, and giving each car its own character. Others were part of the wave, too, including Al and Gil Ayala, Neil Emory and Clayton Jensen of Valley Custom, and Joe Bailon.

Much of the long, low look customizers were trying to achieve during the 1940s was made easier with the release of full-envelope-bodied cars starting in '48 and culminating with the '49 Mercury. In fact, customizing '49 Mercs would make the custom scene more popular than ever—but that's a story for the next chapter.

1

2

3

4

5

6

7

8

9

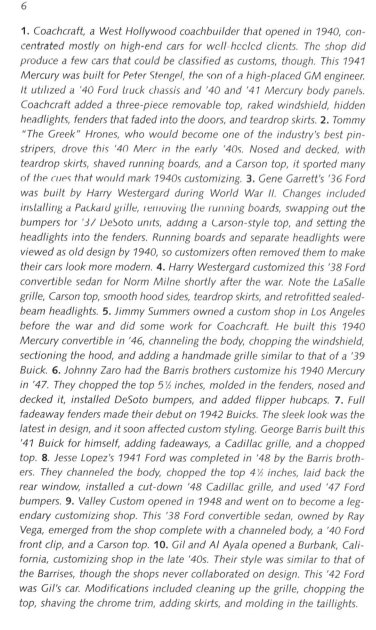
10

1. Coachcraft, a West Hollywood coachbuilder that opened in 1940, concentrated mostly on high-end cars for well-heeled clients. The shop did produce a few cars that could be classified as customs, though. This 1941 Mercury was built for Peter Stengel, the son of a high-placed GM engineer. It utilized a '40 Ford truck chassis and '40 and '41 Mercury body panels. Coachcraft added a three-piece removable top, raked windshield, hidden headlights, fenders that faded into the doors, and teardrop skirts. **2.** Tommy "The Greek" Hrones, who would become one of the industry's best pinstripers, drove this '40 Merc in the early '40s. Nosed and decked, with teardrop skirts, shaved running boards, and a Carson top, it sported many of the cues that would mark 1940s customizing. **3.** Gene Garrett's '36 Ford was built by Harry Westergard during World War II. Changes included installing a Packard grille, removing the running boards, swapping out the bumpers for '37 DeSoto units, adding a Carson-style top, and setting the headlights into the fenders. Running boards and separate headlights were viewed as old design by 1940, so customizers often removed them to make their cars look more modern. **4.** Harry Westergard customized this '38 Ford convertible sedan for Norm Milne shortly after the war. Note the LaSalle grille, Carson top, smooth hood sides, teardrop skirts, and retrofitted sealed-beam headlights. **5.** Jimmy Summers owned a custom shop in Los Angeles before the war and did some work for Coachcraft. He built this 1940 Mercury convertible in '46, channeling the body, chopping the windshield, sectioning the hood, and adding a handmade grille similar to that of a '39 Buick. **6.** Johnny Zaro had the Barris brothers customize his 1940 Mercury in '47. They chopped the top 5½ inches, molded in the fenders, nosed and decked it, installed DeSoto bumpers, and added flipper hubcaps. **7.** Full fadeaway fenders made their debut on 1942 Buicks. The sleek look was the latest in design, and it soon affected custom styling. George Barris built this '41 Buick for himself, adding fadeaways, a Cadillac grille, and a chopped top. **8.** Jesse Lopez's 1941 Ford was completed in '48 by the Barris brothers. They channeled the body, chopped the top 4½ inches, laid back the rear window, installed a cut-down '48 Cadillac grille, and used '47 Ford bumpers. **9.** Valley Custom opened in 1948 and went on to become a legendary customizing shop. This '38 Ford convertible sedan, owned by Ray Vega, emerged from the shop complete with a channeled body, a '40 Ford front clip, and a Carson top. **10.** Gil and Al Ayala opened a Burbank, California, customizing shop in the late '40s. Their style was similar to that of the Barrises, though the shops never collaborated on design. This '42 Ford was Gil's car. Modifications included cleaning up the grille, chopping the top, shaving the chrome trim, adding skirts, and molding in the taillights.

Calori Coupe

Jack Calori started out a hot rodder. He built and raced four 1932 Ford roadsters before acquiring a '29 Ford roadster that would become one of the most famous lakes racers of the day. Calori's cars could be distinguished from most hot rods of the time by their level of detail and finish. Each car was beautifully painted and upholstered, and the engines were polished and chromed. In addition, they were very competitive on the lakes, a fact to which his collection of timing tags can attest.

Jack bought a 1936 Ford coupe in 1947 from the original owner to replace the '29 roadster as a daily driver and, in fact, become the '29's tow car (see bottom left photo, opposite page). Jack's friend, body man Herb Reneau, who was responsible for the work on the '29, saw the car's potential. While stored in his garage, Herb cut off the top without warning. Fortunately, Jack succumbed to the "kustom" allure, and he and Herb went on to build one of history's most stunning '36 Ford customs.

Jack severely stepped the rear of the frame and installed a dropped axle at the front to achieve the right stance, while Herb chopped the top three inches, and added a 1939 LaSalle grille, a clamshell hood, skirts, and '40 Chevy headlights. The bumpers came from a '41 Ford, and the taillights originated on a '41 Hudson. The car is undeniably similar to the Westergard style, but Calori claims he had never heard of Harry Westergard when he and Herb built the car.

Jack didn't give up his hot rodding roots entirely. When he sold his '29, he kept the engine and installed it in the '36. The engine, a 59AB Mercury, was bored and stroked ⅛ inch

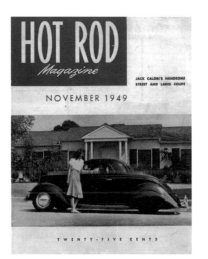

each way, then given a Clay Smith cam, a Lincoln distributor, Eddie Meyer heads, and a Weiand intake. The oil pan, dipstick tube, water pumps, generator case, and oil filler/breather were all chromed, and the heads and intake were polished.

When installed in the '29, the engine had earned Jack no less than a third-place finish at every lakes event in which he competed. Calori tested the engine in the coupe too, running 114.5 mph in a Russetta Timing Association run. The problem with putting the "hot" motor in his custom car, however, was cooling. There was no room for a fan, and the LaSalle grille didn't allow for much airflow. After adding a scoop under the front bumper, punching louvers in the hood, and adding water capacity to the radiator tank, the car still wouldn't cool properly.

Much of the car's fame is a result of its appearance on the cover of the November '49 issue of Hot Rod. Tom Medley spotted the car on the street and arranged an impromptu photo shoot. This exposure inspired many imitators, and earned the coupe a spot in custom history.

Jack traded the coupe in 1950 for a new Mercury. Roger Domini later found it in Washington and owned it for many years. In 2003, Jorge Zaragoza purchased the car and had Roy Brizio Street Rods restore it for the first-ever custom class at Pebble Beach in 2005. There, it won both best in class and the Dean Bachelor award. Soon thereafter, the car went on display at the Peterson Automotive Museum as a living piece of customizing's early days.

–Bill Ganahl

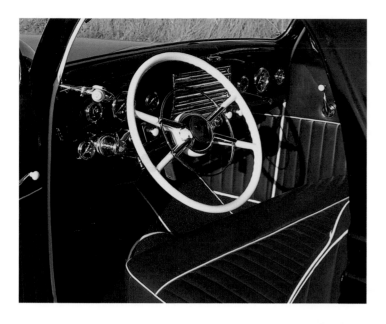

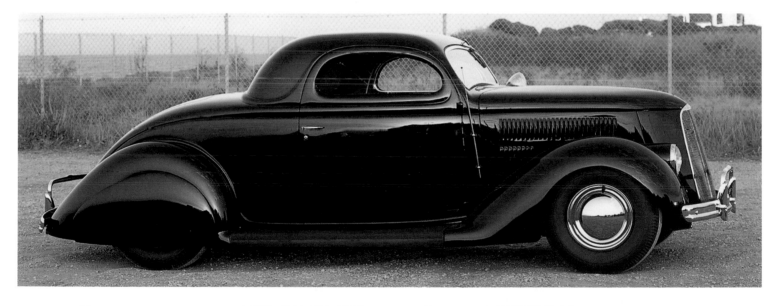

Ohanesian 1940 Mercury

Two key ingredients of a winning custom are a good design sense and quality craftsmanship. In the early days of customizing, many cars had one but not the other. Some cars looked great from a distance, but close examination revealed slipshod metal-work with an excess of lead filler. These cars prompted the then-derogatory term "leadsled." Other cars had quality bodywork, but ungainly proportions and bizarre styling details.

This breathtaking 1940 Mercury convertible sedan, originally built for Harold "Buddy" Ohanesian of Sacramento, gets it all right. The project was started in '43, and progressed gradually as Ohanesian drove the car in between customizing sessions. Harry Westergard performed some of the restyling, then Ohanesian's high school buddy Dick Bertolucci took over.

The hood and front fenders were reshaped to accept a 1946 Chevy grille. Initially, the stock Mercury headlight bezels were painted body color, but by the mid '50s the car sported frenched headlights with an attractive "cove" on their lower edges. The windshield was chopped four inches, with the vent windows and trim cut down to match. All of the stock chrome trim was removed, along with the door handles. The door latches were modified to operate by pushbutton electric solenoids mounted in the running boards. A '40 Packard provided the teardrop rear fender skirts. The rear fenders were molded to the body, along with the taillights and rear splash pan from a '42 Ford. Both bumpers were sourced from a '42 Chevy, and the rear one was modified with molded-in exhaust outlets. The rear license plate was frenched into the decklid and mounted behind a piece of glass—a modification that police occasionally frowned upon at the time.

All of the body modifications are impressive, but the high-light of the car is the beautifully contoured steel top. It was hand-formed by Bertolucci, who utilized the front half of a '46 Chrysler top, the back half of a '41 Buick roof, and his considerable hammer-welding and metal-fabrication skills. The top is removable, but the seams are so tight and the shapes so fluid that it appears to be a solid part of the car. The stock trunk opening was cut down and the rear of the body significantly revamped to accommodate the new top.

The car was severely lowered in back with a C'd frame and de-arched rear spring with reversed eyes and long shackles. A steel plate was mounted under the gas tank to protect it from highway bumps. A dropped axle and straight spring brought the front ride height down. Inside, a '47 Cadillac dashboard was installed, along with custom upholstery. Under the hood, a '46 Mercury flathead was installed to supply the power.

Buddy relied on the Merc as his daily driver for several years, even using it as a tow vehicle for his 1933 Ford coupe Bonneville racer. The car was then stored until the early '70s, when it was acquired and partially refurbished by Louie Martin and Dennis Nash of Sacramento.

Ed Hegarty bought the car in about 1975, and had a more thorough restoration performed in time for an exhibit of his-toric hot rods and customs at the Oakland Museum in '96. The Merc also appeared at the 50th Anniversary of the Sacramento Autorama in 2000, where Bertolucci was an honored builder, and at the first showing of customs at the Pebble Beach Concours in 2005.

Matranga Mercury

Nick Matranga's 1940 Mercury was one of Sam and George Barris's first masterpieces, an innovative and influential car that still inspires customizers today. Sadly, it only existed in its finished form for about a year.

The car was started at Barris's Compton Avenue shop in 1949, but was in the works for over a year, enduring a couple of shop relocations as Sam carefully planned the major modifications and worked on the details.

The standout feature of the Matranga Mercury is its beautiful top chop, measuring five inches in front and seven inches in back. Sam had previously chopped the tops of Johnny Zaro's and Al Andril's 1940 Mercurys, so he had the operation down to a science by the time he did Matranga's car. To avoid a "mail-slot" appearance at the front, the top of the windshield opening was extended into the cut-down roofline so it would match the height of the side windows.

At the time, hardtop rooflines were the latest styling innovation from Detroit. General Motors' Buick, Cadillac, and Oldsmobile divisions introduced pillarless hardtop body styles in 1949 that were well-received by the public. The Barrises and Matranga put their own spin on hardtop styling by cutting out the center door posts of the Mercury and replacing them with smoothly hand-curved ⅝-inch channel stock. The custom side-window trim complemented the graceful arc of the chopped top and completely changed the character of the car. This trick would be copied numerous times on other customs throughout the years.

At Matranga's insistence, the Mercury's handsome front end sheetmetal was left unmodified save for dechroming. Both the front and rear bumpers came from a 1946 Ford. The rear bumper guards were modified to house taillights formed from transparent red Lucite. All four fenders were molded to the body, as was a '46 Ford rear splash pan. Teardrop fender skirts from a 1941 Buick were modified to fit. A deep maroon lacquer paint job finished off the exterior.

The interior was every bit as dazzling. Glen Houser's Carson Top Shop did the upholstery in white and deep red naugahyde with black carpeting. The dashboard was fully chromed, and Nick and friend Jesse Lopez formed dash inserts from red plexiglass.The steering wheel came from a '50 Mercury.

The finished car racked up plenty of show trophies and served as rolling advertisement for Barris Kustom's abilities. Nick enjoyed cruising in his new custom and particularly appreciated its uncanny ability to attract girls, but soon military duty called and Nick shipped off to Korea. Unsure of his future, Matranga sent word back to the States for Barris to sell the car. The new owner was allegedly street racing it on a rainy night in early '52, lost control over some railroad tracks, and hit a telephone pole. The owner walked away, but the Matranga Merc was totaled.

Given its outstanding design and short lifespan, it stands to reason that the Matranga Mercury would be copied. Plenty of beautiful Matranga-inspired Mercurys have been built over the years, but most agree that the most accurate clone was created by the late Duncan Emmons. That car is shown here in front of the NHRA Motorsports Museum. Duncan had the expert help of Bill Hines, Joe Reath, Eddie Martinez, Red Twit, Richard Graves, and his son Duncan Jr., in making this excellent re-creation of custom history a reality.

It's a summertime Saturday night in the 1950s, and the Southern California suburbs are hopping. In the San Fernando Valley just north of L.A., ex-GIs are bent over their crude roadsters doing last-minute checks before heading out at midnight to one of the dry lake beds east of Los Angeles. Their goal is to be first in line for the heads-up racing that starts at dawn. Soon they'll aim their headlights for the excitement of speed and the camaraderie that goes with running the straight, dusty courses. But first, a few of them conduct impromptu light-to-light races down San Fernando Road to check out the clutch and size up the competition.

Over in the bedroom communities of Lakewood, Lynwood, and Compton a few miles west of L.A., cruisers in their late teens and early 20s are "drive-in hopping." It's a ritual that takes off from The Clock drive-in in Bellflower,

down Bellflower and Whittier boulevards slowing for girls, friends, and maybe even a short stoplight race. It's all in the name of blowing off steam.

The drive-ins play host to a traveling circus of "show boats" flaunting their polished custom cars. These hangouts are perfect for setting up some side-by-side racing along Sepulveda Boulevard or over by the oil derricks outside Whittier in Santa Fe Springs. Drive-ins all over Southern California are the social-activity "command centers" for the hot rod and custom car culture.

Occasionally, street racing accidents end up on the front page of the *Orange County Register* in grisly detail. There is safer, organized racing in Orange County, too. It's the abandoned airstrip, which is considered the first organized drag racing venue in the country—Santa Ana Dragstrip.

It's the golden age of the hot rod and custom car, and Southern California is

but also a lot to do with what lay beyond them. World War II changed the world and laid the foundation for the American car-crazy phenomenon that exploded in the 1950s.

Once the hostilities in Europe and Asia had ceased, those lucky enough to make it back wanted to enjoy living the way they couldn't while serving Uncle Sam. Finally home, ex-GIs couldn't get enough of cool cars, all-American burgers and fries, and the girl next door who had grown up since they left. Building a hot rod or custom was a method of self-expression, and for many, the cars provided the means for the social life they desired.

Many GIs also found it hard to let go of the adrenaline rush of enemy action. Something inside them yearned for a little bit of that thrill, but without the potential wartime consequences. Getting behind the wheel of a cool hot rod or custom fulfilled those conscious and

then heads down Pacific Coast Highway to The Clock on Sepulveda in Culver City, over to Tiny Naylor's in Hollywood, onto the freeway to Toluca Lake and Bob's Big Boy, over to Bob's in Pasadena, a straight shot west to Nixon's on Whittier Boulevard, and finally back to The Clock in Bellflower.

For those low on gas money, there's always cruising the boulevard. Chopped 1949 Mercs dressed in either in dark, organic colors or multihued primer, roadsters and coupes with hopped-up flatheads, and groups of buddies in dad's four-door sedan drive up and

the place to be. Decades from now, these scenes will be relived and re-created thousands of times. Hot rods and customs from this period will be revered, copied, and restored to preserve for all time this magical era in automotive history. It could only happen now, under these circumstances, only in this place, only for a while. It is the convergence of many factors, tangible and intangible.

* * *

Why this all came about had much to do with what was happening on this side of the Atlantic and Pacific oceans,

unconscious desires. And with many coming back from the war with some money saved and a job waiting, they had the means to acquire what they wanted.

Also consider that young car enthusiasts were presented with a broadening array of speed and customizing equipment, new-car offerings, and magazines that hadn't been available before the war. *Hot Rod* magazine had been around since 1948, but *Motor Trend*, *Car Craft*, *Hop Up*, and *Rod & Custom* also sprang up in the early '50s, spreading the word about new products and the cars people were modifying. The venerable flathead V-8, the engine of choice for hot rodders, was still around, but it had evolved and found its way under the hood of what many consider to be the quintessential custom car: the 1949-51 Mercury.

These Mercurys were the final evolution of the low fender, high beltline school of design. The new 1947 Studebakers, '48 Oldsmobiles and Cadillacs, and '49 Fords and Chevys all raised their fenders in line with their beltlines, forever changing automobile design. These cars laid the groundwork for the radical Chrysler, GM, and Ford products of 1955 that would incorporate an uninterrupted body without fender, hood, or trunk definition. The 1949-51 Mercurys at least partially held on to the earlier body design language, making them familiar to customizers, and therefore popular as modern versions of the old school of design. This resulted in some of the most memorable custom cars of all time.

Many of the famous Mercs were created, or at least updated, at the Barris brothers' shop in the early to mid 1950s. They included the '49 coupes of Sam Barris, Louis Bettancourt, and Jerry Quesnel; the '50 coupes owned by Buddy Alcorn and Wally Welch; Ralph Testa's '50 convertible; the '51 coupes of Dave Bugarin, Bob Hirohata, and Frank Sonzogni; and Freddy Rowe's '51 convertible. It is a short list to be sure, especially when you consider that this small group of Mercury customs influenced such a large contingent of custom car aficionados that have loved these cars ever since. Imagine the impact they must have had when they were first introduced to the world in the early 1950s!

Meanwhile, for hot rodders, the Russetta Timing Association, established in 1948, and the Southern California Timing Association, which had formed in '37, were still holding speed events at the SoCal dry lakes. Classes were established based on characteristics such as a car's weight, body style, aerodynamics, engine displacement, and number of cylinders. For those who wanted to go even faster, racing on the vast salt flats at Bonneville in Southern

Utah was catching on. The first National Speed Trials for hot rodders was held there in '49, and participants liked the longer runs and faster times.

While Russetta and the SCTA had given structure to the dry lakes, it was

becoming apparent that a body was needed to organize, monitor, and sanction the heads-up racing called "drag racing." *Hot Rod* magazine and its editor Wally Parks, under the auspices of the National Hot Rod Association (NHRA), stepped up to fill the void. Wally founded and became the first president of the NHRA in 1951, all the while handling his editorial chores at *Hot Rod*. The NHRA's mantra was to get it off of the streets and race safely at an organized dragstrip. Wally eventually left Petersen Publishing Company (*Hot Rod*'s publisher) in 1963 due to the increasing demand for his time at the NHRA.

The formation of the NHRA was an important step toward respectability, but much work needed to be done. When night fell and cruisers gathered at the drive-ins, the scene often became loud and rowdy, and sometimes got out of control. This caused concern for city fathers, police, and neighboring residents. Street racing was a frequent occurrence, and so were accidents. It was illegal, dangerous, exciting, and fun—a sure cocktail for disaster. But this wasn't the only thing drawing the ire of parents and the constabulary.

Some hot rodders and custom owners adopted a look, brought back with them from the war. They wore leather

jackets, blue jeans, and T-shirts with cigarette packs rolled into sleeves. It has become a cliché, but at the time it was meant to convey an antisocial, edgy distinction from what was acceptable. The look was part of the point of the whole hot rod and custom car phenomenon: To create a different lifestyle for adolescents from that of their parents. It was teenage rebellion. It was the beginning of the youth culture.

Though similar in appearance and ideology, there were differences between hot rodders and custom owners. Hot rodders bought their parts from speed shops and performed most of the work on their cars themselves. The custom crowd sought out the expertise of shops that performed mild-to-wild body alterations. And therein lies the difference and the rub.

Some rodders felt disdain for custom cars because they were "low and slow" and most of the work was performed by outside shops, not the owners themselves. They derided customs as "lead barges" or "lead sleds" due to their sometimes abundant use of lead as a body filler. Custom owners shot back at hot rodders with names like "shot rods" and "Ricky racers." Rodders tended to be "gearheads" that weren't as interested in the aesthetics of their cars as custom fans. Custom guys concentrated on looks and cared little for performance. These two groups are intertwined in our modern view of their activities, but they were actually quite different and could be antagonistic toward each other.

Some feel that the custom car was a

direct offshoot of the hot rod. That view doesn't jibe with the vastly different approaches the two factions had toward their cars. Yes, some rodders drove customs and vice versa, but it wasn't the norm. Owning two cars was beyond the reach of most hard-working young men. And the abilities required to master engine and chassis modifications, as well as body customizing and fabrication, were rarely found in a single person, or even among a whole peer group.

That's where the custom shops came in. Barris Kustoms was the best known of the early custom shops. Located in Lynwood, California, the shop was in what some call "the nest" for its concentration of custom-related enterprises. Gaylord's Custom Upholstery, which specialized in Carson-type tops, was just around the corner from Barris Kustoms, and Larry Watson, Ed Schelhaas, and Dean Jeffries were also located within the nest.

Also in the L.A.-area were Link Paola, Jimmy Summers, the Carson Top Shop, Gil and Al Ayala, and Valley Custom. Northern California had its players, too. Gene Winfield operated out of Modesto, and Joe Bailon and Joe Wilhelm worked in the Bay Area.

By the mid 1950s, Dean Jeffries, Von Dutch, Ed "Big Daddy" Roth, Junior Conway, Dick Jackson, and Larry Watson were all plying their custom painting and/or pinstriping talents either at Barris' or within the nest. Some, like Von Dutch, were already established names, and the rest would become famous in the custom car world as the '50s progressed.

For the hot rodder or drag racer who wanted performance beyond the means of a shade-tree mechanic, some of the shops in the nest also catered to hot rodders and drag racers. The Chrisman clan, which included brothers Art and Lloyd and uncle Jack, started their engine building and racing careers in Lynwood, as did Keith Black, who pioneered the development of the Chrysler Hemi engine in drag racing's early days.

Back on the streets, car clubs formed all over the L.A. basin with names like Renegades, Road Runners, and Night Riders. They were fraternities of like-minded rodders or custom owners. Toward the end of the decade, a distinction even developed among dry-lakes racers, drag racers, and the "street" hot rodders who were organizing clubs like the Pasadena Roadster Club and L.A. Roadster Club. Some members of the street roadster clubs raced, but the main point was to bring together owners with similar tastes and to change the public's perception of

them as riotous renegades unable to stay within the bounds of the law and accepted behavior. The clubs also organized social events for their members and hosted car shows that allowed members to showcase their cars to the general public.

With car club-peer recognition, car-show competition, and magazine coverage rewarding the best cars, the level of craftsmanship ramped up greatly. For the most part, hot rods and especially customs were well-built, attractive cars that met or exceeded anything coming out of Detroit.

On the competition side, salt flats and lakes racing were finding limited participation due to their need for flat, barren landscapes. With the topography being unique to only a few areas, there was no possibility for expansion. Thus, this type of racing maintained its tradition of amateur participation, and does so even to this day.

With the NHRA's help, however, drag racing took off. Expanded classes, evolving safety procedures and equipment, and new tracks helped it grow, but even more important was the professional presentation. New, high-compression overhead-valve engines were introduced in Cadillacs and Oldsmobiles in 1949, and this engine design became available in most cars from the Big Three by '55. These faster, more reliable powerplants found favor with hot rodders, especially those who drag raced, and led to the development of new speed equipment and more speed shops to sell it.

Typical early drag racing speeds hovered around 100 mph at the dawn of the dragstrip in the early 1950s, but by the end of the decade speeds were exceeding 180 mph. Events were literally moving quite rapidly in drag racing's development, and not just on the West Coast.

Dragstrips were opening in both the East and Midwest too, helped along by the NHRA's Safety Safari—a group of men paid to organize dragstrips under NHRA sanction. By 1955, the first NHRA "Nationals" was held in Great Bend, Kansas, with drag racers across the country participating.

As the decade progressed, an unspoken, accepted look developed for hot rods and customs, and that look was slightly different for the East and West Coasts. East Coast customs tended to sit higher than their West Coast counterparts due to the bad roads and harsh winters easterners faced. East Coast cars also tended to be less radically modified, but they took on more baroque styling themes when they were heavily customized.

Channeled hot rods found greater favor in the east as owners strived for more sports carlike proportions. Closed coupes and sedans were also built in greater abundance in the east, again because of the more severe weather. Highboy roadsters and coupes that adopted the look of the prewar lakes racers were more prevalent on the West Coast, as were more radical customs inspired by greater competition at car shows. The west drove the trends for hot rods and customs due mainly to the location of the magazines that catered to these cars, but also due to the abundance of craftsmen located in California. Later in the decade, a number of East Coast magazine titles emerged to better cover the local scene, and this only helped spread the popularity of hot rods and customs nationwide.

With a burgeoning national scene, the car show phenomenon also spread across the country. Hollywood, California-based *Rod & Custom* magazine

acknowledged this fact as early as 1953 by featuring an article on a prominent West Coast custom—the Hirohata Mercury—driving cross-country for the annual Indianapolis Custom Show held in conjunction with the Indy 500. During the winter months, these indoor rod and custom shows intensified interest while racing and cruising all but disappeared due to the weather. They also helped spotlight regional speed shops, mechanics, and body shops that catered to the hot rodder or custom car owner.

As the decade drew to a close, customs transitioned away from 1940s and early '50s coupes and sedans with moderate-to-radical body modifications. The new look, featured on late '50s finned hardtops and convertibles, utilized paint techniques and relatively little custom bodywork. Customizing was now in a paint gun. These "mild customs" were popularized by painter Larry Watson and his brand-new, widely publicized 1958 Ford Thunderbird. Custom cars were still in their prime, but with the sweeping changes Detroit made in automobile design— the canted headlights, high fins, thin roofs, and large expanses of glass—mild

customs became distinctive enough with just panel painting or scallops, lowering, cool wheel covers, and some well-done tuck-and-roll upholstery. Detroit was designing beyond the need to customize, but teenagers and custom car enthusiasts still needed to stand apart from their parents and peers.

Hot rods were ending the decade on a high note, too, but they would face a number of challenges over the next few years as America entered the dawn of the factory "muscle car" era.

Hot rods and customs seemingly came out of nowhere at the beginning of the decade to become a cultural phenomenon that encompassed the whole United States. Hot rods and customs appeared in movies, advertising, and television shows. They affected laws and city policies. Their influence reflected the changing importance that the teenage culture would take on as the decades progressed. The car scene didn't just grow in the 1950s. It became a subculture with its own clothes, language, businesses, magazines, events, shows, competitions, and more. It was the golden age of the hot rod and custom car. ⟶⟩⟨⟨

NieKamp Roadster

In 1949, Bill NieKamp was a middle-aged man playing a young man's game. Forty-three years old at the time, he set out to build a hot rod he could enter in car shows and race at Southern California's dry lakes.

A body assembler and painter at the Plymouth factory in Long Beach, California, NieKamp bought a '29 Model A roadster body for $15 and channeled it over '27 Essex frame rails. NieKamp performed most of the work himself, using very basic techniques.

Whitey Clayton fabricated the bellypan, hood, and track nose, while NieKamp made the floorboard and nerf bars. Under the hood, NieKamp installed a 1942 Mercury flathead V-8 with Evans heads, a Weiand intake manifold, a Winfield cam, and a pair of Stromberg 97 carburetors. NieKamp kept close records along the way, and the sum cost of the project came to $1888.72.

Before NieKamp raced the car, he showed it at the inaugural National Roadster Show in Oakland, California, in lakes trim with a passenger-side tonneau and no windshield. The meticulously built rod won the first America's Most Beautiful Roadster award.

NieKamp raced the roadster at El Mirage for three seasons, culminating with a run of 142.40 mph in July 1952. Soon thereafter, he turned down a $2800 offer for the car, opting instead to raffle it off to benefit a racer who had been seriously injured at Bonneville. The winner of the raffle, a young soldier named Dick Russell, drove it as his daily driver and raced it at the Santa Ana Drags before selling it to Delmer Brink in 1958.

Brink decided to swap in a Buick nailhead engine, but never completed the work, and sold the car to then *Rod & Custom* associate editor Jim "Jake" Jacobs in 1969 for $1300. Jake,

who had recognized the car as the very first AMBR winner, restored it in a 1971 series of articles in the magazine. Jacobs' efforts made the NieKamp roadster the first historic hot rod to be restored, a practice that would come into vogue 20 years later.

After the flathead Jake installed died in 1975, he replaced it with a 265-cid Chevy V-8. The small block remained in the car until '97, when the roadster was invited to compete in the first Hot Rod class at the 1997 Pebble Beach Concours d'Elegance. With respect to the car's storied past, Jacobs restored it to its 1950 configuration, installing another flathead, removing the windshield, and adding a tonneau. Now displayed at the Petersen Automotive Museum in Los Angeles, this hot rodding icon is preserved for posterity.

Bonneville, 1951

NieKamp with Jim Jacobs, 1974

1

2

3

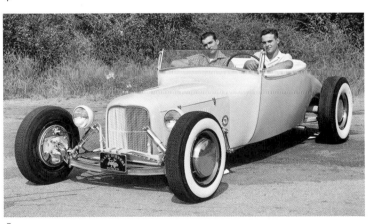

4

5

1950s AMBR Winners

The First and Second Annual Automotive Equipment Display and Hot Rod Expositions were put on by the SCTA in 1948 and '49. Held in Los Angeles, both events were big successes. Meanwhile, in Northern California, Al and Mary Slonaker had promoted a new-car show that included a handful of hot rods in '49. The enterprising couple noticed that the small group of hot rods drew the most spectator interest, and decided to make their next show an all hot rod affair. Thus was born the first National Roadster Show in January 1950. Held at the Oakland Exposition Building, the event soon became known simply as "Oakland."

The couple went all out to make the event a success, even stopping hot rodders on the streets to invite them to the show. They had a nine-foot-tall trophy made and dubbed it the America's Most Beautiful Roadster award (AMBR). The first recipient of the title was L.A. resident Bill NieKamp for his '29 Model A (pp. 42–43). Today, more than 50 years later, the AMBR is still the most coveted award among hot rod roadster builders.

1. The 1951 AMBR winner was Rico Squaglia's red '23 T with a Westergard track nose, hood, and full bellypans. The engine wasn't finished. After the show, Al Slonaker ruled that all cars had to be driven into and out of the building. **2.** Bud Crackbon won the title in 1952 with a tracknose '25 T pickup on a '32 frame. Painted blue with orange scallops, this car ran a 248-cid Merc flathead, and its windshield and fenders were easily removed for lakes runs. **3.** The first '27 T to claim the AMBR award was Dick Williams' '53 winner, which had run 123.636 mph at Bonneville. Painted light blue, it was ahead of its time with a chrome-moly tube frame, setback engine, and rare Kinmont disc brakes. **4.** A patriotic red, white, and blue paint theme helped nab the '54 trophy for Frank Rose and his fendered '27 T. Frank's car featured a custom hood, a hand-formed bellypan, and a 257-cid Ford flathead V-8.

6

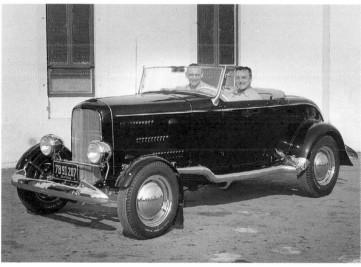

7

8

5. 1955 produced the first tie for the AMBR title. Blackie Gejeian and Ray Anderegg both won with Ts. Anderegg's '27 T started life as a coupe and ran a modified Mercury flathead V-8. **6.** Blackie's shortened '26 T, which had been entered twice before it shared the title in '55, was one of the first rods with a completely chromed undercarriage. **7.** Vic Edelbrock raced this 1932 Ford roadster at the dry lakes, and installed the first Edelbrock intake manifold on the flathead engine. Eddie Bosio bought the car, rebuilt it, and took the '56 AMBR title, making it the first Deuce to win at Oakland. **8.** Jerry Woodward's Thunder Rod '29 red roadster captured the 1957 AMBR title. Quad headlights, an unusual rear-mounted spare, and a drastically abbreviated and channeled body made it a controversial choice. **9.** George Barris' shop built the first two-time AMBR winner, Richard Peters' Ala Kart '29 roadster pickup. The pickup, which won in '58 and '59, featured a fully chromed chassis, a hand-formed bed, and white pearl paint with gold and purple scallops by Dean Jeffries. Built as a dedicated show car, it became one of the most popular AMBR winners ever.

9

Wetzel's Roadster

Bill Hook started building this 1932 Ford roadster in the late '40s, enlisting the famous Valley Custom shop in Burbank, California, to further modify the already channeled body. Valley Custom smoothed the rear wheel arches, added a rolled rear pan, shaved the door handles, and moved the gas filler to the driver-side rear quarter panel. The shop also installed a DuVall windshield and added a Stewart Warner Hollywood instrument cluster. A second Hollywood instrument panel, minus the instruments, was added to serve as the glovebox door. Hook sold the Deuce unfinished in '52 to Dr. Leland Wetzel, who had friend Leonard Carr build the engine and finish the car.

Wetzel spared no expense in building the Ford flathead V-8, equipping it with Evans heads and intake manifold. When complete, he drove the Deuce from his Springfield, Missouri, home to the Bonneville Speed Week and Pikes Peak Hill Climb with his wife, Bertha, to watch the action. Bertha chronicled that trip in the December 1952 *Hot Rod*, noting the varied weather conditions they endured in the roadster.

Dr. Wetzel owned the Deuce roadster for 43 years until Kurt McCormick, a noted Barris custom collector from nearby Webster Groves, Missouri, convinced him to sell it in 1995. When Kurt picked up the car, he reported that it was stone-cold original to the photos taken in 1952.

Kurt had Dave Conrad of Kirkwood, Missouri, perform the complete restoration and change the engine in the process. Kurt opted for another period engine he had on hand, the 1954 Cadillac 331-cid V-8 from the Barris-built Parisienne custom (pp. 70–71).

Kurt had the engine machine work done by Ronnie Simon of St. Louis, then installed the SCoT blower along with other period-correct components. Kurt says the Cad V-8 fit without drilling any new holes into the frame.

Kurt maintained the front nerf bar with encircled "W" that Dr. Wetzel had made. With the exception of the new engine and front tires, the car now appears just as it did in 1952.

Frank Mack T

Frank Mack T When Tom Medley (aka *Hot Rod* magazine's Stroker McGurk) saw this 1927 Model T roadster at the first Detroit Autorama in '53, he was impressed. The show judges agreed, awarding it Best in Show. Tom wrote a feature on the car for the November 1953 *Hot Rod*, dubbing it the "ImMACKulate T." Immaculate it was, as Mack spent more than 3000 hours over three years building the roadster, doing everything but the upholstery himself.

Mack, a Farmington, Michigan, native, pieced the tracknose together from two 1941 Chevy fenders. He fabricated a full bellypan, but left the transmission and driveshaft exposed between the driver and passenger seats. E&J accessory head-lights give the car a look that is distinct from other rods of its era. Hand-fabricated, chrome-plated, ¾-inch nerf bars and early Dayton wheels complete the package.

The suspension consists of a 1938 Ford tube axle and spring setup hooked to a reworked '37 Ford crossmember. In the rear, the stock crossmember bolts to a '34 Ford rear end with 4:11 gears.

The Mercury flathead engine is basically stock, except for a pair of Edelbrock heads that boost compression to 8.5 to 1.

Mack reluctantly sold the car to collector Bruce Meyer in 1997. Never restored, it is a testament to Mack's skills as a

builder and his dedication to automotive maintenance. Preserved in remarkable condition, this unique roadster is an important living example of the history of hot rodding. Fittingly, Meyer showed it at the 50th Detroit Autorama—the place where ol' Stroker first saw it all those years ago.

Early Bonneville

The Bonneville Salt Flats of Southern Utah had been the scene of the World's Land Speed Record attempts since 1935, with names such as George Eyston, Malcolm Campbell, and John Cobb etched in the history books.

In 1949, Robert E. Petersen and Lee Ryan from Petersen Publishing Co., along with Wally Parks of the SCTA, flew to Salt Lake City to meet with the Bonneville Speedway Association. Their goal was to provide hot rodders with a venue to go even faster. The dry lakes had only 1½-mile runs, while Bonneville offered runs up to 13 miles long. As a result of the meeting, the first National Speed Trials was scheduled for August 22–27.

Only 50–60 cars participated in the first speed trials, primarily because the date wasn't announced until a few weeks before the event. The cars raced in classes based on body type and engine size. A supercharger moved a car up one engine class.

Many cars ran faster than they ever had. The So-Cal Speed Shop streamliner of Dean Batchelor and Alex Xydias posted the meet's best time at 193.54 mph with a Mercury flathead V-8, setting the C Streamliner class record. After the pair swapped in a Ford V-8/60, the streamliner ran 155.17 mph, setting the A Streamliner class record. Another notable participant was 17-year-old Don Waite in his rear-engine '27 T roadster. Dubbed the "dumb kid," Waite showed 'em by setting the C Lakester class record at 151.90 mph.

Rodders drove many street roadsters to the Trials. In typical dry-lakes fashion, upon arrival, they removed their windshields, headlights, and, in some cases, fenders. John Browing had the fastest roadster. He qualified at a speed of 140.18 mph and set the C/Roadster class record at 129.69 mph.

Although that first meet was held as a "test," the National Speed Trials caught on. The cleaner, faster salt flats grabbed the thunder from the dry lakes in the early '50s, and many firsts occurred at Bonneville. In fact, the "Two Club" was established there in '54 when Art Chrisman, Bob Rufi, Otto Rysmann, Willie Young, and Jim Lindsley all posted two-way averages of more than 200 mph. No matter how fast the cars, a spirit of cooperation has always permeated Bonneville, as teams have shared labor, parts, and even engines. It is truly a special place to race.

Tom Medley (left) and Wally Parks, 1950

Overnight work in Wendover, Utah, 1951

Don Waite's '27 T, 1950

Fran Hernandez in Bill Likes' 1932 Ford roadster, 1951

So-Cal Coupe

After running a bellytanker and a streamliner at Bonneville from 1949 to '51, So-Cal Speed Shop founder Alex Xydias decided to build a coupe he could run at both Bonneville and the dragstrip. A chopped and channeled '34 Ford coupe that Russell Lanthorne and Jim Gray ran at Bonneville in 1951 fit the bill. Xydias (shown in the coupe on the opposite page) retained the Frank Kurtis nose, installed a supercharged '48 Merc flathead, and finished the car to a high standard.

The rebuilt coupe debuted in 1953 as part of the So-Cal Speed Shop racing team and immediately set records at Bonneville, where it topped 177 mph to set the C Competition Coupe/Sedan mark, and at the dragstrip, turning 121 mph for the NHRA B Modified record. With its dual racing pedigree, *Hot Rod* magazine dubbed it the "Double-Threat Coupe" in a May 1954 cover story.

Later in 1954, the coupe ran with an Ardun overhead-valve conversion and an even more radical chop. The first quarter-mile pass with the 460-horsepower engine produced a record 132 mph. However, tragedy awaited at the next race at Pomona. The clutch blew up at the starting line, setting the car on fire and severely burning driver Dave DeLangton. Dave died a month later. Xydias gave up racing after the tragedy and sold the car to John Moxley.

Moxley ran the car, now called "Miss 400," at Bonneville, setting more records. He sold it to Jerry Eisert in 1956, who raced it until '60, then put it up on blocks. Jim Travis, a long-time fan of the car, convinced Eisert to sell it to him in 1969.

Travis raced the car at the drags and Bonneville in the early 1970s and continued to race at Bonneville until '96, which makes it one of the most raced cars in automotive history. Before Travis retired the coupe, he ran 236 mph at Bonneville with a supercharged Chevy engine.

Don Orosco purchased the car from Travis in 1996. Orosco's shop, DBO Motor Racing, restored it to its '54 configuration (with the Ardun heads) to compete in the Pebble Beach Concours d'Elegance Historic Hot Rod Coupe class in 2001. There, the coupe faced two cars it had raced against at Bonneville in the '50s—Art Chrisman's Model A competition coupe and the Pierson Brothers' '34 coupe. Still a formidable competitor, the So-Cal Coupe won the class, adding another victory to its storied résumé.

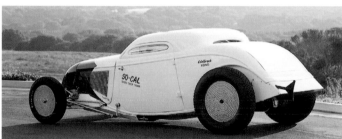

Chopped Mercurys of the '50s

The custom car certainly existed before the 1949-51 Mercurys, but it didn't take off as a cultural phenomenon until these and other postwar cars hit the market. Prior to the '49s, postwar models were just rehashed '42s. Fenders were separate, hoods were tall and narrow, front grilles were usually upright and rectangular, and rear ends dropped off sharply in a rounded bustle.

Then came April 29, 1948, and the release of the 1949 Mercury. Though it did have a modern envelope body, the design wasn't especially progressive, with its dated two-piece V-shaped windshield, thick slabsided body, vestigial fadeaway front fenders, and rounded, fadeaway rear end. Other cars from Cadillac, Oldsmobile, Hudson, and even Ford were more modern in design, but it was actually the '49 Merc's aesthetic quirks that made it so appealing to customizers.

Southern California shops had been customizing 1940-48 Fords and Mercurys for years. The new cars were certainly different, but elements of the old cars remained, making the new Mercs easier to work on than other, more modern new designs. Plus, the frumpy Mercs seemingly begged for bodywork. These cars presented themselves as blank automotive canvases.

Mercury changed the cars slightly for 1950, then more significantly for '51. The '50s received a different front-end treatment, new hubcaps, and revised trim all-around. The '51s got an even bolder grille, extended rear fenders with upright taillights, and a more modern, reshaped rear window. Coupes were the preferred body style, but a few convertibles and even sedans received the custom treatment.

Magazines such as *Hot Rod*, *Hop Up*, and *Motor Trend* caught on to the growing customizing trend and featured the coolest rods and customs. This led to more business for existing shops and the emergence of new ones. Business was thriving for the likes of George and Sam Barris, Valley Custom, the Ayala brothers, Joe Bailon, and Gene Winfield, and much of the work was devoted to 1949-51 Mercs.

The first known 1949 Merc to be chopped was Sam Barris' car done at the Barris shop in 1950. Others soon followed, including many of the cars shown here, and the trend reached its high point with Bob Hirohata's tasteful '51 (pp. 56–57) done by the Barris shop.

There's no telling exactly how many 1949-51 Mercs were actually chopped and customized in the 1950s. Barris' shop completed maybe 35-50 cars, and the total probably isn't more than a couple hundred. By '57, the '49-51 Mercs had largely been upstaged by newer, sleeker Detroit designs that required less work to turn heads.

Just as the 1932 Ford is the quintessential hot rod, the 1949-51 Mercs are the ultimate customs. A few custom car fans recognized that fact as early as the 1970s, and since then, many more custom Mercs have been built in that classic '50s style. But it was those select few Merc customs built in the early to mid '50s that created an aesthetic all their own. Those Mercurys, built by legendary artisans, propelled the hobby forward more than any type of car in the history of customizing.

1

2

3

4

5

6

1. Stock 1949 Mercurys were tall and thick, with more ornamentation at the front than most customizers would allow. Interestingly, the design was originally intended for the first postwar Fords, but Ford Motor Co. thought the car was too big and moved it up the line to Mercury. 2. Sam Barris' coupe is recognized as the first chopped 1949 Mercury. Sam customized the car in 1950, chopping the top four inches, replacing the stock dip in the door with a continuous flowing line, lowering the car four inches, frenching the headlights, and making his own taillights and grille. 3. Gil and Al Ayala built this '49 coupe for Louie Bettancourt in 1950. Notable features included the slanted B-pillars, rounded hood corners, extended headlights, "full fadeaway" fenders, and pieces from a '54 Ford grille. 4. Johnny Zupan purchased the Bettancourt car and took it to the Barris shop for updating in 1956. Changes included adding scooped fender skirts and more chrome, swapping wheel covers, and spraying on two-tone gold paint with Dean Jeffries-applied pinstriping. 5. Among the first 1949-51 Mercury convertibles to be chopped (an easier process than on coupes) was Ralph Testa's '50. The car also used horizontally mounted '49 Buick taillights and a Henry J grille. 6. Frank Sonzogni was a full-time policeman and part-time customizer at the Barris shop. Frank built his '50 Merc during off hours in 1954, adding molded-in scooped skirts. The Sonzogni car is shown here with John Zupan's '49 (center) and Buddy Alcorn's '50 (right, see pp. 78–79). 7. Fred Rowe's '51 convertible was chopped by the Barris brothers in 1953. Unlike most customs, it boasted a hot rodded flathead Ford engine. Rowe's car is shown here on the set of Running Wild, where it appeared with the Hirohata Mercury. 8. Dave Bugarin's '51 coupe came out of the Barris shop in '55. Unique features included '54 Packard taillights, '53 Buick headlights, and a hardtop look for the chopped roof.

7

8

Hirohata Mercury

The Hirohata Mercury is the quintessential chopped Merc and easily the most famous custom of all time. It's a masterpiece of "just right" customizing alchemy; ostentatious yet elegant, sinister yet inviting. It represents the pinnacle of chopped Mercury styling, built after most professional customizers had acquired a full range of metalworking skills but before many of the styling excesses of the 1950s would take over.

The car was originally built by Barris Kustom in 1952 for Bob Hirohata. It was the first 1951 Mercury chopped; the top came down four inches in the front and seven inches at the rear, with the stock rear window leaned forward at a graceful angle. The center door posts were removed and replaced with handsomely curved ⅝-inch U-channel stock, a reprise of the treatment the Barrises first used on Nick Matranga's '40 Mercury.

Up front, the hood was dechromed and reshaped to extend into the modified grille opening. The grille bar was hand-formed, with wraparound parking light moldings fashioned from 1950 Ford parts. Headlights were frenched with trim rings from a '52 Ford. The bodysides were reconfigured with tapered fadeaway fender lines that dipped into hand-formed functional scoops adorned with chrome teeth from a '52 Chevy grille. The stock Mercury fender skirts were modified to mount flush with the body. Handsome 1952 Buick Riviera sidespears split the Ice Green and Organic Dark Green two-tone paint job. The flamboyant colors were a definite departure from customs up until that point, as most wore dark metallic colors. Taillights from a '52 Lincoln were frenched low into the rear fenders.

The car was lowered in front with cut coil springs and in back with a C-sectioned frame, de-arched springs, and two sets of 1¼-inch lowering blocks. Custom rolled-and-pleated upholstery adorned the seats, side panels, headliner, and even the inside of the ashtray. Von Dutch applied the pinstriping on the dash, and Hirohata made his own laminated plastic teardrop dash knobs.

Soon after it was completed at Barris', Hirohata had Dick Lyon replace the Mercury's flathead with a new 1953 Cadillac engine. Hirohata and a friend then took the car on a cross-country trip, introducing California customizing to other parts of the country. They drove to Indianapolis to see the Indy 500 and attend custom car shows in Indiana and Michigan. The trip was chronicled in the October 1953 issue of *Rod & Custom* magazine. Hirohata used masking tape to protect the Merc's vulnerable surfaces from rock chips along the way.

Later, the Merc was repainted in Lime Green and Organic Green two-tone, and featured in the 1955 movie *Running Wild*. Hirohata then sold the car and it changed hands a couple more times. In 1959, 16-year-old Jim McNiel bought the

Bob Hirohata checks the trunk-mounted fuel-filler cap.

well-worn Merc off a used-car lot for $500, refurbished a few details, and drove it throughout high school. McNiel used the car regularly until 1964, then put it into storage.

Over the years, the car's legend grew as McNiel kept the car under wraps and out of public view, always turning down any offers to sell (some of them quite lucrative). Finally, in 1989, Pat Ganahl, then editor of *Rod & Custom*, learned of the car's location and coaxed McNiel to bring it out of hiding and restore it with parts and materials donated by the magazine's advertisers. The restoration was a drawn out process, as McNiel worked meticulously and on his own schedule, but the exterior of the car was completed in 1996—just in time for the car to be shown at a historic display of rods and customs at the Oakland Museum of California. The crowning touch was a gorgeous repaint in the original colors by former Barris employee Herschel "Junior" Conway. After the museum show, veteran stitcher Eddie Martinez was called upon to precisely re-create the original custom upholstery. Its resurrection was a long time in the making, but the quintessential custom Mercury is now back in top form.

Mamie Van Doren and George Barris on the set of Running Wild, 1955.

Ernst Chevy

In 1951, Barris Kustom Automobiles was fast developing a sterling reputation. The custom scene was vibrant, Sam and George Barris were doing some of their best customizing work, magazine exposure was bringing in plenty of business, and the Lynwood, California, shop was gaining nationwide fame. The word even spread to the most unlikely of car guys: Larry Ernst, a Toledo, Ohio, Catholic priest with a strong affinity for customs.

Ernst showed his enthusiasm by purchasing a brand-new 1951 Chevrolet Bel Air hardtop coupe and driving it to California for the Barris treatment. Ernst delivered the car with two main instructions: customize it and keep the Continental kit. Although they didn't want to retain the Continental kit (a decidedly East Coast custom cue), the Barrises made the best of it. To make the add-on accessory look integrated, Sam extended the rear fenders 12 inches rearward and 1½ inches downward, and molded the Continental spare's shelf into the body. Sam completed restyling the rear end by working in '49 Ford taillights and their characteristic windsplits, and routing the exhaust through the rear bumper, which received a '49 Chevy front license plate guard.

The rest of the car was given equal consideration. Sam chopped the top 2½ inches at the front and six inches at the rear, laying back the A-pillars 2½ inches in the process. The result was beautiful, and the Ernst Chevy is widely recognized as the first hardtop known to be chopped. Barris Kustoms also swapped out the two-piece windshield for the one-piece unit from a '51 Oldsmobile and cut it to fit. Most of the chrome was shaved from the body, including the door handles and all the trim on the hood and trunk. Up front, Barris Kustoms replaced the grille opening with the graceful, rounded unit from a '50 Merc, installed the grille from a '51 Meteor (Ford's Canadian brand), and added '49 Chevy bumper guards to the stock bumper. Lowering the car by cutting the front coil springs and slightly flattening the rear leafs gave the car the right stance, and purple and orchid paint provided the shine.

The result was a truly spectacular car. It received ink from a host of magazines (though they were discreet about the owner's name and occupation), and won a trunkful of trophies. Styles and trends changed quickly in those days, and many custom owners updated their cars to keep pace. Father Ernst followed the trends and soon brought the car back to the Barris shop for a second round of customizing that would make it flashier. This time, the Barris boys rounded the front hood corners, reworked the side trim, installed scoops in the rear fenders, altered the taillights, and painted the car in a two-tone burnt orange/metallic green scheme.

A teenager named Burns Berryman saw the car at a drive-in in 1952 and immediately fell in love with it. Burns located the car again in 1980 and bought it. The car was in very rough shape, but Burns set about restoring it anyway. He chose to return it to its first Barris design because that's the way he remembered it. After a 10-year odyssey, the car had regained the look it sported in 1951, though Burns did retain the rounded hood corners.

Another custom fan, Keith Ashley, liked the second Barris version so much that he had a clone of it built. As you can see by the accompanying modern and historic photos, both versions are and were tasteful examples of the art of customizing from one of history's most respected shops.

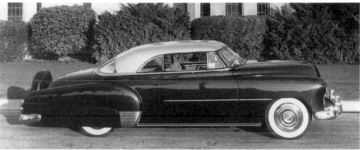

Actress and Playboy Playmate Jean Moorehead with Father Ernst's Chevy.

Father Ernst with second version.

Sam Barris with original version in progress.

1950s Rodding Activities

Street racing in the Los Angeles area got so bad in the late 1940s and early '50s that the police would stop any car that looked like a hot rod and cite it for every equipment violation they could find. In the minds of the authorities, street racing was such an epidemic that they sought legislation to put it to an end.

The favorite hangouts were drive-ins like Bob's Big Boy and the 'Wich Stand where young men and their hot rods would challenge each other to a drag race, or "dig out," at some remote location. Of course, the constabulary took a dim view of this activity. But not all cops were the opposition. Some policemen backed hot rods and legitimate racing at the dry lakes. Some were even members of the Southern California Timing Association.

Organized efforts to displace this outlaw image included heavily promoted reliability runs. The most famous reliability run was put together by the hastily formed Pasadena Roadster Club. Made up of a number of SCTA clubs specifically for the occasion, PRC organizers didn't want to use an existing club name for fear that the name would bring with it a stigma. Roadsters from far and wide came to participate in road rallies without racing or any exhibitions of speed. Their goal was to show the world (and the police) that they weren't all bad. It helped.

Other clubs agreed to join the fight for their reputation by doing good deeds like changing flat tires or getting gas for stranded motorists. After performing their deeds, rodders would give out club cards that said "You have just been helped by the XYZ Hot Rod Club." Members agreed to take no gratuities.

1

2

3

4

5

1. One club that participated in reliability runs was the Pasadena Pacers, shown here checking out a passing roadster pickup. **2.** The lack of sophisticated repair equipment didn't deter these hot rodders. Here they're changing a fragile transmission that required the entire rear end be removed first. **3.** The Rose Bowl parking lot was the gathering and sign-in cite for a few reliability runs. The object of a run was to follow a given route and return without breaking down or missing a turn. **4.** High school shop teachers were recruited by law enforcement to teach the finer points of the hot rod to young students in hopes of helping to deter outlaw street-racing activity. **5.** This period publicity shot shows Hot Rod editor Wally Parks discussing the new fender-law requirements with California Highway Patrol officer Art Pollard, who was also a hot rodder. **6.** Corner gas stations were popular hangouts for car nuts. Here, two '29s and a '32 are gathered at a Shell station. **7.** Early hot rod clubs liked to line up and show off their hardware. Not much has changed.

6

7

Early drag racing

The first organized drag race was held at Goleta Airport in Santa Barbara, California, in spring 1949. Backed by the Santa Barbara Acceleration Association, the impetus was a grudge match between two Los Angeles street racers. Fran Hernandez, in his nitro-powered '32 Ford, faced off against Tom Cobbs in a supercharged '29 roadster. Fran won.

Drag racing took off when C.J. Hart, Creighton Hunter, and Frank Stillwell convinced the Santa Ana airport authorities to allow them to hold a drag race on the far west runway. They had to agree to stop racing if the airport needed the runway.

Hart developed a unique starting system, utilizing a rolling start to save on driveline wear and tear. Each driver would stage behind the starting line and apply the brakes. When signaled by the flagman, the drivers would match each other in a slow roll, and when they reached the starting line, the flagman would give them the signal to take off. The first car to cross the finish line, as determined by a pair of judges at the end of the quarter-mile strip, was the winner. If the start wasn't even, they would rerun the race.

Elapsed time (E.T.) wasn't recorded, only top speed. Speed was determined by a timing device attached to rubber hoses that stretched across the dragstrip. The elapsed time between hoses was translated into miles per hour. It wasn't very sophisticated.

J. Otto Crocker introduced his more sophisticated Chrondek electronic timing equipment at the 1953 Southern California Championships at Pomona. Elapsed times, which had been sparingly used before, were also reported. Dragstrip operators were quick to pick up on Pomona's excellent system, and within two years all drag racing followed suit.

As speeds increased and cars were further stripped of unnecessary components, accidents became a problem and safety rules were needed. Safety hubs on rear wheels, scatter-shields around clutches, seatbelts, and roll bars were all required by 1957.

The success and popularity of the Santa Ana drag races spawned several others in the Los Angeles area. Soon Saugus, Long Beach, Fontana, Colton, Riverside, and San Fernando all hosted drag racing. The phenomenon then spread across the country, thanks largely to the efforts of Wally Parks and the NHRA Safety Safari in the mid 1950s.

Chrisman Model A Sedan

Jack Chrisman's stylish sedan was a formidable competitor in the early days of drag racing. The black-and-white photo on the opposite page shows the car at its best, smoking the tires as it leaves the starting line at the Santa Ana dragstrip in 1954. The famous Von Dutch-striped radiator-shell insert and five-inch chop made this car easy to spot. The power was routed from the Chrysler 354-cid Hemi engine to the '40 Ford rear end with 4:11 gears.

Prior to receiving the Hemi, Jack's '29 saw daily service with a stout Ford flathead V-8. On weekends, he removed the jets from the four Stromberg 97 carburetors (thus increasing flow), filled the fuel tank with a mixture of nitromethane and alcohol, and ran as fast as 117 mph in the quarter mile. After Jack installed the Chrysler engine and a LaSalle transmission, the miles per hour jumped to 129. The stronger engine and gearbox led to a consistency that allowed driver Art Chrisman, Jack's nephew, to dust all comers in the A/Fuel Coupe and Sedan class in 1954.

Early drag cars became obsolete all too soon. When smaller coupes with similar powerplants came along, their performance spelled the end of drag racing success for the Chrisman sedan. Jack sold the car in 1958 to move up to dragsters, where the team would find more success. The Chrisman team won the NHRA World Championship in 1961.

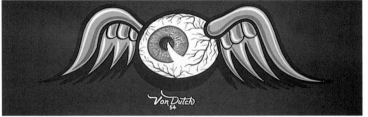

Almost 50 years later, the Chrisman sedan returned to the Chrisman family. Jack's son Steve bought it and had Jim Travis restore it. Art Chrisman again built the powertrain, now with a Turbo 400 transmission, and a 392-cid Hemi with 354 heads and dual quads. Artist Dennis Jones reproduced the Von Dutch grille-shell insert working from photos. Beautifully restored, the '29 Model A has come full circle.

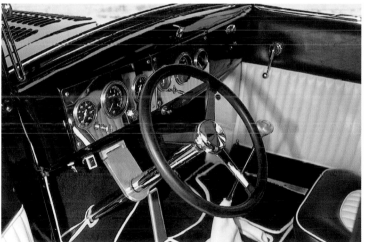

Golden Rod

Golden Rod As the hot rod culture grew in the 1950s, East Coast cars didn't receive the ink that their West Coast counterparts enjoyed, mainly because the hot rod publishing industry was located in California. However, the East Coast scene was still vibrant, and developed a distinct style of its own. One car that did receive magazine coverage was Jack Lentz' *Golden Rod*, which appeared on the October 1961 cover of *Car Craft*. With its deeply channeled body and low stance, Jack's car was a prime and beautiful example of the "East Coast look."

Jack, a body shop owner from Bedford, New Jersey, purchased the 1932 Ford roadster in '53 for $75, intending to restore it as a stock classic. Instead, he decided to put his bodyworking skills to the test and spent the next 18 months turning it into a smooth hot rod.

Jack started by modifying the front end with a dropped and filled axle. He moved the crossmembers to accommodate a '49 Merc flathead V-8 and a '40 Ford transmission, then chromed all of the front-end components, except the front axle and spring.

To lower the car, Jack removed the floorboards to channel the body eight inches over the frame, then sectioned the grille shell five inches to match. His true genius, however,

came through in the bodywork. He smoothed the doors and cowl, removed the windshield stop ridge, added a curved windshield, contoured the door hinges, frenched the exhaust pipes into the rear panel, filled the rear wheelwells, and recessed the license plate. The trunk received a lot of attention, too. Jack cut the decklid in two and molded the top portion into the body, leaving only a 14-inch high opening. He wired the trunk to a remote release that he accessed from a dash control. To top it all off, he painted the body with 20 coats of gold lacquer.

Up to this point, Jack did all the work himself. However, he wasn't an upholsterer, so he had Richmond Hill Auto Top Company do the interior. The finished car appeared in several period magazines, garnering praise for its clean design and beautiful finish. Those traits earned it a lot of car-show booty as well.

The *Golden Rod* remained on the East Coast all of its life. Never fully restored or repainted but still immaculate, Murray Smith showed the car in the Hot Rod class at the Pebble Beach Concours d'Elegance in 1999, a testament to Lentz' original work. Soon thereafter, it found another good home. Skip Barber, of racing-school fame, bought it for his personal collection.

The Polynesian

Valley Custom of Burbank, California, was one of the most prolific and important shops of customizing's golden era. The shop opened in 1948 and closed its doors for good in 1960. Unlike Barris Kustoms, Neil Emory and brother-in-law Clayton Jensen, the principals behind the shop, weren't overly concerned with promotion and didn't take pictures to document their projects. Thus, Valley Custom cars are not as widely remembered as Barris cars of the day.

One car for which there is plenty of documentation is Jack Stewart's *Polynesian* 1950 Oldsmobile. The buildup was extensively chronicled in a 47-page article in the 1954 *Motor Trend Custom Cars Annual*.

Jack Stewart was stationed in California while in the Air Force and got a taste for the vibrant Southern California customizing scene. When he was discharged in 1951, he planned to move back to his home in Canton, Ohio, but he had some ideas for a custom car and knew SoCal was the place to get it done. The '50 Oldsmobile 88 Holiday hardtop best fit his ideas, so he bought one and looked for a shop that could realize his vision. Valley Custom was the right choice. The shop incorporated Jack's ideas and added their own "less is more" philosophy to create a beautiful custom.

Jack envisioned a sectioned body and a chopped roof, but Valley Custom convinced him that only sectioning was needed. Jack also wanted the design to play off modern aviation, with long fenders, air scoops, and recessed head- and taillights. Valley Custom made these ideas reality.

Valley Custom started by sectioning the body four inches. A complicated process, sectioning involves removing a horizontal section of metal out of the body—as well as the interior, firewall, and engine compartment—and welding it back together. The Polynesian was sectioned four inches at strategic points all around the body.

According to Jack's vision, Valley Custom gave the rear fenders a new shape, with a straight, rather than sloped, top contour that led into angled taillight housings. New, larger taillights were chosen from a 1947 Studebaker. These were inset and trimmed with perforated metal. Scoops were cut into the leading edge of each rear fender and the openings were also filled with perforated metal grilles. The rear bumper was heavily modified to accept exhaust outlets and a recessed license plate mount. New, larger skirts, hand-formed to echo the fender shape, completed the back end of the car.

Jack wanted the front-wheel cutouts to be perfectly circular. Valley Custom obliged, using the wheel hubs as center points to scribe and cut new ones. The front grille opening would act only as an air scoop; there would be no grille. Valley Custom designed an airplanelike inlet with the bumper raised two inches to bisect it. They formed the front fascia to allow the bumper, a modified '46 Olds unit, to be inset. The shop also frenched the headlights and trimmed them with the same perforated metal used elsewhere on the car.

Jack chose a maroon-toned metallic-purple lacquer, dubbed Orchid Flame, for the color. Valley Custom sprayed on the paint, then finished the car with simple, straight trim pieces.

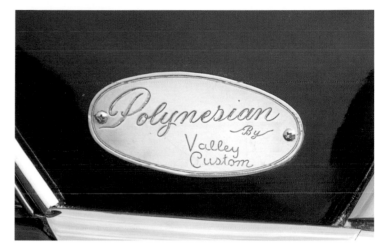

Jack took the completed car back to Ohio with him and
eventually sold it to a new owner who updated it with fins.
Gene Blackford of Cuyahoga Falls, Ohio, tracked down the
car in 1971 and immediately cut off the tailfins. It wasn't until
2004, when officials from a local Concours d'Elegance called
the Glenmoor Gathering announced that the 2005 show
would feature customs that Gene decided to restore his long-
dormant classic. The restoration took right up until the 2005
Gathering, but the car had indeed returned in all its beautiful
Valley Custom glory. Jack Stewart, the original owner, was
even on hand to witness the rebirth of what is widely recognized as the most beautiful car Valley Custom ever built.

The Parisienne

The Parisienne Most customs of the 1950s were built by or for young guys, often to impress their buddies and attract girls. Occasionally, however, an older fellow built a custom. In the case of Milton Melton and his *Parisienne* Cadillac, the resulting car blurred the line between a custom and a coachbuilt classic.

Milton Melton was a middle-aged supermarket executive from Beverly Hills in 1954 when he took possession of a brand-new $5738 Cadillac Eldorado. He immediately drove it to Barris Kustom Autos for a unique customizing treatment. The Barris crew's main task was to section the car three inches. They took the metal out of the hood, the tops of the doors, and the rear fenders. The Barris guys also modified the hood with integral scoops on each side, chopped the windshield 1¾ inches, fabricated frames for the vent windows, and cut down the side windows.

The other radical work involved the rear portion of the 129-inch-wheelbase brute. The Barris shop laid back the housing for the Continental spare at an angle, sinking it into the decklid. This required pancaking the decklid and lengthening the fenders a full 20 inches to make the Continental kit appear integral. The extra length extended the car to almost 19 and a half feet! In the process of lengthening the fenders, the Barris crew removed the Cadillac's characteristic rear fins and relocated the stock taillights in new, lower, openings. They also modified the rear fenders with '54 Packard-style bulges at the leading edges, and reworked the side trim by adding chrome-trimmed air scoops below the bulges. Finally, the exhaust was routed through a modified '55 Pontiac rear bumper in four shotgun-style outlets.

Prior to shipping it off to famous coachbuilder Bohman & Schwartz for a custom-built top, the Barris shop cut down the front seat four inches and added rolled-and-pleated upholstery to the dash pad. At Bohman & Schwartz, the *Parisienne* received a two-piece top, done in the "sedanca de ville" style similar to town cars of the early 1900s. Maurice Schwartz built the top using an oak frame with sheetmetal panels covered with padding. The rear portion was bolted to the car, and the front portion was clamped in place for easy removal. Bohman & Schwartz also added a pair of cast-bronze landau irons to the top and painted the car white.

The completed car made its debut at the 1955 International Motor Review in Los Angeles, dazzling classic and custom enthusiasts alike. The story goes cold from there until noted hot rod and custom collector Kurt McCormick found it in *Hemmings* in 1978 and bought it sight unseen for $2500. The car sat until '93, when Kurt restored it to the form shown here. Kurt took a couple of liberties with the restoration, installing a 1960 Cadillac 390-cid engine bored to 396 inches, lowering the car 2½ inches, removing the tuck-and-roll upholstery from the dash, and adding English wool carpeting in the interior and trunk. Kurt made all the changes in the true spirit of the car, only adding to this historic custom's stately coachbuilt demeanor.

Pisano/Ogden Buick

By the mid 1950s, customizers were gravitating toward new cars that required less radical bodywork to turn heads, but well-executed earlier-model customs still retained their appeal with many enthusiasts. This '41 Buick convertible, originally built by drag racing brothers Tony and Joe Pisano in the early 1950s, held its own against the chopped '49-51 Mercurys and modified late models that were on customizing's leading edge.

The focal point of the car is the five-inch-chopped windshield and Carson top by Gaylord's Upholstery. The Carson top is so named since the design originated at the Carson Top Shop, but the term was soon applied to any custom-made lift-off top that mimicked the original Carson top design. Carson tops gave a much more rakish profile than the stock convertible tops and their bulky folding mechanisms could achieve.

Other than the chop, the body modifications were subtle. The stock Buick's busy headlight trim was discarded and the headlights smoothly frenched into the front fenders. The car was nosed and decked, and the door handles, taillights, and fuel-filler door were removed. Front and rear gravel pans were molded in, and the stock bumpers were swapped out for '41 Lincoln units. The front bumper guards were removed, and the rear bumper guards were modified to house custom-made Lucite taillights. A '49 Chevy license plate guard was also fitted to the rear bumper, and twin spotlights were added to the windshield posts. Under the hood, a 331-cid Cadillac engine was installed.

By 1956, the Buick belonged to Herb Ogden, who was in the Army and stationed in Southern California. Ogden brought the car to Barris Kustom for a freshening, after which it appeared in a couple customizing magazines of the day. The Buick migrated with Ogden back home to Virginia when he was discharged from the military in the late 1950s. Ogden sold the car in '63, and from there the story gets fuzzy as the Buick went through several different owners.

Around 1982, enthusiast Barry Mazza discovered the Buick in the Washington, D.C., area, and acquired it in very tired condition. He performed a full restoration over the next 10 years. Barry made a few changes from the car's previous forms, but made sure the alterations would be period-correct and enhance the car's appeal. Mazza molded the rear fenders to the body, added fender skirts, and removed the rear fender guards. The longer sidespear trim on each rear quarter came from a '41 Buick Roadmaster coupe. The front bumper received a '49 Chevy license guard and bumper guards with Lucite parking lights to match the rear. After the bodywork was finished, Tommy the Painter at Black Oak Auto Body in Wayne, New Jersey, applied the black lacquer paint.

The Buick had a big-block Chevy engine when Barry got it, so he installed another era-correct 331-cid Cadillac engine. Bob Ecstandt stitched the black and white tuck-and-roll interior, and Barry had the entire dashboard chrome-plated. Custom collector Kurt McCormick talked Barry into selling the car in 1996, and the Buick now holds a place of honor in Kurt's collection. The Buick was displayed at the first gathering of historic customs at the 2005 Pebble Beach Concours d'Elegance, where it still held its appeal 50 years after it was built by a pair of drag racing brothers.

A young Herb Ogden shows off the "kick and pull" method for opening the Buick's doors—latch buttons were hidden under the rocker panels.

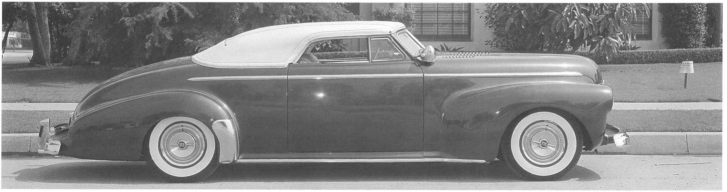

This shot, taken around 1956, shows off the Buick's fabulous profile. Note the hood louvers, chrome rear-fender guards, and '56 Buick hubcaps.

McGowan Brothers' Roadster

Even from the beginning, not all hot rods were built in California. Bobby and Frank McGowan were a pair of Branford, Connecticut, teenagers in 1955, a time when old Fords were cheap and plentiful. Bobby and Frank paid $7.50 each for a bare-bones 1931 Model A roadster and another $7 for a wrecked '40 Ford coupe. Then they bought a '32 Ford pickup from a local car club for another $20. As part of the deal, they had to give back the pickup body, which was fine with them because they only wanted the chassis. So, for $42, they acquired all of the chassis and body ingredients necessary to build a rod.

Local fabricator Charlie Hilde did the chassis work, which included Z'ing the '32 rails and fabricating hairpin radius rods to replace the stock wishbones. Jack Crump, a body man from just up the road in Guilford, hammered the '31 into first-class shape. Bobby bought a new Ford flathead truck block and outfitted it with a set of Edmunds finned-aluminum heads, a dual-coil ignition, Fenton cast-iron headers, and a

McCulloch supercharger for some substantial yet dependable horsepower. The '40 Ford donor supplied the transmission, rear end, brakes, and dash. The dual master cylinders came from a '54 Ford.

After the body was painted multiple coats of 1953 Buick Tahitian Red, local boy Jim Tyrell added tasteful pinstriping. Final touches included '50 Pontiac taillights, Chevy-truck headlights, and Stewart-Warner gauges.

The brothers raced their rod at the local dragstrip and showed it a few times, capturing the attention of the East Coast press. Despite the high profile, the car was mostly their daily driver.

The roadster stayed in the family for nearly 40 years before Bobby reluctantly sold it to collector Gordon Apker in 1995. Gordon had it professionally restored, insisting that authenticity be maintained. The restoration turned out so beautifully that the Model A was one of nine cars invited to represent the inaugural Historic Hot Rod Class at the prestigious Pebble Beach Concours d'Elegance in 1997.

La Jolla

Harry Bradley is one of the most respected custom car stylists in history. A well-known designer for General Motors and Mattel's Hot Wheels brand, Harry kept his hand in the custom car arena throughout his storied career. The car featured here, known as *La Jolla*, was not only Harry's first custom, it was his first car.

Harry acquired a 1951 Chevy Bel Air hardtop in '54 when he was still in high school in La Jolla, California, (hence the car's name). Part of the deal was a promise to his parents that he wouldn't modify the car. But as Harry put it in a 1985 article in *Super Rod & Custom* magazine, "They had gotten to me—'they' being Pinin Farina, Harley Earl, Joe Bailon, the Barris brothers. My parents didn't have a chance against the likes of them." Harry immediately began an extensive customizing process.

Every panel of the body received some customization. Harry dechromed the hood, then had friend Herb Gary pancake it, a process that involves molding in the hood, then cutting out a smaller panel from the flatter top portion. Harry installed an electric motor and twin screw drives to open and close the new hood.

After the top was chopped about three inches, Harry straightened the doors' upper lines and reskinned them. He modified the A-pillars to match the doors' new shape and installed custom-made one-piece glass in each door. To match the new windshield opening, Harry had new lower moldings cast in lead and chrome plated. The sheetmetal around the backlight was replaced with a piece cut from a '49 Plymouth that was narrowed and sectioned. The new opening was fitted with a '53 Pontiac windshield cut to fit.

Up front, Harry frenched the headlights, installed a '49 Merc grille opening, and fashioned a grille from copper. He also smoothed the bumper, removed the bumper guards, and added a '49 Chevy license plate guard. Out back, he pancaked the trunk as well and chose to utilize a continental kit. To work it in, he extended the rear fenders and installed hand-cut clear taillight lenses. The rear bumper came from a '52 Pontiac.

Perhaps the most unique elements of the *La Jolla* are the "floating" rocker panels. To make these, Harry and Herb cut new rockers and 1½-inch thick frosted-white Plexiglas to match. They installed the Plexiglas, then added the new rockers over the top. This created a more flowing line into the rear fenders. For an additional touch, Harry added LEDs at the leading edge of the plexiglass panels, causing them to glow like a lens at night.

At the time, lowering a custom usually involved installing lowering blocks that harmed handling characteristics. To avoid any handling and ride penalties, Harry lowered his car by channeling it behind the rear seat. To do so, he cut the frame ahead of the rear springs, raising the rear end 3½ inches within the body and thus lowering the rear suspension. Simple suspension modifications were made to lower the front end.

Stricken with polio at a young age, Harry couldn't drive a conventional car, so he had friend Floyd Martin make hand controls for the throttle and brakes. Under the hood, Harry installed a new 283-cid Chevy V-8 engine. For paint, he chose a deep chocolate-ebony candy pearl color.

The *La Jolla* is unique among custom cars in that Harry

owned it for more than 45 years, driving it much of the time. It followed him through college, family, and his automotive design career. Harry eventually sold the car in 1999 to noted custom collector Jack Walker. Jack worked with Harry to restore the car, adding two Bradley-approved changes. For the inside, Jack had Harry design a new rolled-and-pleated interior, which was rendered in white and light lavender by Bob Sipes. And outside, instead of brown, Jack had the car painted dark purple, a color that Bradley favored even in the '50s. The car toured the custom auto-show circuit for a while before retiring to Jack's stable of historical customs.

Buddy Alcorn Mercury

In the 1950s, it was not uncommon for finished customs to be remodified and updated to keep pace with quickly changing automotive fashion. This was especially true if the vehicle changed hands, since the new owner usually felt compelled to put his own stamp on the car.

This '50 Mercury was originally completed for an unknown owner in 1952 by Gil and Al Ayala. The two brothers performed the initial restyling, including the top chop, rounded hood and deck corners, and door handle and chrome removal. The top was chopped four inches in the front and a full 7½ inches in the rear, achieving a tapered slope with almost fastback proportions. The Mercury's signature doorline hump was reworked into a smooth "full fadeaway" body line, rear quarter panels and taillights from a 1952 Olds were grafted on, and the car was finished in a deep maroon color.

Buddy Alcorn then bought the car and brought it to Barris Kustom Autos in 1955, where Sam and George and crew updated it with new trim, taillights, and a deep eggplant-colored paint job.

The 1950s' best customizers were highly skilled at blending bits and pieces from various cars into a cohesive new design. There was no set template for all of this, no professional design degrees involved; these self-taught designers simply relied on their own innate design intuition. The Alcorn Mercury utilizes trim pieces from a variety of cars, each artfully blended into a harmonious whole. The headlight bezels are '52-54 Ford/Mercury items, which were extremely popular with customizers for their "frenched" appearance. The grille bar is a narrowed '52 Olds item with two extra teeth added. The front bumper is from a '51 Mercury, and the rear bumper is a '52 Ford piece with molded-in exhaust outlets.

Both bumpers sport '55 Pontiac bumper guards. A '55 Chevy trim spear forms the upper section of the side trim, while the lower part is an inverted '53 Dodge piece that borders a hand-formed scoop adorned with '54 Mercury teeth. Taillights were taken from a '55 Plymouth, and hubcaps are '56 Mercury units modified with bullet centers and color-keyed paint. To the credit of the Ayalas and Barrises, none of these additions and alterations looks tacked-on.

The Alcorn Merc, like other pre-1956 customs, exhibits an incredible amount of skilled labor, which was one of the reasons this style of custom almost became extinct. Traditional customs were falling out of fashion as the '50s progressed and Detroit's dreamboats got lower and flashier. For about the same cost, a car enthusiast could buy a new 1957 model fresh off the showroom floor, lower it, perform a few simple trim swaps and give it a wild custom paint job, and end up with a car with as much appeal as a heavily modified seven-year-old Mercury—with a fraction of the time and effort.

Buddy later traded his Mercury to Barris employee Dick "Peep" Jackson for Jackson's mildly customized '57 Ford. Jackson updated the Merc with a pinstriped two-tone paint scheme, then traded it away for a '57 T-Bird. Although it was one of the best-executed customs of its time, the Alcorn Merc's style had fallen out of favor. The car sat on a used-car dealer's lot, changed hands a few more times, then deteriorated as it sat outside exposed to the elements for many years. Noted Barris collector/restorer Kurt McCormick acquired its remains in 1998, then embarked on the grueling restoration process. The job was completed in 2002, and aside from mechanical updates and a few modern creature comforts, the Alcorn Merc appeared as it did in its original Barris form.

Moonglow

Most of the famous customs of the 1950s were professionally built by shops that specialized in customizing. The Ayala brothers, Barris Kustom, Valley Custom, and others honed their metalworking and design skills over time, and built truly high-quality, beautiful cars. It was rare that a custom car owner did the work himself, and rarer still were well-done homebuilt customs. The *Moonglow*, a '54 Chevy Bel Air built by commercial artist Duane Steck of Bellflower, California, endures as the most famous, and certainly the best homemade custom ever built.

Duane initially customized the car in his spare time over the course of 12 months in about 1956. He did most of the work himself, but he wasn't above a little help from his friends. With the aid of welder Ben Cook, Steck chopped the top 3½ inches, then he and his brother made a Plexiglas rear window. Duane heated the Plexiglas in his mother's oven to get it to conform to the right shape, then he and his brother burned their hands on it while running it out to the car. The top chop, combined with suspension alterations that dropped the car a total of seven inches, gave the Chevy a sinister look.

By the mid 1950s, more and more customs suffered from too much customizing. Not so with the *Moonglow*. Duane only made changes that enhanced the look. At the front, he frenched a pair of '52 Ford headlights, removed the chrome grille surround and bumper guards, added 10 extra teeth to the '54 Chevy grille, and shaved the hood trim.

In back, Duane extended the rear fenders by forming copper tubing and sheetmetal into sharkfin taillight housings. He filled those housings with '56 Chrysler taillight lenses turned upside down. Duane also shaved the trunk trim, and modified the stock bumper with bumper guards from a '56 Chevy to which he added integral backup lenses.

Duane had Del's Trim Shop cover the interior with powder blue and white upholstery in the stock pattern, and had the car painted to match. Larry Watson applied the pinstriping, and hubcaps with Olds flipper bars were added. The completed car appeared on the cover of the January 1957 *Car Craft*. This would become the car's most famous form, but, like other custom owners, Duane soon made changes to stay abreast of evolving trends and keep the car fresh for the show circuit. Over the next few years, the car received hooded headlights, a lowered rear bumper with the exhaust routed through it, Buick portholes in the rear fenders and hood, and two different paint jobs: one a metallic silver with white pearl scallops, the other a brilliant candy blue.

In the early 1960s, Duane traded the *Moonglow* for a sports car and within a few years it was crushed. Despite his considerable talent, Duane never built another notable custom, but the one he did build continues to inspire custom fans to this day. At least six clones of the *Moonglow* in its various stages have been built (including the white car shown in the color photos, which was built by Charlie Brewer of Hamilton, Ohio, in the early 1980s). That's an amazing legacy for any car, but it's even more impressive considering this car was built in his driveway by an unknown artist who would never build another custom.

Blue Danube

By the time Lyle Lake arrived from Florida in the mid 1950s and became shop foreman at Barris Kustom Autos in Lynwood, California, the gang at the shop had pretty defined roles. Sam Barris was the artist, designing the look for clients' cars and often executing it. George Barris was the front man, getting the shop's name out there.

As part of his efforts to tout the Barris name, George worked for Petersen's Trend Books, snapping pictures and writing articles on customizing techniques. Since Lyle worked at the Barris shop, George thought it would be a good idea to use the Buick the shop was building as Lyle's personal car in an article on the cost of customizing. So, camera and invoices in hand, George and Lyle documented everything along the way.

Lyle's 1951 Buick Riviera received extensive bodywork. Lyle and the Barris crew chopped the top three inches in front and six inches in the rear ($700), laying the rear window down to match the roof angle. This created a low, lean look that was complemented by several bodyside modifications. The crew shaved the doors and added pushbuttons ($50), installed handmade skirts ($20) and functional rear brake scoops ($55 each), and reworked the side trim using stock trim up front with straight trim running from the rear bumper to the middle of each door ($20 each). The trim choice was a curious one because many non-Buick customs of the day utilized Buick side trim for its unique, swoopy shape. Nonetheless, it worked, especially with the paint.

The face was also quite unique. Instead of a complete bumper, Lyle chose a rolled front pan flanked by two bumperettes made from '51 Chevy parts welded to Cadillac bullets ($80). The shop cut the grille from lengths of tapered tubing ($115) and rounded the hood corners ($10 each) to match the grille opening. The nose was dechromed ($25) and a California Custom Accessories headlight shade kit ($50) was frenched in, visually extending the fenders.

Some interesting touches were incorporated into the rear as well. Lyle added frenched taillights made by splicing two '54 Merc lenses together and installing them upside down ($65 each). The bumper was taken from a '53 Oldsmobile ($80) and the exhaust was routed through it ($70). Finally, thanks to the $190 lowering job, rollers were needed under the rear end to prevent the bumper from scraping on the ground ($20).

Barris applied the three-tone blue paint scheme ($250), with the top a sky-blue metallic, the main body pearl blue, and the bottom ocean blue mist—thus the nickname *Blue Danube*. Dean Jeffries, who worked at the Barris shop at the time, added white and copper pinstriping ($20). A set of 1956 Lincoln hubcaps ($15 each) completed the look. The total bill? $2000.

The *Blue Danube* garnered a lot of attention, appearing on the cover of *Trend Book 143 – Restyle Your Car*. It also showed up in the March 1958 issue of *Custom Cars*, and in an episode of the television show *The Twilight Zone*.

Unable to find the original, noted custom collector Jack Walker contacted Lyle Lake and learned it had been crushed. So Jack commissioned Kenny Baker and Dick Huckins to build the clone shown here in 1998. The original may be gone, but the Barris article on the car provides us a glimpse today of the price of admission for the best in 1950s customizing.

The original Blue Danube *in 1957.*

Junior's '50 Ford

In 1954, Herschel Conway was a 16-year-old car lover with lots of imagination and, as it turned out, a wealth of untapped ability. Already a devotee of the custom scene, he helped his brother Herb work on his 1950 Ford. The car had been lowered and given a straight bar grille before Herb bought it. After the brothers leaded in the door handles and decklid, and molded in the front pan, Herschel bought it and attempted to modify a pair '51 Merc skirts to fit.

Herschel had given the skirts their proper shape, but needed them welded together, so he approached friend Dick Jackson, who worked at Barris Kustom. Dick suggested they ask Sam Barris to do the welding. Sam did the job and told Herschel he had done a good job of forming the skirts. He even offered the shop's painting services for the car if Herschel would prep it. Sam and George Barris were so impressed with the job young Herschel did prepping the car that they offered the teenager, who they would give the nickname "Junior," a job at the shop after school. The Barris shop sprayed on a gold enamel paint job, and Junior immediately started entering it in shows. He won a few awards, but then rear ended someone and had to redo the front end. This lead to a second round of customizing that would make the car one of the more notable "semicustoms" of the day.

A semicustom is a car with some bodywork, but not any of the more radical procedures, like a top chop or sectioning.

Junior's car received a lot of attention all-around, but the top was not chopped and no sectioning was done.

As a teenager with little money to spend, Junior made a deal with Sam. Sam would fill and peak Junior's new '51 Ford hood and smooth out the holes in the bumpers if Junior would help Sam paint his house. That was just the beginning of the work on the redone front end. Junior added a pair of '53 Mercury bumper bullets and molded in a Mercury grille opening, and the Barris shop made the grille from metal rod and backed it with chrome mesh. The shop also molded in a pair of '55 Chevy headlights, added scoops to the hood, and rounded the hood corners.

Like the front, the rear bumper was smoothed and fitted with '53 Mercury bullets. Junior had the Barris crew add a finlike kickup at the trailing edge of the rear fenders, into which they frenched '56 Buick taillights. The stock taillight openings were then fitted with hand-formed frosted-plastic backup lights. The inside of the trunk, as well as the interior, was given maroon and eggshell-white upholstery by Jack's Top Shop of Los Angeles.

One Barris customizing trick at the time was designing side trim, often used from other cars, that would work for that particular custom. George designed the trim, which utilized a combination of '55 Ford pieces on the bottom, '53 Dodge parts on top, and gold mesh in between, and Junior installed it. Three gold-plated teeth were added to each fender skirt.

Later, Junior had the Barris crew fashion different rear fender skirts. These were made from '57 Mercury Turnpike Cruiser skirts with scoops cut at the leading edge. Lakes pipes were initially installed to exit from the bottom of the front fenders. Later they were moved to exit just behind the front wheels.

A few other notable details were incorporated. The Barris crew removed the center bar from the windshield and made the doors, hood, and trunk pushbutton actuated. Junior made the hubcaps, using Olds caps with bullet centers and Lincoln Continental fins, and had portions of them gold anodized. Under the hood, Junior installed a Mercury engine with a mild cam, Fenton heads and intake manifold, and Stelling & Hellings air cleaners.

George painted the car in 28 coats of "Sam Bronze," a translucent lacquer named in honor of his brother Sam, and laid out the design for the pinstriping, which was applied by Dean Jeffries.

Junior called his 1950 Ford semicustom *Teardrop* and entered it in many shows, winning more than 40 trophies. The car appeared in the 1959 movie *T-Bird Gang*. Junior sold the car to Johnny Zupan in '59. Johnny subsequently traded it for a hot rod, and from there, the car's fate is unknown. Junior's story is known, though. He built upon the skills he learned at Barris Kustoms to open Junior's House of Color in 1960 and eventually become one of the world's best automotive painters.

Dream Truck The story of the *Dream Truck* is a mix of insight, good luck, and the persistent leadership of Spencer Murray. Murray, the first editor of *Rod & Custom* magazine, gathered together and focused on a single project an improbable array of the best craftsmen of the 1950s customizing art. Starting with his daily driver, a '50 Chevy pickup, Spence set out to create a wild custom whose development could be regularly depicted in the pages of *Rod & Custom*.

The construction of the *Dream Truck* was covered in dozens of articles, starting in the September 1953 *R&C*. The project progressed through most every custom technique in its five-year odyssey, inspiring a generation of custom fans.

The project started with custom modifications, performed by a who's who of customizers, on a factory-fresh 1954 Chevy truck cab. Sam Gates chopped the top 3⅜ inches and sectioned the body 5⅓ inches. Neil Emory and Clay Jensen of Valley Custom finished the chop and sectioning work, and hand-formed the beautiful dashboard. Curly Davis finished the dashboard, integrated it into the door design, and widened the rear window. After Gene Winfield radiused the front-wheel cutouts and sectioned the hood, Barris Kustom added quad headlights, scoops to the roof and hood, and front and rear grille openings formed by molding together '54 Studebaker front pans. Bob Hirohata added the clear front and translucent red rear turn-signal lights. Later, Bob Metz

formed the wild scratchbuilt canted fins. Each of these craftsmen proved integral in the development of the truck.

The *Dream Truck* was given several mechanical upgrades with the aim at making the truck perform as well as it looked. To lower the truck, the rear spring perches were relocated, and an airbag suspension was installed and hooked to a semi-elliptical front-spring setup. Most importantly, the *Dream Truck* was the first vehicle to receive a documented small-block Chevy engine swap. The new-for-'55 V-8 would soon become a milestone engine in the rod and custom world.

As the project evolved, different versions and paint jobs emerged. First shown in gray primer with white scallops, the

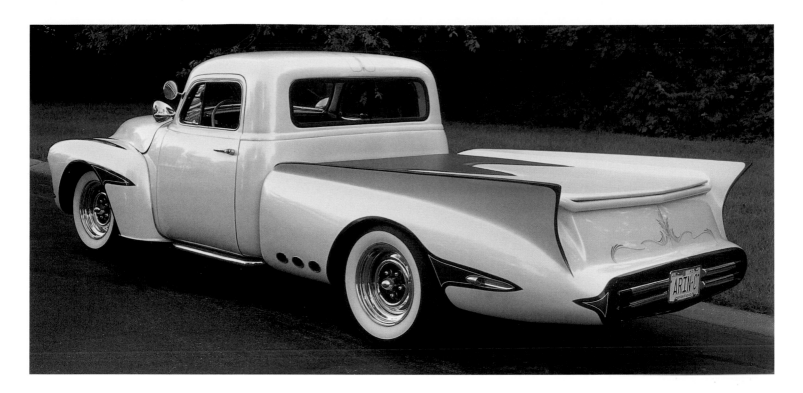

truck progressed to metallic lavender with Dean Jeffries-applied scallops, then to bright white with scallops, and ultimately to metallic lime gold with a fresh burgundy red scallop design. Each version was enjoyed by uncounted numbers of custom fans as Spence campaigned the truck at car shows across the United States.

This history might have been enough to cement the *Dream Truck* in custom car lore, but more was yet to come. In 1958, a tire blew on the pickup that was towing the *Dream Truck*, causing the iconic custom to flip end over end. After the horribly damaged vehicle was trailered back to California, George Barris displayed it—with the mangled bodywork—at car shows. Soon thereafter, Spence parted it out and sold the banged up vehicle to a buyer who never fully paid for it.

The *Dream Truck* disappeared until the late 1970s, when, after a decade of searching, Bruce Glascock found its worn-out hulk in California. Bruce acquired it, and asked Spence to help him guide the restoration. After months of difficult work, the *Dream Truck* was returned to its white paint livery and placed on the Darryl Starbird show tour. In 1986, Bruce sold the truck to custom car collector Kurt McCormick who rebuilt and modified the drivetrain and front suspension, then presented the truck again to the custom car world.

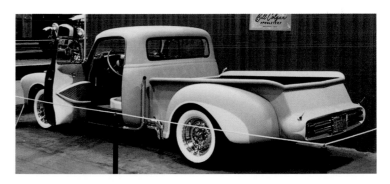

The *Dream Truck* has since been displayed at many venues across the United States, including a major cultural presentation at the Oakland Museum and, later, at Starbird's Rod & Custom Car Hall of Fame Museum in Afton, Oklahoma. Thanks to Bruce Glascock, Kurt McCormick, and Spence Murray, the combined effort of the 1950s' best customizers is well-preserved.

–Mark S. Gustavson

1

2

3

TV and Movie Rods

Although the original growth of the California hot rod movement was spurred by young World War II vets, the great burst of hot rod movies came nearly a decade later, beginning in the mid 1950s, as a reflection of the preoccupations of a younger generation of hot rod enthusiasts. The kids who comprised this new audience had been toddlers or just entering grade school in 1945. Ten or 12 years later, they were old enough to drive and, like the first-generation rodders, they came to the party with plenty of disposable income.

American business catered to these youngsters in many ways, of course: clothing, music, food, radio, television (remember rod-loving Kookie on *77 Sunset Strip*?). And then there were "teenpics," movies shot in a week to ten days by independent producers for $80,000 to $100,000, and usually released in pairs as double bills. Fast and gaudy, they became wildly popular at drive-in theaters, America's "passion pits."

Major Hollywood studios were slow to recognize the new audience demographic, partly out of cultural ignorance, partly because of inbred disdain for "exploitation pictures." Other, smarter moviemakers, who had heretofore existed on Hollywood's fringe, grasped that teenagers wanted to see hyped-up representations of themselves on screen. The most successful and visible of the hip independents, American-International Pictures (AIP), didn't even own traditional studio facilities. Instead, AIP leased space on an as-needed basis, and set up cofinancing and distribution deals with box office-savvy inde-

pendent producers like Roger Corman and Alex Gordon. AIP took a fat cut of each picture's gross, and used the profits from one movie to finance the next. This was assembly line filmmaking, granted, but it had energy and verve, and paid young audiences the attention that other, larger studios weren't providing

After science fiction, the hot rod/juvenile-delinquent thriller was the most popular teenpic genre. AIP's enormous success inspired Allied Artists, Howco, Filmgroup, and other indies who released hot rod pictures with metronomic regularity. By the late '50s, the B-picture units of Universal-International, Columbia, and even high-hat MGM had made their way to the dragstrip. A few stars emerged—Mamie Van Doren, John Ashley, Yvonne Lime, Brett Halsey—but the main appeal for audiences was the vicarious pleasure of witnessing rebellious, middle-class kids dismiss their parents as "square," and rip up the streets with their rods. The thrill of speed was complemented by rock 'n' roll, gang tussles, occasional comic relief, and lots of well-filled sweaters. Nobody claimed this stuff was art, but it sure was fun.

4

5

6

7

1. Hot Rod *(1950) is probably the first picture of its kind, arriving during the relatively early period of rod activity. The star, "Jimmy" Lydon, had gained fame in the 1940s playing squeaky-clean Henry Aldrich.* **2, 3.** *In "Mr. Kagle and the Baby Sitter," a 1956 episode of TV's Ford Theater, a hot rod becomes the chariot of eloping oldsters Charles Coburn and Fay Holden. Actor and T-bucket father Norman "WooWoo" Grabowski (far left, photo 2) was featured.* **4.** *June Kenny and Gene Persson are about to collide with a giant spiderweb in this sci-fi teen thriller from 1958.* **5.** *Chuck Connors, later TV's Rifleman, starred in* Hot-Rod Girl *as a cop whose attempt to set up a legal dragstrip is temporarily undermined by some bad apples. AIP released it in 1956 on a double bill with* Girls in Prison. **6, 7.** Dragstrip Girl *(1957) featured racer "TV" Tommy Ivo (photo 7, seated in passenger seat), who began his movie career in 1945, at age nine. He worked steadily until he turned his back on acting in 1962, to pursue racing full time.* **8.** *Dragnet star Jack Webb gets the facts about Tom Pollard's '29 roadster.* **9.** *Parents disapprove of hot rodding in* Teenage Thunder *(1957), but relent when the kids win races and act like good sports. Robert Fuller (second from right) later starred in TV's* Wagon Train *and* Emergency! **10.** *William Bendix (left) gets nervous when Junior wants to buy Jim Griepsma's '34 coupe in a 1956 television episode of* Life of Riley, *a show that often featured hot rods.*

8

9

10

Grabowski T

In 1952, Norm Grabowski, who had just been discharged from the service, set out to build a hot rod. He bought a 1931 Ford Model A V-8, but swapped the A body for a shortened '22 T touring body to which he added a radically shortened Model A pickup bed. He further modified the car by mounting the front axle forward of the front crossmember, suicide-style. This type of car, soon to be known as the "T bucket," would emerge as one of the most popular in hot rodding history.

For the right stance, Norm removed 20 inches from the rear of the frame, then Z'ed the rear rails using the removed sections. He extended the front of the frame five inches, installed the steering column in a nearly vertical position, and channeled the body six inches over the frame. For motivation, he installed a 1952 Cadillac V-8 with a GMC 3-71 supercharger. Final touches included a black paint job, red rolled-and-pleated upholstery by Tony Nancy, and false rails to cover the highly cobbled frame.

A movie executive spotted the car when it was at Valley Custom for chassis work and asked to rent it for his studio. It appeared in a few movies and television shows in 1955 and '56. After an actor damaged it, Norm decided that if his car was going to appear in movies, he would be the only one to drive it. And so began Norm's career as a Hollywood stunt driver and bit player.

Ever the tinkerer, Norm made several changes using studio money to offset the cost. He repainted the body '56 Dodge Royal Blue with flames and pinstriping by Dean Jeffries, swapped the blower for four Stromberg 97s on a Horne manifold, added the skull shift knob, and had a top made so he wouldn't be recognized as the stunt driver.

In this dress, Norm's T became a television star on 77 Sunset Strip. Set in Dino's Lodge on Sunset Boulevard, the show centered on valet/detective Gerald Lloyd "Kookie" Kookson, played by Ed Byrnes. Kookie combed his hair a lot, apprehended criminals, and drove Grabowski's T. Between its Hollywood career and a photo in the April 29, 1957, issue of Life magazine, Norm's T became a symbol of the public's growing acceptance of hot rodding. It also helped spawn a fiberglass-body aftermarket for for rodders who wanted similar cars (see 1968-vintage ad above).

Norm sold the T in 1959 to show-car enthusiast Jim Skonzakis, who modified it twice, the last time to a radical and controversial guise. The car still exists, but not in its most influential configuration. Fortunately, Franco "Von Franco" Costanza built a highly accurate replica of the car as it appeared on 77 Sunset Strip. That car, now owned by John LaBelle, is shown in the color photos on these pages and is the best living tribute to one of hot rodding's most important and iconic cars.

Life *magazine, 1957*

Circa 1960

Circa 1965

Ivo T

"TV" Tommy Ivo earned his nickname as a child actor in the 1940s and '50s, appearing in films and on the *Mickey Mouse Club*. When he turned 16 in 1952, he startled the local Burbank, California, Buick dealer by plunking down cash to buy a new car. He promptly went to the local strip to see what it could do. The Buick proved to be extremely slow, but the '55 Century he bought three years later was very quick. Tommy won his first time out in the '55, setting an A/Stock Automatic record at Pomona.

Winning whetted Ivo's appetite to go faster, and he soon set out to put a hopped-up engine in the lightest car he could find. Inspired by Norm Grabowski's recently built T-bucket, Tommy built a T-bucket of his own using a desert-derelict 1925 T touring body that he shortened to become a two-door. He shortened a Model A truck bed even more to house the battery and fuel tank. With the help of noted Buick engine builder Max Balchowsky, Tommy assembled and tuned the engine, a 402-cid Buick nailhead V-8 first equipped with four twos, then with Hilborn fuel injection. Tony Nancy, another hot rod legend, did the upholstery.

A feature in the August 1957 issue of *Hot Rod* revealed that this combination of light weight and more-than-ample torque netted 21 trophies in as many trips to the strip. The little T was exceptionally quick in the quarter-mile, running E.T.s of just under 11 seconds with top-end speeds of 119

mph. It was also beautiful and found its way into several TV shows and movies.

Tommy sold the car after only a year and went on to become one of drag racing's first touring professionals and a major contender in Top Fuel drag racing. After its retirement from drag racing, Ivo's T was reworked a couple of times; once by George Barris, who added square headlights. It served as a 1960s show car, and, along with Grabowski's T, as the inspirational prototype for thousands of fiberglass "Fad Ts." After sitting untouched for years, Jack Rosen, who had received the car from his father Hy, had it restored it to its original configuration. Ron Jones performed the restoration, doing justice to the quality work a young speed-obsessed actor did all those years ago.

1

Satan's Angels

Like their hot rodder counterparts, custom car enthusiasts have always gravitated toward one another, forming clubs of like-minded enthusiasts. By the mid 1950s, Southern California custom car clubs such as the Cut Outs and the Renegades, both of Long Beach, were thriving. In Northern California, the premiere custom club was the Satan's Angels.

Established in 1953, the club required its members to have a car either in progress or completed with no less than three body modifications. Members' cars had a distinct and similar look, mostly because the majority featured custom work by noted Bay Area customizer Joe Bailon. Club members themselves also took on a similar appearance. In addition to their club jackets, members adopted an unofficial uniform of black slacks and red suede shoes when gathered as a group at public functions.

At the club's height, members numbered close to 30, and the group was remarkably prominent in the custom car scene. At the 1957 Grand National Roadster Show, the Satan's Angels had no less than 12 cars on display, and a high percentage of club members' cars graced the pages of the hot rod and custom magazines of the day.

The group fizzled out in the early 1960s, as most members were pulled away by marriage and career obligations and the custom scene in general waned. Some members stayed in the hot rod and custom world. Frank Livingston, club president from 1955 to '57, would remain a lifelong enthusiast who owned several magazine-quality customs over the years. Member Jerry Sahagon went on to become one of the best custom upholsterers in the business.

The original Satan's Angels left a strong impression that persists even today. The club was reformed by a group of Bay Area enthusiasts in 2000, and shortly thereafter, Frank Livingston rejoined the club he had helped make famous almost 50 years earlier.

2

3

4

1. *This 1957 photo shows members (left to right) Duke Chavez, Stan Medeiros, Sonny Morris, Eddie Dameral, Nelson Passas, Ronnie Leal, Jerry Sahagon, Bob Johnson, and Frank Livingston posing with their customs in the parking lot of the Oakland Exhibition Center.* **2.** *Sonny Morris's Blue Mirage 1950 Mercury was extensively customized with a wild pancaked and peaked hood, scooped and hooded headlights, front and rear tube bumpers, and a '55 Plymouth grille. Interestingly, a top chop was not among the modifications.* **3.** *The Blue Mirage also boasted gold-plated bumper guards, '55 Plymouth taillight lenses turned sideways, and the all-important club plaque.* **4.** *Stan Medeiros's 1950 Chevy hardtop featured Olds flipper hubcaps, fender skirts, '55 Pontiac rear bumpers, and '56 Olds taillights in reworked rear fenders.* **5.** *Jerry Sahagon's 1951 Chevy coupe wore an unusual grille/bumper treatment crafted from two '54 Buick bumpers, round rod, and seven '53 Mercury grille teeth. Other customizing touches included scoops above the headlights and in the rear fenders, shaved door handles, reworked trim, and Olds Fiesta hubcaps. The candy apple red paint job was Joe Bailon's first.* **6.** *A young Jerry Sahagon shows off his Chevy's white tuck-and-roll interior. Jim Cook did this stitching, but Jerry would go on to open his own upholstery shop, Sahagon's Custom Car Concepts.* **7.** *This dazzling gold 1951 Chevy fastback belonged to Frank Livingston. Bernie Shanklin performed the initial bodywork, which included a 1955 Plymouth grille, '51 Frazer taillights in extended rear fenders, and a '51 Pontiac rear bumper. Later, Joe Bailon updated the car with scoops over the head- and taillights as seen here. Frank's Chevy also sported one of the first candy paint jobs, a Brazilian Gold and Tropic Tangerine two-tone. Painter Mel Pinnoli mixed the colors from printer's ink toners, and the paint faded quickly.* **8.** *Satan's Angels activity hit its peak in 1957, when the club had 12 cars on display at the Grand National Roadster Show in Oakland. Front and center in this shot are Frank Livingston's Chevy fastback and Ronnie Leal's '53 Chevy hardtop.*

5

6

7

8

1

Grapevine

Larry Watson was one of the most prolific and influential pinstripers and custom car painters of the late 1950s and '60s, so his own rides were naturally at the fore-front of custom automotive fashion. His first mild custom, a '50 Chevy two-door sedan called the *Grapevine*, was also one of the best.

Like many customs of the 1950s, the *Grapevine* went through multiple stages of modification. Ed Schelhaas of Bellflower, and later Jay Johnston of Compton, were enlisted to do the bodywork. To start, the stock trim and bumper guards were removed, '56 Buick side trim was installed, and a '53 Chevy grille shell (with 13 '53 Chevy grille teeth) was added. The Pacific Custom-stitched interior featured heart-shaped tuck-and-roll inserts on the carpet and seats.

The roof was left unchopped, but a truly ground-scraping stance was achieved via reworked A-arms up front, and a C'd frame and de-arched springs at the rear. The total drop amounted to nine inches in front and eight inches in the rear. Full length lakes pipes made the car appear even lower. The look was unbeatable, but steep driveways and speed bumps could be a problem, not to mention the frequent tickets from the police. This style vs. practicality/legality quandary led to the development of hydraulically adjustable suspension

2

systems in the early '60s.

Larry sold his Chevy in early 1958 and put the cash toward a brand-new '58 Ford Thunderbird, which he immediately customized with a severe lowering job and a panel-painted finish. The progression of the *Grapevine* is one example of how quickly fads changed and how restless most young '50s customizers were; the three distinct versions of the *Grapevine* Chevy shown here span less than three years.

3

4

5

1. *A young Larry Watson stands beside the Grapevine in its first form, before the grille shell was molded in and '56 Olds headlights were added. Sharp eyes will note that the stock '50 Chevrolet front bumper has been inverted for a subtle custom effect and the two-piece Chevrolet windshield has been replaced with one-piece Oldsmobile glass. This shot is from late 1956 or early '57.* 2. *The rear view shows off the reshaped fenders and inverted '54 Mercury taillights.* 3. *Larry and girlfriend Elaine Sterling pose with the Grapevine in its 1957 version. Notice that Larry managed to squeeze another four '53 Chevrolet teeth into the grille opening. Door handles were now shaved and scoops were added to the leading edges of the rear fenders.* 4. *This open-trunk shot reveals Naugahyde upholstery with fitted tools, flares, and first aid kit. Notice that the trunk floor was reworked for rear axle clearance.* 5, 6. *In early '58, Larry revamped his Chevy with a wild free-form scallop paint job. The skirts were removed and spotlights with painted-on hearts were added. Note the subtle bodyside crease that leads into the rear fender scoops. In this form, he renamed the car The Heartless.*

6

The Aztec

One of the most famous radically designed customs of all time emerged from the Barris Kustom shop in 1958, but it wasn't "officially" a Barris car. That's because two part-time Barris employees, Bill Carr and Bill DeCarr, spent two years building the car after hours.

Bill Carr was a car nut who had moved out to California in the early 1950s to be close to the hot rod and custom scene. He took a part-time job at Barris Kustom and bought a '55 Chevy convertible with a couple hundred miles on it that he mildly customized. Carr soon became disenchanted with the mild look and began dreaming of a more radical design. He talked to DeCarr, a longtime Barris metalworker, and George Barris about more-radical customizing ideas. George helped with a few sketches and soon the two Bills were hard at work on a car that would become known as the Aztec.

By the mid 1950s, Detroit's car had become lower and wider, taking some thunder away from traditional customizing techniques. For a custom to stand out, it had to have more radical and sometimes more baroque work done to it. Such was the case with the Aztec.

Bill and Bill started by undoing the mild customizing done earlier, then moved on to the radical new design. They reworked the front fenders to accept a set of dual headlights from a 1957 Mercury Turnpike Cruiser. The unique front-grille opening was created by molding together two widened '53 Studebaker lower-grille pans, one inverted over the other. This trick was used at the rear as well, only with a smaller opening. The Bills then mounted modified '57 DeSoto bumpers with '57 Olds license plate frames front and rear. They used metal mesh to fill the front- and rear-grille openings, as well as the areas between the headlight surrounds and the fenders. The hood and trunk were pancaked and two

scoops were added to the length of the hood. These scoops were also filled with metal mesh. A lot of metal shaping was necessary to smooth everything out in front and to create the widow's peak that flows from the center of the hood.

In back, the fenders were extended 18 inches with modified 1955 Studebaker Hawk fins worked in at a canted angle. The sides received '57 Mercury Turnpike Cruiser skirts modified with scoops that were filled with mesh screens. Custom trim was made from mild steel bar and extruded aluminum panels. The doors were shaved and given rounded corners.

Though the two Bills did most of the work, several key customizing figures of the day helped complete the car. Bob Hirohata lent a hand by making the taillight and backup light lenses from red and clear Lucite. Sam Barris chopped the windshield frame 3½ inches. Bob Houser of the Carson Top Shop made the three-piece top and stitched the white Naugahyde and copper Frieze-type velour upholstery. The upholstery extended to the headliner, dash top, trunk, and even the underside of the hood. Junior Conway prepped the car for paint, which was sprayed on in 30 candy tangerine coats by George Barris. Dean Jeffries did the pinstriping.

The completed car was a hit. It appeared in numerous magazines, and Bill Carr drove it to shows all across the country, meeting his future wife at one of those events. Bill eventually sold the Aztec to a man named Bobby Wilcoxson, who had robbed a bank in New York to raise the money to buy it! The car was impounded by the FBI, then bounced around from owner to owner. It was impounded again when the owner of the shop where it sat was arrested for drug violations. Eventually, however, Barry Mazza of Fort Pierce, Florida, realized a lifetime dream by buying the car and restoring it to the form shown here.

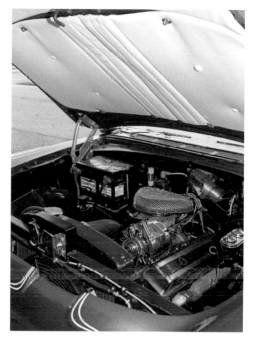

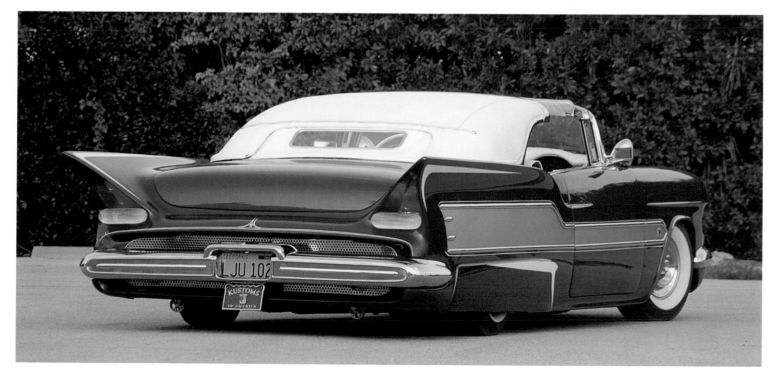

Custom Paint

When the pioneer of many custom paint trends says he feels partially responsible for killing off the custom car, you think he's kidding. But that is what Larry Watson said, and when you think about it, he's right.

Just before and after World War II, stock automobiles possessed heavily crowned body surfaces with square shoulder transitions, big proportions, and thick chrome accents. Customizing changed those proportions through chopping, channeling and/or sectioning, and lowering—along with other custom treatments like trim changes and frenched headlights. These modifications were performed to make each car a "one off."

But in the last half of the 1950s, Detroit's cars transitioned from soft and doughy to slick and slim. The elements customizers had been changing were now already there. Tops were thin, there was lots of glass, and the bodies had a sectioned profile right from the factory.

Meanwhile, an artist that went by the name Von Dutch was reinventing the age-old craft of pinstriping by applying free-form pinstriped designs to motorcycles and a few cars. Young enthusiasts Larry Watson and Dean Jeffries soon picked up on Von Dutch's designs and added their own ideas. What started as a few accent lines around a grille opening or headlight quickly blossomed into multicolored flame and scallop designs that wrapped around the entire car.

Watson was still in high school when he did his first stripe job, and soon he had cars lined up in his driveway when he got home from school, waiting for his touch. Jeffries started working out of George Cerny's shop and later Barris', adding his own wild designs to customer cars. Before long, the two young painters had their own shops.

In 1958, Watson changed everything again when he bought a brand-new Ford Thunderbird and introduced another form of custom painting. The combination of panel-painting and heavy body outlining set the mold for many customs to come. Watson's T-Bird also made use of another paint trend that was sweeping the custom scene: candy colors. Many painters had started experimenting with candies in about 1956. These translucent colors applied over gold or silver metallic bases were tricky to apply and they weren't perfected until about '58.

Soon, a lowered new car with paneling, body outlining, or other custom paint was enough to qualify as a custom. Chopping tops, frenching headlights, and all the other expensive, time-consuming body modifications became unnecessary. These mods were still being performed, but their popularity had lessened. In addition to Watson and Jeffries, George Barris, Dick Jackson, and Junior Conway were also creating customs with paint. All these men were pillars of the custom car community, so what they did was gospel.

Then, in the early 1960s, customs began to incorporate more sculptured surfaces that would be hidden if they were panel painted or scalloped. So, the trend moved away from paneling and toward solid candies and pearls. Though custom paint jobs have always elevated cars into the custom category, without the traditional scallops, paneling, or flames, the

Continued on page 102

1

2

3

1. The scallops on this 1957 Chevy are typical of Larry Watson's style. He would outline body transitions with a one-to-two-inch band of paint, then outline that with pinstriping. In many cases, scallops were added to hide areas where trim or badges had been removed and the resulting holes filled. This allowed the customer to keep the factory paint while turning his car into a mildly shaved and scalloped custom. This Chevy was customized by merely adding Dodge Lancer wheel covers, scalloping the body, installing Appleton spotlights, and swapping in a Corvette grille. 2. Jerry DeVito's wild San Jose-based 1957 Ford was called The Maze, for obvious reasons. The over-the-top scalloped paint job was applied by Bob Hendricks. Multiple colors were shot over a green base, then pinstriped in white. Other mild customizing tricks on the car included peaked fins, tunneled custom taillights, peaked rear roof scoops, and a rolled rear pan. 3. Dean Jeffries stripes around the flames on a 1957 Chevy. Flame painting could be seen on race cars and airplanes at least since the '20s. Its application on hot rods and customs was popularized by Von Dutch starting in the early '50s. Though they were more commonly seen on hot rods, some customs had wild flame jobs. 4. Dean Jeffries outlines the scallops in white on Joe Zupan's Barris-built 1956 Ford F-100 pickup, while John Chavez's '55 Olds with '56 Packard taillights sits in the background. "Jeff's" scallops contained more decorative motifs than Watson's, which tended to be straightforward outlining without the flourishes, reverse details, or hints of flame licks. Note also the cool hand-painted shirt Jeff is wearing. 4

5

Continued from page 100

distinction between a custom and a merely lowered new car became blurred.

When muscle cars such as the 1961 Chevy 409s, '62 Ramcharger 413 Dodges, and '63 427 Ford Galaxies hit the streets, they featured the same slick, sculptured bodies, but they now had big horsepower. So the trend changed again. Car enthusiasts started searching for more power and chasing quarter-mile times, diverting their attention from customs. One-of-a-kind looks became less important.

By the mid 1960s, metalflake paint jobs were part of the custom scene. The effect was achieved by suspending tiny metal flakes in a clear carrier and shooting it over metallic base coats. Watson also introduced two more paint creations: cobwebbing and lace painting. Cobwebbing involved shooting a panel with unthinned toner that came out stringy and made interesting patterns. Lace painting was done by laying down a piece of lace fabric as a mask, spraying over it, then removing the lace to reveal an intricate pattern. These techniques would be used on numerous custom vans, but that's a story for another book. By the late 1960s, the "ponycar" had become popular, Watson had quit painting in '66 to pursue an acting career, and the custom car had almost completely faded from the scene.

While it may have portended the demise of the custom car, "Watson-style" custom paint is strongly regarded for its flashy colors, interesting applications, and customizing ease. These paint schemes were works of art applied to the body of a car, and their effect can still be felt today.

6

5. Larry Watson performed his first flame job on Lowell Helms' 1950 Ford sedan. Besides the shaved door handles and trim, Helms' custom received '56 Olds headlights and a molded-in '53 Chevy grille opening, a lowered stance, and lakes pipes. The fades in this flame job were done by shooting the bronze first, then coming back in with silver. When Lowell decided he didn't like the silver, Watson went to a 24-hour auto parts store to get a white spray bomb. The quick fix at 3:00 A.M. was to cover the silver with the white spray paint. Watson roars with laughter over this episode today. **6.** Larry Watson tapes Al Lazurus' 1955 Chevy prior to shooting green "seaweed" flames. The name originated when Al cruised through a local drive-in and someone yelled, "Look at the seaweeds on that Chevy." Most flame jobs up to this point didn't feature the sinewy flame licks common in today's flame paint jobs. Most either utilized the "crab claw" type of flame licks, or the almost ragged short licks popularized by Von Dutch. Lazurus' Chevy changed that. An expert pinstriper, Watson would outline his scallops and flames to clean up any minor tape pulls or ridges created from the thickness of the newly applied paint. **7.** Jack James' 1957 Buick Special was Watson's fourth flame job, and one of his last using enamel paint. Enamel flames required a different technique than lacquers. Watson had to apply layers of different colors, then use rubbing compound to blend the layers together, creating a fade effect. James' Buick featured one of the most extreme flame jobs ever, with Watson's "seaweed" flame licks. The car was brand new and had no modifications other than lowering and Buick accessory wire wheels. Watson ended up in the hospital after spraying the Buick due to the effects of the lead in the enamel.

7

8

9

8. *This shot of Larry Watson's 1958 Ford Thunderbird custom is an outtake from the cover shoot for the 1959* Custom Cars Annual. *The publication named the car "Custom of the Year." The nitrocellulose lacquers of the era gave a lot of depth and exhibited really clean colors, but they didn't hold up well under the UV rays of the sun. This was the first of many Watson paint jobs to feature "paneling"—each body surface was inlaid with a complementary or contrasting color that stayed within the panel itself.* 9. *The first lacquer paint job on Larry Watson's 1958 T-Bird started to fade from sun exposure, so Watson did further paneling in purple and silver to hide the sun fades. The outlining accentuated the subtle body sculpturing of the stock sheetmetal. Body modifications were almost nonexistent, yet the car screams late-1950s custom.* 10. *Another way to panel a custom was to merely outline the trim and outside edges of the body. In the case of this 1958 Impala, the rear pillar was shot with the same gold used for the outlining. A subtle white pinstripe was run around the edges of the gold. Even the Impala badges and original trim were left intact.* 11. *Once Larry Watson had sold his award-winning '58 T-Bird, he headed over to the local Cadillac dealer and purchased this brand-new 1959 Series 62 coupe. Besides the custom interior and lowering, Watson applied one of his signature panel jobs over the base white factory paint. He also painted the top silver, and later ran chrome tape stripes over it, covering them with clear to hide the ridges. Within a year Watson would trade in his '59 for a used (but desirable) '57 Cadillac Brougham. That's Larry with photographer James Potter's daughter.*

10

11

Roubal Drag Roadster

In the 1950s, many a street roadster was subjected to its owner's quest for faster quarter-mile times. Drag racing, like roadster racing on the dirt before it, turned many fully equipped streeters into bare-bones race cars that were no longer legal to drive on the street. Southern California racers Jerry Norek, Bob Brissette, "Boof" Palmquist, and Tony Nancy piloted such cars. Some exceeded 150 mph in the quarter-mile.

This 1932 Ford roadster was first assembled by Bob Roubal of Long Beach, California, in 1956. He stuffed in a 1953 Cadillac 390-cid engine, painted the body candy-apple red and the frame black, then sold it to Bill Deming in '57, who added the roll bar. Deming soon sold the car to Bob Cash, who had Von Dutch paint the grille insert white with gold

stylized "Bob + Don" lettering (Don was Cash's brother). Cash, who owned a gas station in Buellton, California, also installed a set of Halibrand wheels (he was a Halibrand dealer) and swapped the Caddy engine for a 301-cid small-block Chevy with four two-barrel carburetors. In Cash's hands, the roadster set a B/Roadster record of 130 mph at the first Winternationals in Pomona, California, in 1961. Cash raced the roadster for close to a decade, until it was made obsolete by lightweight cars with fiberglass bodies and tubular frames.

The roadster changed a few more times until 1999, when Ralph Marano of Westfield, New Jersey, bought it. Ralph gave it a new lease on life, restoring it to the guise it wore when Bob Cash raced it. Now, however, the fit and finish far exceeds anything seen at the dragstrip in the 1950s or '60s.

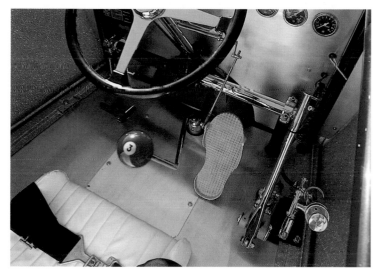

CHAPTER 3: THE 1960s
Challenge from Detroit

The decade of the 1960s was a strange period for hot rods and customs as both would witness a demise in popularity. Many factors created the right climate for nearly ending customizing and hot rodding, and much of it had to do with what was going on in Detroit.

Production cars were becoming more stylized, with thinner roofs, shorter body sections, and more sculpturing than anything that had been available through most of the 1950s. With slim, tall fins; lots of glass; and tighter body sections, they took on a look that was a natural progression of American automobile design. The look was hard to match by customs based on 1940s and early '50s cars. Even the radical customizing trick of body sectioning—mostly seen on 1949-51 Fords because of their slab sides—couldn't change the heavily crowned fenders, tops, and body sections that looked old compared with the latest from Detroit.

As production cars became more modern in appearance, they were also developing a wallop under the hood. The auto manufacturers were fighting it out in NASCAR and drag racing, and they met the challenge with increasing

also grabbed attention from hot rods and especially custom cars. In addition, numerous new-car options became available that were unheard of just a few years previous, swing-away steering wheels, disc brakes, and eight-track tape players among them. These items seemed futuristic from a 1950s perspective, but they were widely available on new cars in the '60s.

On the track, drag racing was becoming more sophisticated, and therefore more expensive. The era of the dual-purpose hot rod that served as both daily transportation and a race car was over. To stay competitive at the dragstrip, many hot rods were modified to the point that they could no longer be driven on the street. This was especially true in the Gasser classes, which originally came about for hot rodders who couldn't afford the more expensive race-car-only classes that required racing fuel and supercharging or fuel injection. But this wasn't the only turning point for hot rods in drag racing.

In 1965, the American automakers changed drag racing, as well as the perception of their products by young fans, in a big way. In the Modified Stock category, the factories battled it

Funny Car, the Gasser classes started allowing late-model bodies. Many of the more popular Willys, Austins, and English Fords were switched over to sleeker and more Funny Car-like Ford Mustangs, Chevy Camaros, and Plymouth Barracudas. It was another sign that the old was fading.

Custom cars and hot rods were, in part, a reaction to the bland fare coming from Detroit in the 1940s and early '50s. But by the '60s, U.S. automakers were creating machines that matched or exceeded customs in terms of looks and hot rods in performance. And while it was once a problem for a younger person to afford expensive equipment, young men of the '60s had easier access to credit and could therefore buy new cars.

For those with gasoline running through their veins, other automotive interests emerged that pried them from the seats of their rods and customs. Volkswagens and their offshoots, dune buggies, became popular beginning in the mid 1960s. *Hot Rod* and other enthusiast magazines ran ads selling fiberglass kits and how-to articles to go along with them. Some have likened the air-cooled VW engine to Ford's flathead because of its simplicity and the proliferation of aftermarket parts that became available.

Volkswagen was also partially responsible for another automotive diversion: the van craze. It started with VW "hipple vans" and spread to their American counterparts. The van movement wouldn't really take off until the 1970s, but it definitely began in the '60s.

By the late 1950s, car shows had become popular with custom owners, and their interest spawned the show car circuit of the '60s. But even in the '50s, a car wasn't eligible to compete a second year unless it had new modifications that distinguished it from its previous iteration. As a result, many of the wonderful customs of the '50s were slowly degraded from a styling standpoint with unnecessary changes in the name of competition. Canted headlights and more baroque styling features were turning the once beautiful cars into overdone statements that should have been left alone. This, too, began a gen-

cubic inches and engine configurations that were previously available only through speed shops. With the dawn of the muscle car era, you could drive off the showroom floor and take on anything, including the average homebuilt hot rod.

Besides muscle cars, Detroit began offering "personal luxury" cars—personified by the Buick Riviera, Pontiac Grand Prix, and Ford Thunderbird—that

out a quarter-mile at a time. In the interest of speed and better weight distribution, they altered the wheelbases of their factory entries, supercharged the engines, and modified or sometimes completely eliminated stock frames and suspensions. This ultimately produced the Funny Car, which took the limelight away from the older cars running in the popular Gasser and Fuel Altered classes.

Soon after the introduction of the

eral decline of the custom car genre.

But it didn't stop there. As the decade progressed, wacky show rods proliferated the show car scene. Ed "Big Daddy" Roth was one proponent of the genre with his wild fiberglass creations. As Ed tried to outdo himself each show season, his custom show rods went farther over the top, though they usually held some charm. Other rod builders got into the act, too, which led to ever-stranger creations. By the 1970s, this would manifest itself in such odd concepts as motorized toilets, Coke machines, and pool tables.

Another factor in the decline of customs in the 1960s was Hollywood. Some of the famed customizers of the '50s moved slowly away from building customs for individual customers to the more lucrative television and movie work. George Barris was the most notable of these, but Dean Jeffries also did customizing and stunt work for Hollywood, especially after moving his shop next to the Hollywood freeway adjacent to Universal Studios. Larry Watson actually became an actor, appearing in more than 150 television shows from the 1960s through the '80s. Even Von Dutch got into the movie scene, doing two cars for the Steve McQueen movie *The Reivers* and setting up timed explosives for numer-

ous movies. These were four of the key figures from the 1950s custom car era.

Not everyone had abandoned the traditional custom car. In the Midwest, Darryl Starbird and the Titus brothers (Jerry and Elden) produced customs based on both newer and older cars throughout the 1960s. In Northern California, Art Himsl and Rod Powell customized cars and did elaborate custom paintwork, carrying on the traditions of two other Northern California

customizers from the 1950s: Joe Bailon and Joe Wilhelm. But the custom was slowly evaporating from the car scene.

The enthusiast magazines provided perhaps the greatest evidence of the custom's decline. By the late 1960s, only *Rod & Custom* magazine was fea-

turing any sort of custom car, and the majority of these tended to be modified Corvettes with flared fenders, extended duck tails, and bubble hoods. Some of the last customs featured were based on later Rivieras and Chevrolet Impalas, but it was questionable whether they actually improved upon the stock designs. It seemed as if the end of the custom car was near.

Meanwhile, the hot rod world was changing with the times even though its numbers were dwindling. The overhead-valve engine, headed by the small-block Chevy V-8 that had made its debut in 1955, had pretty much eliminated the Ford flathead and even some of the earlier overhead-valve engines. Automatic transmissions were getting lighter and more efficient, and were finding their way into more hot rods. As the trends changed to thinner white sidewall tires, hot rodders followed as well.

As the decade progressed, stylistic changes in drag racing, like the use of magnesium wheels and raised front ends for weight transfer, appeared on street roadsters and coupes. A similar phenomenon had happened in the 1950s when Indy roadster characteristics such as hairpin radius rods and larger diameter tires in back and smaller

in front were adopted by hot rodders.

On the club scene, groups like the L.A. Roadsters, Bay Area Roadsters, and Early Times found their way into *Hot Rod*, *Popular Hot Rodding*, and especially *Rod & Custom* magazines with their high-quality cars and club gather-

ings, now called rod runs. Some of these club runs were combined to produce larger gatherings like the Roadster Roundup, which still continues today. Over the years, members of each of these clubs worked at numerous West Coast hot rod publications. This helped keep the hot rod fires fanned even as actual participation in rodding waned.

As the decade drew to a close and drag racing became more of a professional endeavor, engine and chassis builders and component manufacturers started businesses to cater to the latest speed equipment and service needs. Many of these businesses also made hot rod components. Kent Fuller, Dragmaster, Andy Brizio, Cal Automotive, and Speed Products Engineering (which would later become The Deuce Factory, specializing in street rod components) all supplied drag racing components or services, and advertised T-bucket kits. Others offering T-bucket kits were Ted Brown, Bird Engineering, and Total Performance in Connecticut. Some of these enterprises would lead off the second coming of the hot rod in 1970.

Though the 1960s ended on a down note, some new and exciting developments were in the works for the hot rods of the '70s, while the custom car would slowly begin to make a comeback as its old self. A new era and a new generation of enthusiasts were about to burst onto the scene to remember and preserve the old and bring on the new. ⚒

Jade Idol

Jade Idol By the early 1960s, one-upsmanship had caused many customizers to employ radical modifications that too often resulted in overdone, overly ornate, baroque styling statements. It took a keen eye to make wholesale changes yet maintain a cohesive design. The *Jade Idol*, a '56 Mercury built by Gene Winfield for Leroy Kemmerer of Castro Valley, California, has withstood the test of time to remain an attractive example of '60s radical customizing even today.

Working from his Modesto, California-based shop, Winfield performed so many body modifications that the car was no longer recognizable as a Mercury. The major work involved sectioning the car four inches, replacing the rear quarter panels with '57 Chrysler units, and creating completely new front and rear treatments.

A lot of thought and effort went into making the radical changes work. Winfield lowered the car by cutting the front coil springs and adding lowering blocks in the rear. To match the Chrysler rear-wheel cutouts, he grafted a '57 Dodge's flared front-wheel openings into the Merc's front fenders. He also reshaped the front fenders to house canted dual Lucas headlights, which he highlighted with gold trim rings taken from '59 Imperial hubcaps. Winfield left the car's smooth body sides unadorned, but tacked a pair of wide metal appliqués onto the roof.

Winfield completely fabricated the front and rear treatments. He made the front grille surround and rolled pan from round rod and sheetmetal, then cut five rectangular bars to form the grille. He crafted the unique nerf bar-type front and rear bumpers from 1½ x 3-inch rectangular tubing and added

rubber inserts. At the rear, he fashioned a new grille opening and rolled pan and molded them into the rear quarters. Along the way, he inset the license plate and reshaped the trunk. The taillights were made by hand and trimmed with chromed vertical blades. Rectangular rear grille bars were added to match the front.

As a show custom, the interior received the full treatment, too, including a gaugeless dash (the gauges were relocated to the steering hub) with a television mounted in the center. Custom swiveling bucket seats were installed up front and a wraparound lounge-type seat was added in the rear. The seats were upholstered in white-pearl pleated Naugahyde and green-velvet button-tufted upholstery, and the floor was covered in shag carpeting.

In addition to its stylish customizing, the *Jade Idol* earned acclaim for its unique paint job. Searching for a signature look, Winfield sprayed on a blended white pearl, gold, and emerald green paint scheme. It was the first application of what would become a Winfield trademark.

Outfitted with chrome reversed wheels, the *Jade Idol* stormed the show circuit, winning too many trophies to count. Within a few years, it was involved in an accident while in Bill Cushenbery's care. Since the top was crushed (see photo on opposite page), Cushenbery cut it off and installed a new one. He also removed the roof appliqués and repainted the car, applying a toned-down but faithful version of Winfield's original fade.

Fast forward to 1978, when Jerry Rehn of Salinas, California, found the car in a state of disrepair and had it

restored. Jerry changed some elements along the way, adding Buick wire wheels, Stewart-Warner gauges (now in the dash), numerous electrical controls in the full-length center console, and another blended paint job, this time by Rod Powell.

In the early 1980s, Jerry sold the car to Bob Page who had it repainted in a light pearl mint green color with subtle shading. Page sold the car to Billy Belmont of Belmont Rod & Custom in Dedham, Massachusetts. In Belmont's care, the *Jade Idol* was chosen to be a part of a 1996 exhibit at the Oakland Museum of California, where it took its rightful place among a select group of history's most important hot rods and customs.

Eclipse

In the late 1950s, Ray Farhner was a Midwest custom shop owner looking to make a splash. He decided the best way to demonstrate what his shop could do was to build a wild show vehicle that would straddle the line between custom and hot rod.

Farhner enlisted young Doug Thompson to design and help build an elaborate show vehicle based on a 1932 Ford roadster pickup. Working from Farhner's Independence, Missouri, shop, the pair put an estimated 4500 man hours and $4400 into a unique pickup that earned Ray Farhner Kustoms accolades as one of the country's top custom shops.

To lower the pickup, Ray channeled the body six inches over the frame, reversed the front spring, and installed a three-inch dropped front axle. A four-inch top chop helped visually and literally lower the truck further.

Practically no body panel was left unmodified. The grille area was completely fabricated to house quad canted Lucas headlights and a grille made of '58 Ford grille mesh and '58 Cadillac teeth. Ray and Doug set the headlight pods on either side of the grille and faired them into the hood panels. They also molded in the grille shell, hood, front fenders, and running boards; cut a new hood opening; and smoothed over the louvers. Handmade L-shaped nerf bars and dual spotlights completed the front-end styling.

Doug's original plans called for a box-shaped bed, but Ray used a pair of modified '59 Chevy rear quarter panels as the bed sides for a more sculpted look. The duo molded a pair of '29 Model A fenders (turned backward) into the Chevy quarters, and incorporated a rolled pan with an inset license plate. The rear fascia was filled with 1958 Cadillac grille teeth and

'59 Caddy taillights, and wraparound bumperettes were set into the pan. At the top of the bed, Doug and Ray grafted in exhaust tubing to house twin antennas, and below that they ran exhaust pipes made from Ford Model A driveshafts. The bed floor was done in Philippine mahogany, and Ray finished it off with a tonneau cover.

Art West of Kansas City stitched the white Naugahyde upholstery, adding blue buttons and carpeting. The upholstery extended beyond the custom bucket seats to the padded dash, padded step pads on the running boards, and even the bed and engine compartment. West also upholstered the custom top, which featured four-inch overhangs front and rear.

Underhood, Ray installed a hot 1953 Cadillac V-8 bored ⅛-inch over and fitted with an Isky cam, Jahns pistons, Edelbrock manifold, triple Stromberg 97 carbs, and a '39 Ford transmission with Lincoln Zephyr gears.

A set of 1956 Chrysler wire wheels and 22 coats of Moonglow Pearl lacquer, a light blue color, completed the exterior. Ray dubbed the pickup the *Blue Angel* and competed at the 1960 NHRA show in Detroit, where it beat out the *Ala Kart* for best of show. Ray even took the pickup to Oakland to compete in the '60 Grand National Roadster Show.

Within a couple of years, Ray had changed the paint to a darker shade of blue and the name to *Eclipse*. At about this time, Ray started his own show series, and the *Eclipse* became a regular featured custom at Farhner's shows.

Eventually, the *Eclipse* was relegated to storage until custom collector Jack Walker bought it from Ray in 1979. Ray sold the pickup with the stipulation that Jack would have Doug

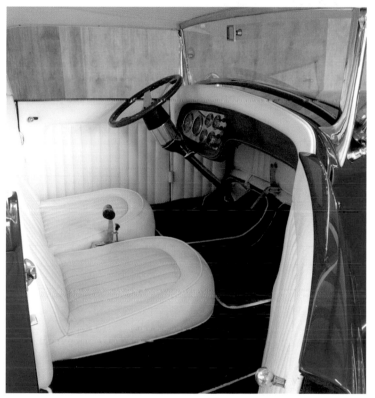

Thompson restore it and let Ray use it on his show circuit again. Jack agreed, and Doug set to work on the pickup he had helped create years earlier. Doug made some changes along the way. He removed the step pads and tonneau cover, made a walnut box for the inside of the bed, and cut a Plexiglas bed floor that would allow a view of the rear end. He also upgraded the truck with modern components, including a Ford 302-cid V-8, a Jaguar independent rear suspension, a Super Bell front axle, and disc brakes.

Jack leased the *Eclipse* to Farhner for two years, then took it on his own extended tour that included a trip to Europe and six years at Darryl Starbird's National Rod & Custom Car Hall of Fame Museum in Afton, Oklahoma. The pickup was restored again in the mid 1990s, and Jack sold it to Mark Moriarity of Mound, Minnesota, in 2005, just weeks after Ray Farhner passed away.

Predicta

In early 1960, Wichita, Kansas-based Darryl Starbird set out to construct an adventurous and futuristic vision of the classic two-seat Ford Thunderbird. Starting with a wrecked '56 T-Bird, Starbird created a sleek, graceful, and powerful personal custom like nothing seen before.

The design began with two 1959 Buick rear quarter panels that Starbird welded to the T-Bird. He left the shape of the doors mostly intact, but continued the edge of the rear quarter fins along the tops of the doors, across the front fenders, and into the front grille shell where they formed the upper lip.

Starbird used steel tubing to define the shape of the front fenders, rolled pan, and headlight panel, then covered that with handformed sheetmetal. In the grille shell, he installed dual headlights fitted with frosted lenses. The grille itself went through several different designs, starting with polished copper tubing surrounding many painted '59 Cadillac taillights. Later, chromed spheres were added front and rear, and finally, Starbird settled on horizontal aluminum grille bars.

Starbird used a '56 T-Bird hood as the trunklid. He populated the rear grille with 28 more '59 Caddy taillight lenses, 22 of which he painted white. The other six were painted translucent red and wired to act as the taillights.

Perhaps the most striking feature of the car was its Plexiglas bubbletop, a first for custom cars. With only the mounting ring to define its perimeter, the top was heated and blown into shape with compressed air, then attached to the mounting ring with small screws. The ring, in turn, was attached to two hinges bolted to the body. Starbird added a body-color

metal windsplit that started at the rear, conformed to the top, tapered to a point, and had twin antennas at the leading edge.

The interior appointments consisted of upright bucket seats and dual-cantilever dash pods upholstered in white-pearl Naugahyde with rhinestone buttons. A speedometer, ignition and light switches, other controls, and a television were mounted on the chromed center console. Starbird added a center-mounted tiller that made it possible to steer the car from either seat, and added pedals to each side.

In the engine compartment, the firewall was chromed and new inner wheelwells were fabricated, and three underhood gauges were added to aid engine tuning. For power, Starbird installed a 1957 Chrysler 392-cid Hemi engine mated to a Chrysler automatic transmission. He first fit it with Hilborn fuel injection, but later switched to multiple single-barrel Falcon carbs that proved to be more tractable. Virtually every

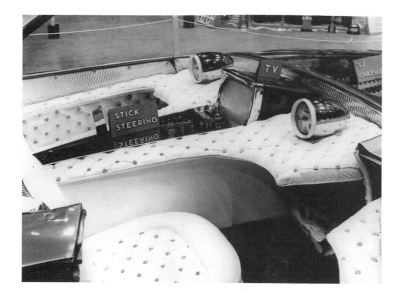

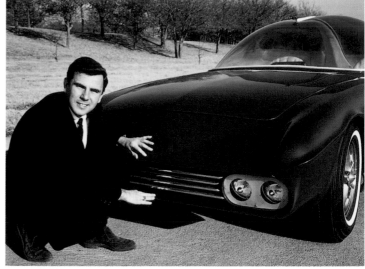

Circa 1963

removable part on the engine and suspension (still the original T-Bird setup) was chrome plated.

After less than two months of intensive construction, Starbird trailered the car to California to compete in the 1960 Oakland Roadster Show. *Motor Life* magazine chose it as the best custom of

Mid 1970s

the year. Starbird drove the *Predicta* regularly, racking up more than 30,000 miles. He even ran it down a dragstrip in late 1960, crossing the finish line at 101 mph.

Like most famous customs of the era, the *Predicta* went through several changes, many while still painted in its original metallic blue. Then, in 1963, model-kit manufacturer Monogram purchased the car to produce a scale model kit. Starbird restyled the car for Monogram by flaring the wheel openings, rounding out the front-grille shell, installing new grilles front and rear, recessing the bubbletop into the body, installing new recessed seats, and painting the car candy red. In 1970, Monogram gave the car away as a contest prize. Ironically, the contest winner was Darrell Zipp, a design engineer for rival kit-manufacturer Revell. Zipp eventually traded the car for a motorcycle, and the new owner painted the car metalflake silver and installed a blower.

In the late 1970s, Starbird discovered the car, bought it, and restored it to its original splendor, removing the windsplit. The *Predicta* now sits proudly in Starbird's Rod & Custom Car Hall of Fame Museum in Afton, Oklahoma.

–Mark S. Gustavson

Circa 1980

The Grasshopper

One of the most influential custom shops of the 1960s was located in Detroit and operated by two talented brothers, Mike and Larry Alexander. Mike and Larry originally built *The Grasshopper* 1931 Model A pickup in late '58 as their shop truck, but over the next few years it became too nice for chasing parts. In fact, it won awards at many custom shows and served as a rolling calling card for their business throughout the '60s.

The custom work on *The Grasshopper* was relatively subtle by Alexander Brothers' standards, but still quite involved. They chopped the top 2½ inches, swapped the '31 fenders for '29s, installed a larger '32 Ford pickup bed, and replaced the stock Model A grille shell with a reworked '32 Ford unit.

The "A Brothers" had an ability to adapt disparate parts into a cohesive design. On *The Grasshopper*, they incorporated a set of '42 Dodge truck headlights, taillights made from '47 Kaiser interior lights, and '54 Chevy side trim for the edging on the running boards. They also outfitted the handmade dash with Chrysler gauges set within a surround made by welding two large U-bolts together. Reflecting on the truck, a modest Mike said, "I don't know what all of the fuss is about. It was just a stock A-V8 pickup truck that we used every day. It only had a few minor changes done to it."

The brothers closed their shop in 1969 and went on to separate careers. Over the years, they lost track of *The Grasshopper*, which eventually ended up in the hands of pinstriper Don "the Egyptian" Boeke. Don sold the pickup back to Mike so he could restore it.

Mike revised the truck with many modern mechanical updates but retained its vintage appeal. He replaced the frame with a reproduction Model A unit, and sent the original '51 Ford flathead to Motor City Flatheads. Motor City added electronic ignition and gave the Offenhauser heads, dual Stromberg 97 carbs, and Edmunds manifold a better-than-new luster. A Ford C4 automatic replaced the '39 Ford transmission, but inside Mike maintained the look of the original by installing a gennie floorshifter.

Mike is quick to credit the many talented artists he enlisted to rebuild the truck. The Gaffoglio family, Bob Hedrick, and Kenny Pfitzer of Metalcrafters, Inc. in Fountain Valley, California, were instrumental in the rebuild. Little John, also of Fountain Valley, stitched the upholstery, and Paul Hatton, who did the original tailgate lettering and pinstriping, reprised his work. Final details were handled at Special Projects in Plymouth, Michigan, with the help of Ken Yanez.

From the outset of the restoration, Mike wanted to finish in time for the 50th Detroit Autorama in February 2002. He accomplished his goal, and *The Grasshopper* appeared with many of its former shopmates in a special tribute to the Alexander Brothers.

Golden Indian

Aside from talent and vision, timing and location are the major contributors to the making of an iconic hot rod or custom. Southern California's unique blend of artistic talent, car culture, and automotive media makes it the backdrop for many of the best-known cars. But for one teenager in 1960, Detroit provided all the talent and inspiration he would need to build a landmark custom.

Mike Budnick was just 18 years old when he bought a new 1960 Pontiac Ventura and used it to cruise historic Woodward Avenue. A chance meeting with another Pontiac owner who drove a car mildly customized by the Alexander Brothers inspired young Budnick to take his Ventura to the Alexanders' shop for a little personalization. As it turns out, the combination of a lively cruising scene in Detroit with the immense talent of the Alexander Brothers produced the *Golden Indian*, a unique example of advanced 1960s custom styling.

The transformation began in January 1961 with the traditional nose, deck, and shave treatment. Fresh out of high school, Budnick didn't have the money to complete the project all at once, so the car was in and out of the "A Brothers" Littlefield Street shop over the next two years. In that time, it received a complete overhaul.

The design wasn't planned. Instead, the A Brothers would mock up their ideas in cardboard and let Budnick give the thumbs up or down. Mike Alexander told *The Rodder's*

Journal, "Mike Budnick basically turned us loose." Whereas most customs of the day utilized parts from other cars, the *Golden Indian* would feature many handmade custom cues.

Other than the roof, every body panel received some type of work. Up front, the A Brothers removed the bumper and replaced it with a fabricated rolled pan. They tucked in the front fenders to meet the pan, flared and radiused the wheel openings, and rounded the hood corners. Chrome tubing formed the grille, and sheetmetal was handformed into the unique extended headlight housings.

Out back, the A Brothers extended the rear end with a new sheetmetal rolled pan and inserted an aluminum bar grille to match the front. They removed the stock taillights and created new lenses from red plastic with white plastic trim bars.

Rear fender work was needed to match the work done on the rear end. The fenders received integrated scoops, and the upper trim piece was cut to end at the car's trailing edge instead of wrapping around. The A Brothers also sunk the lower side trim into the body, rounded the doors, and added dual sunken antennas to the driver-side door. Custom mixed candy lime-gold paint and chrome-reversed wheels with two-bar knockoffs gave it the right look, and a lowered suspension gave it the right stance.

Inside, the Alexander Brothers farmed out the rolled-and-pleated pearl-white Naugahyde upholstery work to a local

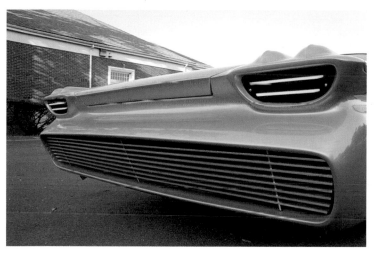

shop called Ray's Kustom Trim. The A Brothers made swiveling front bucket seats and set them on polished-aluminum channels. Gold carpeting, a padded dash, chromed moldings, and a '63 Grand Prix steering wheel added to the look.

Underhood, Budnick added chrome touches, Offenhauser valve covers, and Royal Pontiac air cleaners.

The car appeared on the cover of the November 1963 issue of *Rod & Custom*, then changed hands several times over the years, until it wound up in the possession of Lou Calasibetta of Stillwater, New Jersey, in '87. Calasibetta, owner of the Old Stillwater Garage, kept the car in mothballs until inspiration struck him in '99 at the 50th Annual Grand National Roadster Show. The show's tribute to George Barris started Calasibetta thinking. He figured the Alexander Brothers deserved a tribute of their own, and the 50th Detroit Autorama, set for January 2002, was the perfect venue. He called Bob Larivee, the Autorama's producer, with the idea, and gave the Old Stillwater Garage the task of returning the *Golden Indian* to its former glory.

Two and a half years later, the impeccably restored *Golden Indian* appeared at the 50th Detroit Autorama among a handful of other Alexander Brothers cars. Popular with showgoers, the display was a fine tribute to one teenager's dream and the talent of Detroit's finest customizers.

The Avenger

As the hot rod show circuit gained popularity throughout California in the late 1950s, entrepreneur Don Tognotti was in the thick of things around the Sacramento area. He built cars, ran a speed shop, and promoted regional shows.

Don bought a 1932 Ford five-window coupe for $200 in 1960 and built it for show and go. Along the way, he kept detailed "build sheets" noting the price (many of those prices are listed here) and date of all the parts and work. Don altered the frame considerably, extending it four inches, vertically narrowing the rails, and pinching them in front. He chopped the top three inches and channeled the body ten inches up front and eight inches out back to create one of the first wedge-channeled rods. The resulting rake created an aggressive stance that enhanced the overall look. He made the unique insert for the cut-down grille shell from ⅜-inch clear plastic rod and simple metal mesh. The chromed firewall (Don paid $22) reflects the highly finished engine.

The engine of choice was a 1951 Chrysler Firepower 331-cid Hemi ($200) with four Stromberg 97 carburetors ($70). Don mated the Hemi to a '37 DeSoto transmission and chose a '42 Ford panel rear end ($28.60) and driveshaft. The custom-bent headers ($220) are a work of art, as they sweep gracefully from the engine around the frame and under the car to the rear with nary a muffler or weld in sight.

Don had the interior finished in black with the stock dash replaced by tuck-and-roll padding to match the header panel. He placed the speedometer, temperature gauge, and fuel gauge between the seats on the floor. The upholstery cost him $250.

Don painted the car Aztec Golden Copper and dubbed his $4056.22 creation *The Avenger*. The coupe won its class at the 1961 Grand National Roadster Show, then embarked on a series of shows. It also saw plenty of action at the dragstrip. After its first magazine appearance in the July 1962 issue of *Car Craft*, Don sold the car to Bob McCloskey, who modified it. The reworked coupe appeared in the September 1962 *Rod & Custom*. Well-preserved, it also appeared in magazines in the '70s and '80s.

Ken McBride of Seattle bought the coupe in 1996, and restored it with the help of the build sheets that Tognotti had delivered to him. After the restoration, the car was displayed at the prestigious 2001 Pebble Beach Concours d'Elegance in the Hot Rod Coupe class. Fittingly, *The Avenger* once again did show duty, though it will probably never make another run at the dragstrip.

Little Deuce Coupe
In 1955, 15-year-old Clarence "Chili" Catallo paid $75 for a '32 Ford coupe that became his ticket to the hot rodding scene he so loved.

Scraping together pennies by working in his parents' market in Taylor, Michigan, Chili had Bill Wanderer build and install a 344-cid Olds V-8. Chili rounded out the driveline with Olds parts, including a Hydra-Matic transmission and a chromed '55 rear end. Local customizers Mike and Larry Alexander did the bodywork. The A Brothers sectioned and channeled the body, added a quad-headlight fiberglass nose, made a special rolled rear pan, altered the frame, and covered the cobbled frame rails with polished-aluminum fins. Topped with a blue-lacquer paint job, Chili dubbed the car *Silver Sapphire*.

Chili drag raced the car, turning 12.9 seconds at 112 mph in the quarter-mile, then hauled it out west when he turned 18. He landed a job sweeping floors at George Barris' shop in Lynwood, California, and traded his labor to have the crew there tear down the car, chop the top, and repaint it.

By 1961, the car was an all-out show rod. It now featured a 6-71 blower, three Stromberg 97s carbs, chrome-reversed wheels, a padded and tufted Naugahyde roof insert, and scads of chrome plating.

By campaigning the coupe on the West Coast show circuit, Chili caught the attention of *Hot Rod* magazine, and the car appeared on the July 1961 cover. Its greatest fame, however, came in '63, when it appeared on the cover of The Beach Boys' album *Little Deuce Coupe*.

Chili sold the car, now known as the *Little Deuce Coupe* at the height of its popularity. It went through three owners by 1963 when Ray Woloszak bought it. Ray changed the car over the years, installing a Chrysler 440-cid engine, and took it on the auto-show circuit. When Chili's son, Curt, saw it at a Detroit custom show in '97, he convinced Chili to buy it back.

Now back in Michigan, Chili and Curt began restoring the coupe to the way it looked in the *Hot Rod* magazine shoot that was used for the Beach Boys album cover. Unfortunately, Chili passed away before the car was ready to return to the limelight. Curt forged ahead, however, enlisting the help of many of the men who originally worked on the car, as well as General Motors. Recognizing the blown Olds engine as a significant part of the company's history, GM helped Curt with the engine and drivetrain rebuild.

The restored car appeared at the Pebble Beach Concours d'Elegance in 2001 and at the 50th Detroit Autorama in 2002. After many changes, the *Little Deuce Coupe* now looks like it did when The Beach Boys made it one of the most famous cars in the history of hot rodding.

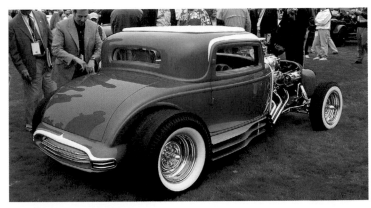

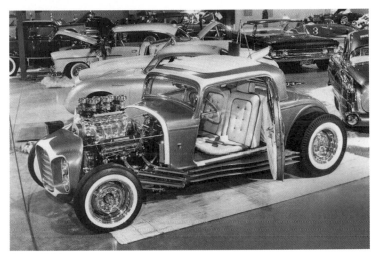

Circa 1961

Prior to final restoration as it appeared on the 1997 custom auto-show circuit

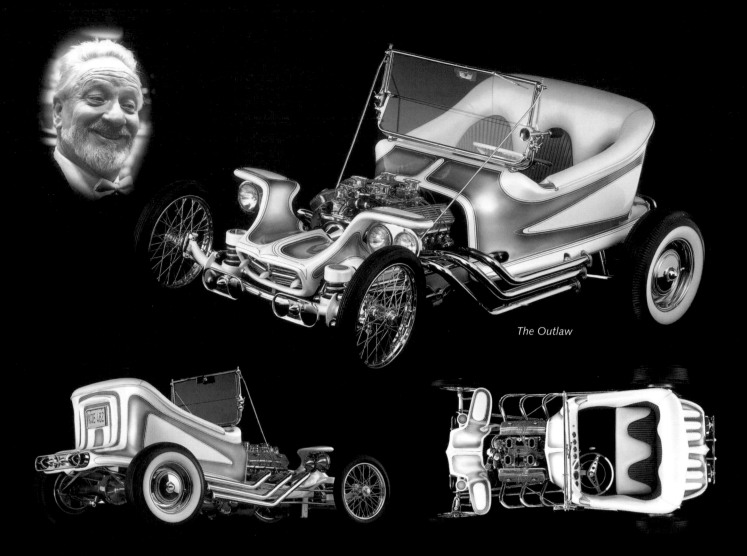

The Outlaw

Ed "Big Daddy" Roth

Perhaps no single character better personifies the often cartoonish irreverence and perverse genius of the hot rod and custom scene better than Ed "Big Daddy" Roth.

Born in Beverly Hills in 1932, Ed built several hot rods for himself in the 1950s and gained a reputation as a pinstriper and painter of bizarre, airbrushed monster T-shirts. He became enthralled with the possibilities of fiberglass after seeing a photo of Henry Ford hitting a '41 Ford's prototype soybean plastic decklid with a sledgehammer to demonstrate the strength of alternate building materials.

Ed built his first fiberglass-bodied car, the *Outlaw*, in 1959 and set the hot rod and custom world on its ear. A radical T-bucket with a handmade fiberglass body and nose, the Outlaw was a serious departure from Detroit production-based bodies, and it expanded the boundaries of what a hot rod could be.

Ed opened his own shop/studio in 1960. Roth and his crew churned out about a car per year for a decade. The first car put out by the shop, the *Beatnik Bandit*, is generally considered Roth's masterpiece. Built that first year, the *Bandit* featured a free-form, bubbletopped fiberglass body over a radically shortened '50 Olds frame. An outlandish "monostick" lever controlled the throttle, steering, and braking. A heavily chromed, blown Olds engine filled the engine compartment.

The *Mysterion*, built in 1963, featured wild asymmetrical styling, a handmade chrome frame, and twin Ford 390-cid engines. Roth Studios built the *Druid Princess* in '66 as one of its last four-wheeled cars. The body featured a Cinderella-style carriage cab, and a four-barrel carb was hidden under the faux blower on the 383-cid Dodge engine.

Roth traveled with his custom rods to shows nationwide, where he sold cartoon-monster T-shirts. Ed's most famous monster character was Rat Fink, a slobbering, fly-ridden rat conceived as a twisted version of Mickey Mouse. The "Big Daddy" moniker came from Revell executive Henry Blankfort, who thought it would be a good marketing hook for Revell's line of Roth car and monster kits.

Ed's public persona was something of a loony pied piper. Through his T-shirts and Revell model kits, he became an off-beat role model for thousands of car-crazy boys. His influence extended well beyond the hot rod and custom world, though, as he became a counterculture icon, whose vehicles were eventually recognized as rolling works of sculptural pop art.

Roth gradually gravitated toward custom trikes and motorcycles as the 1960s came to a close. Later, he returned to car building and was a fixture at custom car shows until his death in April 2001. He is warmly remembered for his significant contributions to hot rodding and popular culture, his gleefully iconoclastic attitude, and his seemingly boundless creativity.

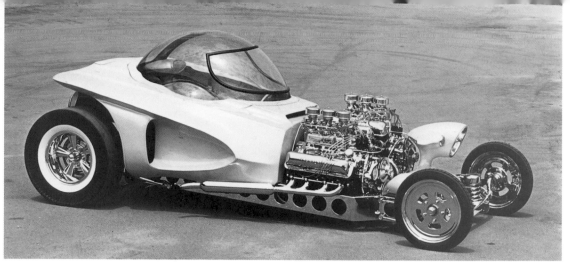

Mysterion

Druid Princess

Beatnik Bandit

Marquis

Marquis As the 1960s dawned, leading customizers pushed the styling envelope further than they ever had. They began to rely more on fabrication than repurposed parts from American cars, and, in some cases, bodies were completely fabricated. The resulting cars owed little to Detroit styling.

One of those customizers was Bill Cushenbery, a Wichita, Kansas, native who had moved to Monterey, California, in the late '50s to be closer to the custom scene. Cushenbery quickly established himself in California with the *El Matador*, a highly modified '40 Ford.

Cushenbery created his next major show car for Monterey-native Gene Boucher. Cushenbery dubbed the car the *Marquis*, and employed radical customizing techniques to create a car whose origins were virtually unrecognizable.

Starting with a 1956 Ford Victoria hardtop, Cushenbery sectioned the body six inches and replaced the rear quarter panels and trunklid with '59 Buick units. The Buick quarters were modified to fit, given flared wheel openings, and topped with small double "V" fins at their trailing edge. Cushenbery completely fabricated the rear fascia. In it, he placed canted '59 Pontiac taillights and a grille assembly consisting of flat bars set in metal mesh backing.

The front end was modified drastically. Cushenbery pancaked the hood and gave it a sculpted asymetrical peak that continued into the hand-formed grille opening. The fenders were reworked to accept quad canted Lucas headlights and bullets to act as bumperettes. A rolled front pan was molded in, and the grille was made from horizontally mounted flat bars set in metal mesh. In lieu of chrome side trim, Cushenbery sculpted peaked, arching character lines for the front fenders and doors.

Inside, Cushenbery installed handmade seats and a full-length center console. The gold and white fabric and Naugahyde upholstery was done by Manger's Auto Trim in Castroville, California.

Don Mathews, also of Monterey, applied the Candy Pagan Gold paint, which was offset by a white leatherette padded top, also done by Manger's. Two and a half years in the works, the *Marquis* made its debut in 1962. It claimed numerous awards, and was featured in several publications, including *Car Craft* magazine and Petersen's *20 Top Customs* Spotlite book.

Boucher stopped showing the *Marquis* after about a year, and it remained in his garage for the next 13 years until Cushenbery fan Bud Millard, of Millbrae, California, purchased it. Bud kept the car in storage until the mid 1990s, then began a frame-off restoration. Work stalled and the car sat for a while, but in 2000, Bud finally found the right people to complete the restoration.

Bud had some changes made along the way. He had the suspension airbagged and modern luxuries added. Power door openers, a billet steering wheel, digital gauges, and a contemporary sound system replaced the original components. Cushenbery had once confided in Bud that he didn't like the flared rear fenders. So, Bud had the flares removed and the radius of the rear wheel openings reduced. Bill

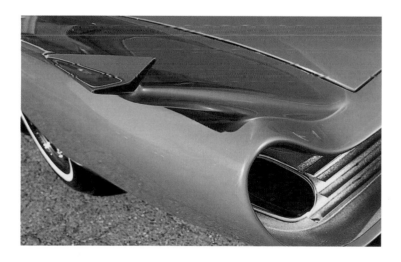

Reasoner applied the new Candy Pagan Gold metalflake paint, Jerry Sahagon refinished the interior, and John Aiello of Acme Builders in Antioch, California, completed the work.

Unfortunately, Cushenbery died in 1998 and was unable to see his creation restored. The *Marquis* returned to the show circuit in 2000, once again winning awards. It then spent time at both the Petersen Automotive Museum in Los Angeles and The Harrah Collection's National Automobile Museum in Reno, Nevada, where it appeared as a tribute to one of customizing's most creative builders.

Limelighter

As customizing progressed into the 1960s, the elaborate scalloping and panel-painting techniques of the late '50s gave way to vibrant, single-color candy finishes or carefully blended fades. Custom bodywork returned to the forefront, advancing beyond top chopping and trim swapping to free-form restyling. The *Limelighter*, originally built by Bill Cushenbery in 1964 for Frank Gould of Hollister, California, illustrates both of these trends.

Starting with a 1958 Chevy Impala hardtop, Cushenbery completely reconstructed both the front and rear fascias. Up front, the stock bumper, grille, and headlight trim were replaced with Lucas headlamps deeply tunneled into peaked "pods," a wildly sculpted rolled pan, and a hand-formed grille shell backed with expanded metal mesh. Out back, the rear bumper and taillights were replaced with tunneled hand-made taillights and a rear rolled pan with integrated exhaust ports and a "grille" that matched the front-end design. In addition to shaving all of the stock trim, Cushenbery molded in and resculpted the Impala's trademark roof scoop and "pitchfork" faux side scoops. The radical bodywork was topped off with a dazzling candy lime-gold paint job with subtle emerald-green fade accents.

Inside, the stock dashboard was replaced with an airplane wing strut supporting two 1950 Nash instrument pods. The wild steering wheel was actually a stock piece from a '60 Oldsmobile. A hand-fabricated center console held the radio, various control switches, and a '57 Oldsmobile instrument panel. The *Limelighter*'s original build cost came to approxi-mately $10,000, a substantial sum at the time.

Like so many famous customs, the *Limelighter* changed hands several times after its glory days on the show circuit and eventually fell into disrepair. After years of tracking its whereabouts, Bud Millard of Millbrae, California, was able to acquire the remains of the car in 1998. He sent the car to Bill Cushenbery, then living in Bakersfield, California, to have him restore the car he originally built more than 30 years earlier. Sadly, Cushenbery soon fell ill and passed away before he could begin. Bud then sent the car to OZ Kustoms in Oroville, California, for the restoration work.

Bud took several creative liberties with the restoration and had the OZ crew incorporate several updates. The top was chopped two inches, an LED third brake light was added to the roof scoop, and the taillights were converted to LEDs as well. The grille detail was altered by the deletion of the Lucite parking lights and the addition of a slim chrome grille bar.

The original *Limelighter* retained its stock '58 Chevrolet 348 engine, but Bud had OZ drop in a 1996 Chevrolet 350-cid small-block V-8/700R automatic transmission combination. The now-scarce Astro chrome slotted wheels and U.S. Royal Master tires were replaced with chrome-reversed wheels on radial whitewalls. A modern airbag suspension system was installed for an even lower ride height. Inside, digital gauges and modernized upholstery were added. Despite the changes, the overall essence of the *Limelighter* was preserved, and the restored car stands as a living testament to Cushenbery's pioneering techniques.

Circa 1985

Goulart Olds

Ray Goulart of Stockton, California, bought a used 1950 Olds Holiday convertible in 1959 for use as a family car. After a couple of years, he decided to turn it into a custom. Though familiar with the custom car scene— his brother owned a famous '50 Ford built by Gene Winfield —Ray had no formal training in auto design or bodywork. So, how did he create one of the more beautiful and successful custom show cars of the 1960s? According to Ray, "OTJ—on the job training," and access to parts from a friend's junkyard helped him turn his Olds into a showstopper.

To start, Ray added a hardtop roof from a 1951 Chevy, but modified it with a '53 Chevy sedan rear window. He drove the car in this form for a couple of years, then gave it the complete customizing treatment. He lowered the car by stepping the frame in back and reworking the A-arms in the front. Adding hand-rolled rocker panels gave the car an even lower look and served to hide the '50 Olds frame.

The car is often said to have a European flavor, and Ray confirmed that the 1958 Ferrari 250 GT affected some of his styling decisions. The rear fenders are especially Ferrari-like. To achieve the look, Ray reshaped and extended the fenders by grafting in '53 DeSoto fenders from the center of the rear-wheel cutouts back, then radiusing the wheel openings. The fenders resolve into hand-formed taillight housings into which Ray inserted '58 Olds taillight lenses turned upside down. Ray wrapped the rear end with a rolled pan made from the sides of a 1947 Nash hood, then made the bumper by cut-

ting away the bottom half of a '56 Buick bumper and splicing the top of a '59 Chevy license plate guard into the middle.

At the front, Ray fabricated an oval grille opening and filled it with multiple chromed steel bars. This grille was changed after a year on the show circuit in favor of four chromed metal rods. He made the front bumper by cutting away the top portion from a '55 Olds unit, then used the lower portion of the Olds bumper to make the front roll pan. For headlights, he frenched in a pair of '59 Chevy units vertically. Ray reworked the front-wheel openings by cutting them higher into the fenders, tapering them at an angle behind the wheels, and radiusing the edges. Vents were also added behind the front wheels

Underhood, Ray installed a 1959 Buick 401-cid V-8 mated to an Olds three-speed manual transmission. He added an Offenhauser dual-carb intake and chromed many of the engine bay's components.

The most striking element of the interior is the full-length console Ray added to create four distinct seating positions. He cut down the bench seats into buckets and had the black Naugahyde upholstery done by Scenic Auto Toggery of Modesto, California. The dash received speedometer and tachometer pods made from cut down 1949 Nash instrument pods. The main instrument housing was made from steel and fitted with an assortment of Stewart-Warner gauges.

Though the car is often attributed to Gene Winfield, Winfield only applied the paint, a copper candy for its first year on the show circuit (1964), then a gold-to-red metallic fade for is second year. During that first year, the car also had chrome-reversed wheels with bullet center caps, but they were replaced for year two with beautiful '53 Buick Skylark wires. Following the trend of the day, Ray gave his car a name, *El Sirocco*.

Ray let the car sit after its three-year car show run, and eventually sold it in 1973 to John Moses, who had it painted candy-apple red. Moses sold the car to noted custom collector Kurt McCormick in '83, and Kurt sold it to collector Jack Walker in '85. McCormick, who has owned more than 100 vintage cars, calls it the highest quality car he's ever owned—an impressive compliment for a car built by a man who had to learn customizing on the fly.

Circa 1966

The Ford Custom Car Caravan

As the 1960s dawned, the American custom car scene was in full swing. Sensing the marketing opportunity to grab the attention of hundreds of thousands of showgoers, as well as the media, Ford Motor Company decided to get in on the custom car craze. Under the leadership of Ford Special Projects Division head Jacques H. Passino, the Ford Division conceived the Ford Custom Car Caravan to create and campaign customized and performance-themed Fords.

The Caravan started in fall 1962 and first relied upon cars built in-house, then presented customized factory cars built by commissioned shops to factory specifications. Ultimately, the Caravan adopted privately created custom cars based upon production automobiles.

Initially, the Ford Caravan featured its famed X-car concept vehicles (*Mustang II*, *Cougar II*, and *Allegro*), which were later joined by the Dearborn Steel Tubing-built Thunderbird *Italien* and the George Barris-built Fairlane *Landau Starburst*, in shows presented by the International Show Car Association (Promotions, Inc.). As the Caravan grew and more cars were needed to fill at least three regional Caravans, Ford reached out to additional customizers and eventually either commissioned or adopted the work of the Alexander Brothers, George Barris, Clarkaiser, Bill Cushenbery, Dearborn Steel Tubing, Fostoria Customs, Dean Jeffries, and Gene Winfield.

To meet auto enthusiasts' parallel and growing interest in muscle cars, Ford expanded the Caravan late in the first season to feature performance versions of its '63½ Galaxie hardtops, an early example of Carroll Shelby's Cobra, and a sectioned '62 Falcon built by Holman-Moody. A couple Fairlane Thunderbolts built by Dearborn Steel Tubing were shown in the second season. Successive versions of some Caravan cars were featured as the builders updated their cars. In addition to the ISCA shows, Ford presented its Caravan at Ford dealerships, county and state fairs, shopping malls, and teen fairs.

Early shows featured an AMT slot car track, as well as appearances by longtime racer and Ford "performance advisor" Ak Miller and most of the customizers whose work appeared in the Caravan. As the Caravan matured, Ford approached individual customizers and proposed that if they installed Ford powerplants in their wild customs, their cars could appear under the Ford banner.

The Caravan was widely covered in several dozen custom car magazines. By the third year, the relative number of custom cars had declined in favor of high-performance versions of Ford production cars. Of the original cadre of customizers, only Barris made appearances for the final Caravan season. The Ford Caravan concluded sometime in the 1965-66 show season.

Starting in late 1963, the Lincoln-Mercury Division got involved with its Caravan of Stars, but this program strictly relied upon in-house designs. Starting with the Barris-built but factory-designed Mercury *Super Marauder* and the Ghia-bodied Mercury *Montego*, this Caravan was joined by the Dearborn Steel Tubing-built *Super Cyclone* and the Winfield-built *Comet Cyclone Sportster*. Both Cyclones successfully merged custom and performance themes. The Lincoln-Mercury Caravan was also enhanced by the Barris-built *Comet Escapade*. This car was built to factory specifications and later modified by Barris when part of the factory design was rejected by Lincoln-Mercury executives! A long wheelbase Lincoln Continental that was probably built in-house also joined the tour. Lincoln-Mercury's Caravan was presented in shopping centers and other informal settings, and ended with the conclusion of the 1966 show season.

By the final two seasons, Ford's two Caravans had switched their focus to performance more than customizing, just as enthusiasts had moved away from customs to embrace muscle cars. Still, the Caravans showed that Ford Motor Company was a proponent of custom cars, and Ford's efforts gave work and publicity to customizers at a time when they really needed it.

–Mark S. Gustavson

This 1961 Ford Thunderbird was originally built by George Barris for the model-kit company AMT. Named the Styline Thunderbird *after AMT's line of kits with custom parts, it appeared in the Ford Custom Car Caravan in two guises. This is the second version.*

Dearborn Steel Tubing built the Thunderbird Italien to Ford specifications.

Though more of a concept than a custom, Ford Styling Department built the Allegro concept car in-house and featured it in the Custom Car Caravan.

Dean Jeffries customized a 1964 Ford Falcon Sprint and named it the Python. Ford adopted this car for the Caravan.

Gene Winfield gave a Ford cab-over pickup an asymetrical treatment and named it Pacifica for the Caravan.

Vince Gardner at Dearborn Steel Tubing designed the Coyote from a 1963 Ford Falcon. Detroit's Alexander Brothers applied the candy-lime paint.

George Barris turned a 1963 Fairlane 500 into the Landau Starburst by giving it an alligator-skin-covered Landau-style top with a removable front panel.

The 1964 Mercury Super Marauder was built by George Barris to a factory design for the Mercury Caravan of Stars.

Gene Winfield was commissioned by Mercury to build the 1965 Comet Cyclone Sportster to a Mercury design.

With 4-71 blower, circa 1962

McMullen Deuces

Tom McMullen started hot rodding as a teenager in the late 1950s, became a wiring specialist in the mid '60s, and founded a publishing company in the late '60s. Along the way, he became one of the most important figures in the history of hot rodding and his flamed Deuce roadsters have always symbolized the hobby's unabashed soul.

Tom bought his first rod, a '32 highboy roadster, in 1958. Equipped with a 283-cid Chevy small block and a two-barrel carb, the car performed well, but Tom wanted more. By 1962, the car was a unique combination of power and style. The small block, now 301 cubic inches, featured a GMC 4-71 blower. A Halibrand quick change and a parachute resided out back, and a pressurized Moon tank sat between the front frame horns. Bold flames, laid out by Ed Roth and sprayed on by Tom, combined with Roth-applied pinstriping to give the car an in-your-face look that appealed to youngsters when it appeared on the April 1963 cover of *Hot Rod* magazine.

Tom opened a street rod wiring company at about this time. Lackluster business prompted him to do freelance magazine articles using his Deuce as the guinea pig. He added a Chevy 327 and raced the car at the local dragstrips and El Mirage, where it set an A/Street Roadster record of 167 mph in 1964. Next, Tom installed a wild Ford 427 wedge that made the car too hairy for street use. After starting his next business (building custom parts for Harley-Davidson motorcycles), he lost interest in the car and eventually sold it in 1969.

McMullen founded *Street Rodder* magazine in 1972, and built a new Deuce in '76 as a magazine project car. Dubbed "The Ultimate Roadster," the car used state-of-the-art '70s technology, but lacked the trademark Moon tank and parachute. A genuine steel roadster, this car featured digital gauges, a credit card ignition, full independent suspension, and a 350-cid Chevy small-block V-8 with dry-sump oiling and Moser DOHC heads. Tom sold this car in the early '80s.

Tom built his third Deuce in 1991, again for *Street Rodder*. This one, built using aftermarket frame rails and a fiberglass body, captured the look of the original as it appeared in '64. McMullen drove his final Deuce until he was killed in a plane crash in 1995.

Another version of McMullen's Deuce (color photo) was built in 1997 to commemorate the 25th anniversary of *Street Rodder*. The magazine staff aimed to capture the spirit of the original, although they built it using a fiberglass body and an aftermarket frame instead of a real steel Deuce.

The original Deuce passed through many owners until it reached the hands of Jorge Zaragoza in 2002. Zaragoza had Roy Brizio Street Rods in San Francisco restore the car to the way it appeared when it was on the cover of the April 1963 *Hot Rod*. The restoration took about a year, and the McMullen Deuce is as good, if not better than, ever.

Drag guise, circa 1965

First car, final McMullen version, circa 1967

With 427, circa 1967

Street Rodder staff car at L.A. Roadster Show, 2002

Instant T In the late 1950s, when Norm Grabowski and Tommy Ivo were introducing the hot rod world to the T-bucket, Ted McMullen was learning welding and chassis fabrication on drag cars. As the T-bucket gained more and more popularity, McMullen decided he could build affordable hot rod chassis, kits, and even turnkey rods.

With that concept in mind, McMullen opened U.S. Speed Sport Mfg. in 1962. All previous T-bucket bodies were custom-made from Ford parts, but now U.S. Speed Sport aimed to offer production-line-style bodies and chassis that could be purchased ready to run or adapted to any combination of engine, transmission, rear end, or any other component the buyer desired.

Featured here is the first complete rod the shop built and the car McMullen used for his floor model. The 96-inch wheelbase, box-rail chassis was jig-welded to be geometrically true. The jig also ensured that every chassis the shop built would be the same. The body, a fiberglass unit designed by Wayne Hartmann and based on a 1923 Ford roadster pickup, is the same one U.S. Speed Sport used for its customer cars.

Baubles weren't part of the equation. To maintain simple, clean lines, McMullen and employee Dick Fletcher used the windshield and front and rear lamps from a 1915 Model T.

The engine of choice was a Corvette 283-cid V-8 breathing through an Offenhauser intake manifold with three two-barrel carbs. The wheels of choice were Halibrands in back and chromed steelies up front. Upholstery by Ed Martinez and candy-tangerine paint completed the rod.

When finished, the car was featured in several period magazines, and *Hot Rod Parts Illustrated* dubbed it the *Instant T*. A flood of inquiries followed the magazine exposure, and soon shops everywhere were offering fiberglass T-bucket kits. Just as Norm Grabowski had introduced the T-bucket, U.S. Speed Sport can be credited with offering the first fiberglass turnkey and kit-car "Fad Ts."

Fletcher was to be the original owner, but he left the shop before he could work off the cost of building the car. So, McMullen kept it, modified a few details, and used it as a dragstrip push car. He exchanged the three two-barrel carburetors for dual quads, put on a set of five-spoke wheels with slicks, and had it repainted candy blue.

The Instant T sat in McMullen's shop from 1967 to '95, when Jim Travis offered to restore it. Ted McMullen has since passed away, but not before he saw his hot rod placed in the Petersen Automotive Museum in Los Angeles as a living piece of hot rod aftermarket history.

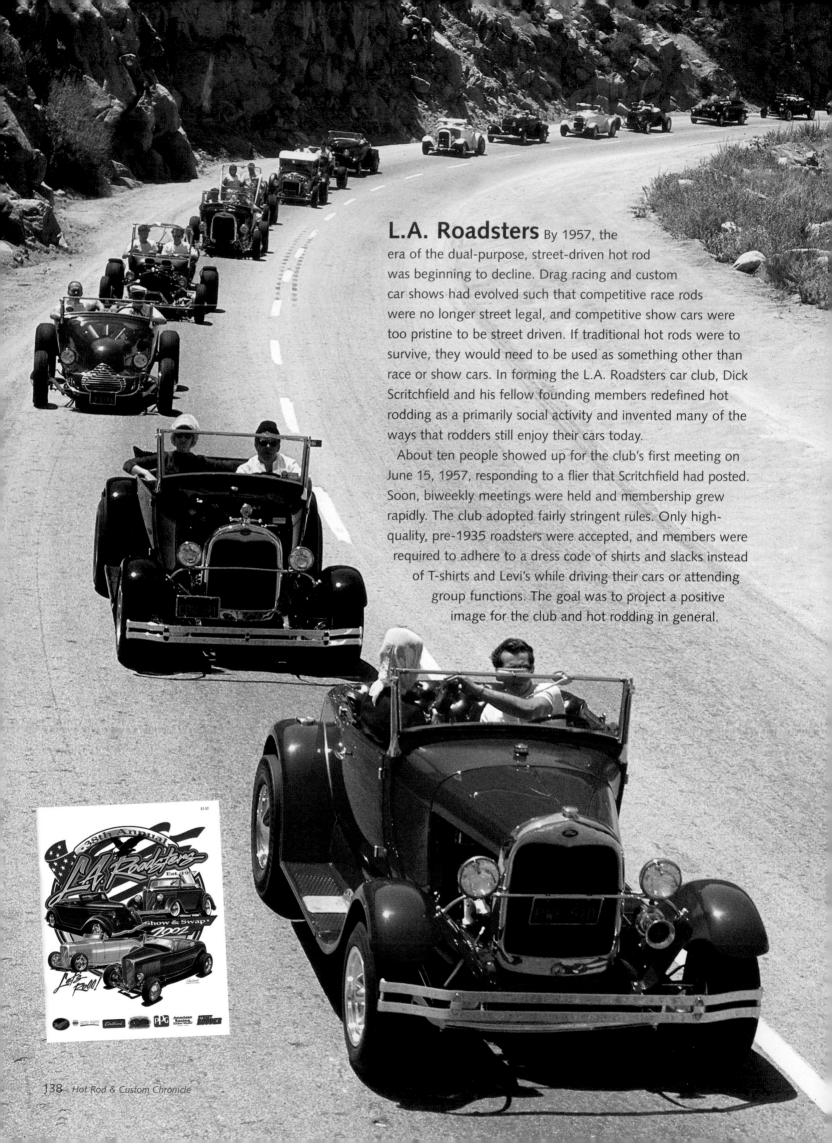

L.A. Roadsters

By 1957, the era of the dual-purpose, street-driven hot rod was beginning to decline. Drag racing and custom car shows had evolved such that competitive race rods were no longer street legal, and competitive show cars were too pristine to be street driven. If traditional hot rods were to survive, they would need to be used as something other than race or show cars. In forming the L.A. Roadsters car club, Dick Scritchfield and his fellow founding members redefined hot rodding as a primarily social activity and invented many of the ways that rodders still enjoy their cars today.

About ten people showed up for the club's first meeting on June 15, 1957, responding to a flier that Scritchfield had posted. Soon, biweekly meetings were held and membership grew rapidly. The club adopted fairly stringent rules. Only high-quality, pre-1935 roadsters were accepted, and members were required to adhere to a dress code of shirts and slacks instead of T-shirts and Levi's while driving their cars or attending group functions. The goal was to project a positive image for the club and hot rodding in general.

As the club flourished, it became a hot rod "rental" source for television and movie productions. The L.A. Roadsters also orchestrated some of the first "rod runs," organized drives to a predetermined site for fun and fellowship. Getting there and back was half the fun. The first "official" "Roadster Roundup" was held in 1966, in Pismo Beach, California. Members of the L.A. Roadsters drove up from the south, and Northern California clubs like the Bay Area Roadsters came from the north to meet in the middle of the state for socializing and games. All of these activities greatly increased the visibility of rodders and their cars to the public.

On Father's Day, June 18, 1967, the L.A. Roadsters held the first L.A. Roadster Exhibition and Swap Meet, a tradition that continues to this day. The club had produced shows earlier in the '60s, but the '67 event was the first to contain a swap meet and be held on Father's Day weekend. The L.A. Roadsters Father's Day show has earned a reputation as a "must attend" event because of the quality of the cars on display and the elusive goodies available at the giant swap meet.

From the inception of the club to the present day, the L.A. Roadsters has always been dedicated to the advancement of well-built, street-driven hot rod roadsters. The club's basic philosophy of simply getting together and enjoying hot rods is as viable today as it was 40 years ago.

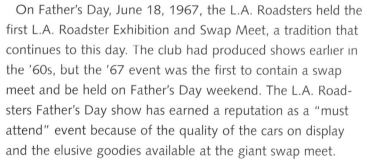

Marasco Roadster Pickup

Ford Model A roadster pickups have always been popular with hot rodders. These vehicles combine the freedom of open-air driving with the utility of a pickup. Plus, from the hot rodder's perspective, they're unusual and, therefore, cool.

Monterey, California, native Dave Marasco built this handsome roadster pickup in 1962 so he could join the Bay Area Roadsters club. It actually started as a coupe, but Dave swapped on a roadster pickup body, which he set back about three inches from stock and outfitted with a Deuce grille. He shortened the stock Model A pickup bed 12 inches and added a unique handmade wooden luggage rack. He also chopped the windshield two inches. For power, Dave installed a 1955 Chevy 265-cid V-8, and left it stock save for an Edelbrock intake manifold and three Rochester two-barrel carbs. A black-lacquer paint job topped with pinstriping by Andy Southard, Jr., completed the project. Southard was a frequent contributor to *Rod & Custom* at the time, and his photos of the finished pickup were featured in the April 1963 issue.

Initially, Dave chose unique chrome-reversed wheels with drilled holes and a stock vertical-bar insert for the Deuce grille shell. Later, he switched to a set of Astro wheels with tri-bar spinner center caps and added a custom-made horizontal-bar grille by Joe Wilhelm.

In 1969, Southard played another role in the pickup's life. Greg Sharp, then a motorcycle officer with the Los Angeles Police Department, attended the Roadster Roundup in Visalia, California. There, he learned from Andy that Marasco's '29 was for sale. Sharp met with Marasco, and within a few weeks the pickup had a new home.

Sharp kept things mostly as Marasco had left them, but added Buick Skylark wire wheels and had Jack Hagemann fabricate a three-piece hood with louvered side panels and lunch-box latches. He also swapped out the tri-power intake for a single four-barrel unit. Sharp showed the pickup at the 1971 Grand National Roadster Show, where it took first place in the Altered Roadster Pickup Class.

After owning the pickup for 34 years, Greg decided that he had done everything he dreamed of doing with it, and the time had come to let it go to an appreciative new owner. He sold it to historic hot rod collector Ross Myers of Boyertown, Pennsylvania, in 2003.

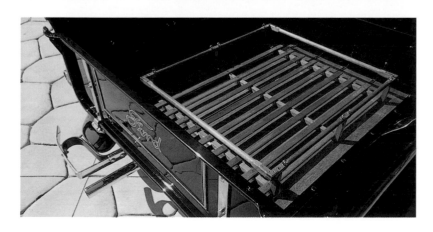

Early Times

The Early Times Car Club was formed in 1964 by ten hot rodders in north Long Beach, California. The group included Joe Barnett, Bill Booth and his brother Tom, Jim Jacobs, Roger Brinkley, John Christopher, Dan Woods, Sheldon Bardin, Allen Barbee, and Don Mabe. They all turned out to be fixtures and trendsetters in the '60s hot rod scene.

Early Times was formed as a reaction to clubs like the L.A. Roadsters that allowed only roadster owners to join. Most members were from a new, younger breed—many were fresh out of high school. These guys weren't from the same generation who had fought in World War II, and they brought fresh ideas to the scene. Founding member Bill Booth's wife Elaine suggested the name "Early Times" after she spotted a neon Early Times whiskey sign in a liquor store. Jim Jacobs designed the club logo, a stylized winged Model T radiator ornament.

Fortuitous geography helped the club grow and develop a style all its own. Most of the original members grew up in the communities of southwest and south central L.A., which were hotbeds of rodding activity. Several members lived right down the street from *Rod & Custom* staffer Bud Bryan, and their close proximity meant frequent coverage in the magazine. With several dragstrips nearby, drag styling heavily influenced Early Times cars, meaning they often had metalflake and cobwebbed custom paint jobs, mag wheels, and pared down, spartan interiors.

Membership had its benefits. Bill Booth explained in 2002: "In the 1960s, only a few shops built hot rods, so you had to do most of the work yourself. That is when a car club came in handy. A wealth of knowledge was shared among club members, and everyone helped each other. When we did need help from machine shops, we usually hung out at J&J Chassis where Dan Woods, Jim Jacobs, Richard Graves, and others all worked. These same guys still build hot rods today. Another member, Jim Babbs, was a great fabricator and radiator builder. Few Early Times cars from the '60s didn't have J&J and/or Jim Babbs workmanship."

The visibility of the Early Times and other rod clubs of the era helped bridge the gap between the specialized, regional rodding of the '50s and the street rodding hobby as it's known today. The club is still thriving, with new and original members enjoying their cars and the camaraderie of like-minded hot rodders.

Tom Hendrickson's 1926 Ford T coupe

Roger Brinkley's 1932 Ford sedan

Mark Morton's '27 Chevy coupe followed by Don Mabe's '29 Ford Tudor sedan and Jim Morris' '25 Buick touring

Dick Rundell's 1929 Ford Model A touring

Dick Knutson's 1915 Ford T-bucket

Don Thelan's 1932 Ford Victoria

Wayne Henderson's 1932 Ford five-window coupe, Danny Eichstedt's "Leg Show" T-bucket, Richard Graves' 1927 Ford T touring (left to right)

Booth '27 T

In 1966, Dan Woods, a fellow Early Times club member, called Bill Booth and told him about a disassembled '27 T touring for sale. Bill greatly admired friend John Monteiro's T touring and wanted one of his own, so he raced over to the owner's house and bought it on the spot. His quick response landed him the car just before another Early Times member showed up to buy it. "We must have had seven or eight touring cars in the club. They were all the rage," Bill recalled.

As a founding Early Times member and devoted hot rodder, Bill used the car to take part in many of the formative hot rod social activities that have become a so important to the hobby. Bill even used the car for several trips around the country.

The trip that was the most fun for Bill and his wife Elaine was the 1970 pilgrimage to Peoria, Illinois, for the first Street Rod Nationals with fellow Early Times members. Other trips, including a jaunt to Boston to visit associate L.A. Roadsters member Ted Wingate, a cruise to New York City and Washington, D.C., and a repeat trip to the Street Rod Nationals in Memphis—all from Long Beach, California—racked up an incredible number of miles of open-air touring.

Like many rodders, Bill changed his car frequently. When he first built it, he assembled all the parts needed, built and installed a Chevy 283-cid V-8, modified the chassis, routed the wiring, and painted the car himself. Along the way, the car underwent several repaints, changing from its original burgundy with black fenders to burnt orange with brown fenders to the brilliant red it is today.

One of the best changes Bill made was installing a Jaguar independent rear end in the early 1970s. The new rear suspension made all the difference in the way the lightweight tub rode. Bill explained: "We would be boogying down the highway and go over a dip, and the rear passengers would all but fly out of the car. The Jag rear fixed all that."

Bill installed a Chevy 350 and a Turbo 400 transmission in the mid 1970s to replace the tired 283. Later, he added steelie wheels with caps and rings and modern radial tires. Bill was in the process of freshening the paint when these photos were taken in 2002, as evidenced by the primered front splash pan. With more than 200,000 miles on it, the touring was still going strong when Bill passed away in 2003. His wife Elaine briefly considered selling the touring, but realized that it had too much sentimental value. She plans to keep it and eventually pass it on to their son Todd.

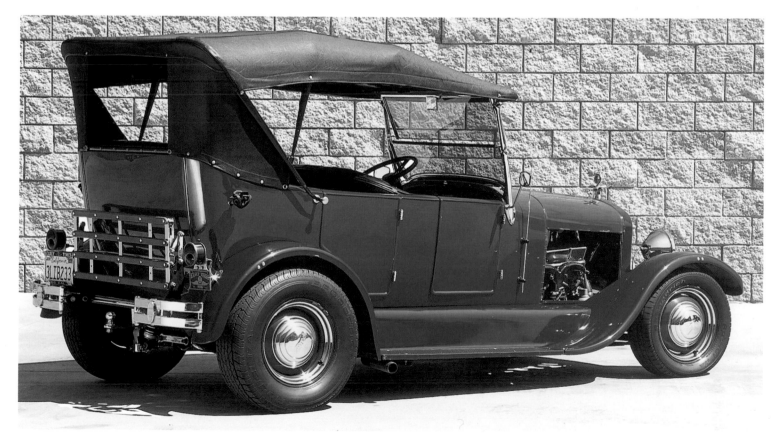

Kendrick Sedan

In 1967, traditional street-driven hot rods were on the wane thanks to muscle cars and later-model street machines, but a number of dedicated builders still kept the flame alive. One of the nicest rods of this period was Phil Kendrick's Deuce sedan. Dave Archer originally built the car in the mid 1950s with a blown flathead. Phil, an Oakland, California, native, bought the car from Dave in the mid 1960s and brought it up to the fashion of the day.

In its late 1960s form, the sedan featured a four-inch chop, unique bobbed and louvered rear fenders, and 40 coats of bright-orange lacquer by Tony Del Rio with pinstriping by the legendary Tommy "the Greek" Hrones. The interior sported swiveling Kellison bucket seats, a Covico steering wheel, Stewart-Warner gauges, and lots of black, pleated Naugahyde. The 265-cid Chevy V-8, bored out to 292 cubic inches, was equipped with Jahns pistons, Edelbrock finned valve covers, and three chrome-plated Stromberg 97 carburetors. Phil routed the power through a '39 Ford gearbox to a Halibrand quick-change rear end. The rear suspension consisted of a chromed Model A spring and Monroe shocks, while the front had chromed and drilled radius rods, a stock spring, and a dropped I-beam axle. Period details included the 15-inch Halibrand wheels on now-rare Goodyear Blue Streak tires, a mirrorlike chromed firewall, and slick handmade drilled nerf bars front and rear.

Phil's impeccably crafted Deuce walked off with the Grand Sweepstakes award at the 1967 San Mateo Auto Show. Phil reworked the car again in about 1970, adding 12-spoke American wheels up front and huge M&H slicks with slotted mags out back. At this time, it also received a pearl-yellow finish with translucent flames. Strange "Super Prune" lettering was also added to the rear body panel with an accompanying prune graphic.

In this guise, the car eventually ended up in the hands of guitar legend and hot rodder Jeff Beck, who shipped it to England in the late 1970s. In '83, Beck decided the damp English climate was too harmful for the extensively chrome-plated sedan, and sold it to a buyer back in the United States. It can still be occasionally spotted at rod events today, though the years have taken their toll.

As shown, this car represents the best of what the 1960s had to offer. Many 1940s and and '50s rods have been restored to their former glory, but so far the '60s remains a largely overlooked era.

TV Customs

By the mid 1960s, participants in the traditional street-driven custom scene had splintered off in many directions. Some custom enthusiasts shifted to muscle cars and drag racing. Two of the original architects of custom car style, George Barris and Dean Jeffries, were pulled into the world of Hollywood.

When 20th Century-Fox and *Batman* producer William Dozier needed a *Batmobile* in 1965 (the pilot episode was to premiere on ABC in January '66), his first call went to Jeffries, who starting working on a '59 Caddy. Jeffries had to bow out when he realized he couldn't meet Dozier's three-week deadline. Barris subsequently accepted the job, probably because he already owned the '55 Lincoln Futura, a bubble-canopy concept car that Barris had saved from the Ford crusher some years earlier by handing over one dollar. With a suitably low, wide chassis, as well as flaring fins, a wide-mouth grille, and swoopy bodyside lines already in place, the Futura was the platform Barris needed to quickly deliver an outlandish, photogenic custom that met the producer's expectations. Inside, the Futura dash was altered only slightly to accommodate prop gadgetry such as a "Bat Phone," "Detect-a-Scope," and an "Emergency Bat-Turn Lever."

Claims about the number of Barris *Batmobiles* vary. Barris' crew pulled fiberglass molds off the original car to make duplicates for car-show tours. Most likely four or five were made, including a drag race exhibition vehicle.

When William Dozier readied another superhero show, *The Green Hornet*, for a September 1966 ABC start, he got back to Jeffries, who was now free to deal with another three-week schedule. Jeffries fashioned the Hornet's intimidating, gadget-packed *Black Beauty* cruiser from a '66 Imperial Crown hardtop sedan. He stripped off the bumpers and other chrome, including the door handles and side mirrors, and added a reshaped, angular nose and a boxed, out-thrust aluminum grille.

Fanciful accessories included rotating license plates, green headlamps, a hidden clothes closet, rear-seat gun storage, and a pop-up "spy scanner" in the decklid. The dash included a hidden phone and other devices. The Imperial's stock 440-cid V-8 and drivetrain remained untouched.

Jeffries built two *Black Beauties*, with car #2 (intended for promotional duty) completed on schedule just three weeks after car #1. Version #1 was a regular on the show, while the promo car appeared in just one episode, "Corpse of the Year," when the Hornet races after an imposter.

Another show that bowed in September 1966, NBC's *The Monkees*, brought more work for Jeffries: the Pontiac GTO-based *Monkeemobile*. Although fondly recalled by car fans, the *Monkeemobile* underwhelmed Pontiac, which had hoped for a marketing splash with a modestly customized, instantly recognizable Goat ragtop. Pontiac even provided the shop with concept drawings (one of which is shown) of a hunky, squared-fendered custom that was clearly a GTO. But Jeffries was responsible not to Pontiac but to producers Bob Rafelson and Bert Schneider, so he went his own way and tweaked the proportions of the concept sketch to more-outlandish dimensions. Up front, the car announced itself with a sharklike nose and repositioned GTO grilles sunk between dramatically

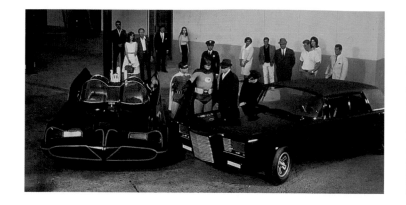

speared front fenders; the "GTO" grille badge remained. The trunklid was removed and the interior was extended into the trunk area to include a third seating row. The windshield was angled upward to meet a '20s touring car-style convertible top.

The stock 389-cid V-8 was fitted with a supercharger and the rear axle was solid-mounted so the *Monkeemobile* would be able to pop wheelies. The car turned out to be too powerful and unruly, so the blower was replaced with a lightweight fake that hid a carburetor.

As with the *Black Beauty*, two *Monkeemobiles* were made, one for practical use and the other for promotion. According to Jeffries, both cars were built within a month.

These cars were a boon for TV ratings and also pulled in huge crowds at custom car shows. Soon, even more-exaggerated, cartoonish rods and customs were being built solely for the show circuit, with no pretense of street drivability. While the TV customs and show rods were popular with the general public, they stole the spotlight from traditional street-driven customs, pushing them further into obscurity.

AMX-400

The rise of the muscle car was a major factor in customizing's demise in the 1960s, as performance began to take precedence over style. But a select few tried to adapt traditional customizing to the new breed of Detroit automobiles. One of the more outlandish attempts to marry muscle car and custom styling traits was the AMX-400, built by Barris Kustom in 1969.

George Barris adapted to the changing times, picking up lucrative work from Detroit and Hollywood when jobs for individual customers slowed down. The Barris Kustom shop's close proximity to the entertainment industry led to a steady stream of projects for TV, movies, and celebrities, while Barris' knack for publicity lured the Detroit automakers.

In the late 1960s, Barris teamed up with the American Motors Corporation to produce a bolt-on customizing kit for the AMX that was marketed through AMC dealers. Through this connection, George got his hands on a factory-fresh 1969 AMX and gave it the full Barris treatment. The biggest modification was the chopped top, which came down 4½ inches. In the process, the windshield posts were raked back two inches, and the rear window was inset between the "flying buttress" rear pillars.

The nose of the car was extended 15 inches and given a wild new look with a radical peaked louver grille. Rectangular headlights were hidden behind three bladelike grille bars, while the hood was revamped with twin scoops and a peaked tip that matched the grille bars' shape. All four wheel openings were radiused, and custom front bodyside flares were added to match the enhanced rear body character lines.

The rear of the car was extended eight inches and reconfigured with a row of 15 louvers that started at the top of the rear window and continued all the way down the trunklid and rear fascia. A novel taillight system featured a full-width light that glowed green during acceleration, amber during deceleration, and red during braking. Body details included a wild set of three-inch-diameter side pipes and a pair of competition-style fuel-filler caps. Both filler caps are just for looks; the actual fuel filler door is at the rear of the car. A two-tone paint scheme in cream-toned Murano Pearl and Rustic Orange cleverly utilized the car's body lines as color breaks.

Since the AMX's stock 315-hp 390-cid V-8 was already capable, no engine modifications were performed. Likewise, the interior was left virtually stock, as it was well-equipped from the factory with power steering, air conditioning, and a tilt steering column.

Total build time was only three months. The AMX-400 toured the country on the ISCA circuit for a few years, and also appeared in an episode of the TV show *Banacek* in 1972 before going into storage. Mike and Lin Geary acquired the car in 2003 in relatively sound condition, with a mere 3300 miles on the odometer, and set about refurbishing it. The car was repainted by Tabz Toys in Lancaster, New York, and Ron Lasker re-created the original pinstriping. After the restoration, the AMX-400 made its public debut at the AMC 50th Anniversary show in Kenosha, Wisconsin, in July 2004.

Restyling muscle cars never really caught on in the hot rod and custom world, but the AMX-400 remains an impressive artifact of an uncertain period.

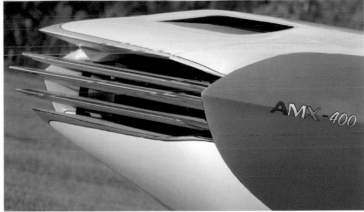

CHAPTER 4: THE 1970s
Rods Revived, Customs Dormant

The 1970s could arguably be considered the most exciting decade in the history of hot rods, while the near-dormant custom was showing signs of rebirth in its original '50s idiom. There are many reasons, but they all lead back to a refocused *Rod & Custom* magazine. Most of the traditional magazines that featured hot rods and customs had moved away from that segment into drag racing coverage, muscle cars, more technical fare, and in the case of *R&C* in the '60s, everything from minibikes to plastic models to slot cars. Now, through the staff's efforts, two developments organized the hot rod scene and ensured its numbers, then and well into the future.

In 1969, the *R&C* staff decided there should be a national event sponsored by the magazine to bring together as many hot rodders and their cars as possible. Besides the fun factor, it would give *R&C* an opportunity to acquire features on cars from other parts of the country, not just Southern California. Since they didn't have the budget to fly cross-country to photograph cars, they tried to meet car owners halfway.

A single, central event would also give the editors an opportunity to talk with their readers and to make contacts for potentially more features. They could take the pulse of what was happening elsewhere, and learn of new trends, shops, and personalities.

The editors decided to locate this event in the center of the country, and the town of choice was Peoria, Illinois. After contacting the city, locating a local club to help with logistics, and flying to Peoria to meet with the mayor, *R&C* proclaimed "All Roads Lead To Peoria" in the June 1970 issue.

Parallel to the event planning were ongoing discussions between the *R&C* staff and concerned rodders about a potential national organization. The goal was to form an organization to help fight pending state and national safety-equipment regulations, legislation related to the safety of homebuilt vehicles, and smog-control devices for hot rods, or "street rods" as they were now called. Also, many rod owners were finding it difficult to get insurance. An organized group, it was surmised,

would attract a national company to insure street rods.

It became apparent that the best place to attempt to start an organization would be at the upcoming event, now dubbed the Street Rod Nationals. So, the National Street Rod Association, or NSRA, was conceived on the eve of the Nationals, just in time to sign up members from all over the country.

More than 600 pre-1948 rods came out for the first Street Rod Nationals on August 14-16, 1970. They showed off their cars and took part in games, but mostly came to party and celebrate the largest gathering of hot rods yet assembled. "Street Is Neat" was the slogan conceived by *R&C*'s Tom Medley, and with a successful event and the beginnings of a national organization, the street rod scene was looking neat indeed. Attendance at the second Nationals doubled, and in recent years, the event has grown to attract more than 14,000 cars. The NSRA has more than 50,000 members today.

The Nationals became a springboard for several milestones that would make street rodding what it is today. A number of publications dedicated to street rods emerged. *Street Rod* magazine first appeared in late 1971, followed by *Street Rodder* and *Ray Brock's Rod Action* in '72. These publications would help spread the word and spotlight new companies and their products.

What about customs? Well, 1971 would mark the end of the continuous string of custom cars to be featured in magazines since 1948. Milo Broz's sectioned '50 Ford coupe was the last custom to be featured. It appeared in *Rod & Custom*, which was the last magazine giving customs any recognition.

For the most part, the few customs that did exist were from the 1960s. And the few being built were either '50s or '60s relics late in their completion, or they were the work of enthusiasts who didn't much care about the current trends.

A couple custom trends did linger, though. Corvettes were somewhat popular with customizers because their fiberglass bodies easily took to modifications. And pickups were being lowered with an occasional rolled pan. But

the traditional custom was dormant.

If there was a significant customizing activity in the early 1970s, it had to be the predominately Hispanic lowriders. They could be found on the streets of East Los Angeles, the San Fernando or San Gabriel Valleys of suburban L.A., parts of Arizona, and in Albuquerque, New Mexico. They tended to be late-model Chevrolets, Pontiacs, or the occasional Oldsmobile or Cadillac. Lowered with dressed-up engines, aftermarket wheels, and wild custom paint jobs, they exhibited excellent craftsmanship—like 1950s customs.

Generally, lowriders had velvet or velour interiors with features like swivel seats, cocktail bars, TVs, and/or elaborate stereos. About all they lacked compared to traditional customs were body modifications, though some had them. They also differed stylistically. Many wore original badges and trim, and they were frequently festooned with such accessories as sun visors, fender skirts, bumper guards, fog lamps, and headlight visors. To avoid problems caused by the lingering Southern California ride height laws from the 1950s and '60s, most also used hydraulic suspensions that could lift or lower the whole car in a matter of seconds. The hydraulics utilized lift gate rams from large trucks attached to the suspension components, and they were powered by an army of batteries in the trunk.

Just as the custom car seemed to fade completely, developments took place in 1973 and '74 that would help rekindle an interest in '50s custom cars.

George Lucas' movie *American Graffiti* was released in 1973 to an enthusiastic audience who connected with the film's nostalgic depiction of teenage activities in the summer of '62. Central to the story were cruising customs and hot rods. For car enthusiasts, what could have been more perfect than the Deuce coupe, chopped Merc, and '58 Impala that were central to the story? *American Graffiti* got people's attention, but there was more to come.

Once again, the magazines played a part. In 1973, *Hot Rod*, not known for featuring customs, ran an article that espoused 1950s customizing as an art form. Examples were included along with a pullout poster by artist Robert Williams. Titled "A Devil With a Hammer and Hell With a Torch," the poster celebrated the accomplishments of George Barris and Ed "Big Daddy" Roth and showed real and imagined '50s- and '60s-style customs.

Then, *Street Rodder* devoted its November 1974 issue to chopped Mercs. Bang! The magazine devoted almost entirely to street rods was featuring a custom Merc on its cover! It was all coincidental, but the 1950s style custom car was being celebrated in different media. Slowly, '50s style customs were coming back.

Back on the street rod scene, numerous fledgling companies were manufacturing components exclusively for hot rods by the mid 1970s. Included among them were Pete and Jake's Hot Rod Parts, The Deuce Factory, TCI, Total Performance, and Super Bell Axle Company. They made kits for engine and transmission installations, suspensions, and disc brakes. The Deuce Factory even had a completely new stamped 1932 Ford frame. These products made constructing a street rod a lot easier and safer. The components were well-made and engineered, and the new rodding magazines, as well as the Street Rod Nationals, provided the means for effective marketing.

As early Ford bodies became more and more rare, fiberglass companies started manufacturing everything from fenders to complete coupe and roadster bodies. Existing businesses expanded their lines, and more companies sprang up manufacture more sophisticated equipment such as independent suspensions and air conditioning systems.

From these companies emerged another hot rod milestone. Shops began specializing in constructing hot rods. Customers could buy any service from chassis fabrication to upholstery to wiring, or opt for a complete "turnkey" rod. Dan Woods' Contemporary Carriage Works, J&J Chassis, Andy Brizio, and Pete and Jake's Hot Rod Repair all were doing hot rod construction and fabrication by the mid '70s.

These were the beginnings of the huge street rod aftermarket industry. It was a slow and steady progression, and

an obvious outgrowth of the Street Rod Nationals and the NSRA.

Customs were slow to this party, and when they finally arrived, it was in a different way than hot rods. The custom car movement had grown from its rebirth in this decade, but the ideas applied to the custom car hadn't changed significantly from the 1950s. The same cars were being customized, the shoebox Fords and 1949-51 Mercs for example, and these cars had more complicated bodies and components than hot rods, making aftermarket bodies and parts less feasible to produce. Aftermarket bodies for typical '50s custom subjects weren't needed anyway because these cars were still readily available and relatively affordable.

Also, most custom modifications have always been unique and labor intensive for each car. Whereas almost every hot rod needed suspension components, making them lucrative to manufacture, customs couldn't benefit from as many aftermarket components because it was too difficult at the time to manufacture custom bodies and the market for such products was much smaller. It also made little sense to make a chopped top for a Mercury or a hood with rounded corners, for instance, because each custom car is a personalized statement, often with different treatments for the various custom modifications.

In the mid to late 1970s, early custom pioneers, like Gene Winfield and Joe Bailon, noticed an increased demand for their '50s-style customizing services —things they hadn't done in maybe 10 or 15 years. Dick Dean, who had been doing customizing work since the '50s, started specializing in chopping the tops of anything, like new pickups, and late-model cars, as well as traditional custom subjects. He advertised in the magazines and became known as the "Top Chop King."

Back in the hot rod world, a new look had taken hold, that of the "resto rod,"

so-called for its use of original components such as lantern-style cowl lights and accessory trunk racks. This gave restorers two reasons to dislike hot rodders. First, rodders were "ruining" original cars by cutting up the frames and bodies and installing late-model engines, air conditioning, and the like. Second, the resto rodders were robbing restorers of their prized original components like headlights, accessory clock mirrors, and greyhound hood ornaments. Original-type mohair upholstery and even stock two-tone paint jobs were showing up with regularity at rod runs and in the magazines.

By the end of the decade, the typical hot rod was a clean, simple traditional or resto rod with modern advances like independent suspensions, disc brakes, rack-and-pinion steering, power windows, power brakes, and tilt steering columns. Like they often had in the past, junkyards provided the components that builder incorporated into their hot rods, only now some different parts were chosen. The quality of street rods was on the rise, and so were participation and the street rod industry as a whole. But a styling shift was on the horizon. The look had its roots in the 1970s, but it wouldn't manifest itself until the '80s.

And while the custom car had begun to return to its 1950s roots in the '70s, it was still loosely organized with very few shows to galvanize its following. The '80s would change that, as several events and organizations would emerge to give custom fans a place to congregate and celebrate. ⤐

NSRA and the Street Rod Nationals

By 1970, it had become impractical for hot rods to do double duty as street/strip or street/show cars. Only a select few rods were nice enough to show or fast enough to race. Yet, many rodders wanted to enjoy their cars. The answer to this problem was simple: drive them! Three *Rod & Custom* staffers set out to help rodders do just that.

Editor Bud Bryan, publisher Tom Medley, and writer LeRoi "Tex" Smith decided that a nationwide rod run would help hot rodders think of their hobby as street rodding. The idea wasn't new. Rod runs had been held before, but never with a nationwide open invitation.

Peoria, Illinois, was chosen as the meeting point for the First Annual *Rod & Custom* Street Rod Nationals due to its central location. The Early Idlers club of Peoria and the Minnesota Street Rod Association agreed to cohost the event and make the local arrangements. *Rod & Custom* printed an article in the June 1970 issue describing the event and inviting all readers to attend. That article also made it clear that exhibitions of speed would not be tolerated.

Going hand in hand with the first Street Rod Nationals was the formation of the National Street Rod Association. The people who formed the nucleus were Cotton Werksman, a rod builder from Barrington, Illinois; *R&C* staffers Tom Medley, Tex Smith, and Jim Jacobs; and two Memphis-area rodders, Vern Walker of Walker Radiator and Gilbert Bugg. As *Rod & Custom* put it, the NSRA was: "An organized body of conscientious early iron hot rodders; a lobby 1) that will

not sheepishly stand by while lawmakers blast away at the very foundations of our sport, 2) who sees the need for and the worth of power in numbers, and 3) whose main meaning for existence is to champion the validity and educational worth of backyard hot rodding." The NSRA charged a $5.00 membership fee, and the Street Rod Nationals helped pull in members.

Held August 14-16, 1970, the first "Nats" drew more than 600 pre-'49 street rods of every description. Although the event wasn't competitive in nature, a few contests were held. A "Streetkhana" featuring low-speed driving games was won by Jim Babbs of Paramount, California, in his pint-sized, scratchbuilt, Subaru-powered C-cab. Orv Elgie of Downey, California, won the "Best Appearing Car" trophy for his '37 Ford sedan delivery.

It wasn't the contests that made the Street Rod Nationals a success. The adventure of driving long distances coupled with the camaraderie of like-minded hobbyists at the event made the Nats a "must attend." Until now, most rodders had only experienced the hobby through their local clubs and the predominantly California-based magazines. Meeting rodders from all parts of the country was an affirmation for all involved.

The second Street Rod Nationals was held in Memphis, the location of the NSRA headquarters, and it drew more than twice as many cars as the first event. By the end of the decade, the Nats had become the largest participant rodding event in the country, and the NSRA had established itself as a valuable organized voice for hot rodders.

Bud Bryan '29 Roadster

Bud Bryan built this roadster in 1968, when he was an associate editor at *Rod & Custom* magazine. The personal project vehicles of rod-magazine staffers often ended up as the subjects of magazine how-to articles, and Bud's roadster was no exception; its construction was documented in a series of articles in *R&C*.

The project started when Bud scored a basket-case body and a rough set of Deuce frame rails for a mere $18. A lot of TLC was needed to bring these components back to life; the frame rails alone had more than 100 holes that needed to be filled. Bud used the front- and rear-frame crossmembers from a Model A, a common trick among hot rodders building Deuce chassis. The slimmer profile of a Model A front crossmember and the higher arc of a Model A rear crossmember provide an additional drop in ride height.

Bud equipped the 276-cid 1948 Mercury flathead V-8 with Weiand finned heads and a Weiand intake manifold with two Stromberg 97 carburetors. He connected the engine to a '39 Lincoln Zephyr three-speed transmission and a Halibrand quick-change rear end. Up front, he installed a straightforward buggy-sprung Bell Auto Parts dropped I-beam axle.

Kelsey-Hayes wire wheels, '40 Ford brakes, and chromed and paint-detailed backing plates were used at all four corners.

Bud and the rest of the *Rod & Custom* staff practiced what they preached. Bud's roadster was a groundbreaking car for the time in that it was one of the first "retro" or nostalgia-styled hot rods. It was deliberately built from vintage components rather than the latest speed parts, and it utilized a Ford flathead for power, rather than some "new-fangled" V-8. Bud and his colleagues at *R&C* were also pioneers in the concept of nationwide rod runs, and their long-distance hauls proved that if you had the gumption and the guts, a flathead-powered roadster could be successfully driven across the country.

Bud's roadster is currently in the capable hands of Julian Alvarez of Garden Grove, California. Julian has literally had a hand in finishing many high-profile street rods, as he was responsible for rubbing out the paint jobs on many of Boyd Coddington's cars and other pro-shop cars of the 1980s and '90s. When it comes to his own cars, however, Julian sometimes prefers patina over perfection, and he has kept Bud's roadster in a well-preserved but mostly unrestored state.

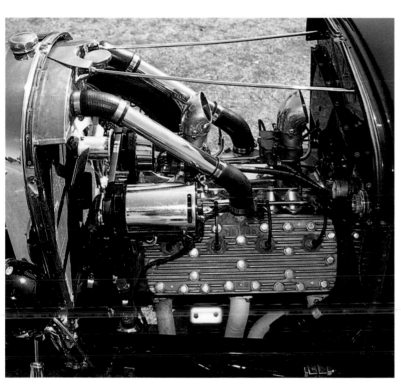

American Graffiti Coupe

Ask any car guy to name his top 10 favorite movies, and George Lucas' 1973 film *American Graffiti* will almost certainly be on the list—usually at or near the top. The movie is well-loved among mainstream audiences for its nostalgic, documentarylike portrayal of 1962 teens, but is especially respected among hot rodders because it gets the cars right. The cars were as perfectly cast as the actors.

American Graffiti revitalized interest in traditional hot rodding by bringing to worldwide audiences the undeniable visceral appeal of a real hot rod in motion. The healthy V-8 rumble, cycle fenders turning with the front tires, night lights reflecting off the chrome-reversed wheels, and bright-yellow paint—all captured the sensory excitement of hot rodding. The eternal coolness of Milner and his coupe has inspired many *Graffiti Coupe* replicas.

George Lucas and *American Graffiti* coproducer Gary Kurtz "auditioned" more than a dozen rods in their search for the right car before purchasing the Deuce that would become the *Graffiti Coupe*. They chose a red, full-fendered coupe mainly because its top was already chopped. Lucas immediately had the car reworked for the movie. The front suspension was rebuilt and chromed. A rare Man-A-Fre four-carb intake, headers, and a T-10 four-speed transmission were added to the existing 327-cid Chevy. The grille shell was sectioned, and the full fenders were replaced by bobbed rear fenders and front cycle fenders. Finally, the car was repainted in bright-yellow lacquer.

The *Graffiti Coupe* endured the typical rigors of film use, then sat for a few years on Universal Studios' outdoor back lot. After Universal had it refurbished in 1979 for *More American Graffiti*, Steve Fitch of Wichita, Kansas, acquired it in a sealed-bid auction. Current owner Rick Figari bought the coupe from Steve in the early '80s and has wisely maintained it in its original movie condition, performing only necessary rehabilitation. Figari, a San Francisco native, often takes it to car shows where it sometimes appears with John Milner himself, actor Paul LeMat.

The California Kid

Among the most significant hot rods of the 1970s was Pete Chapouris' chopped 1934 Ford coupe. It starred in a television movie, bucked the then-dominant resto rod trend, and played an important role in the founding of Pete and Jake's Hot Rod Repair, one of the first modern professional rod shops.

Thanks to *Hot Rod* magazine's Gray Baskerville, Chapouris met *Rod & Custom* staffer Jim Jacobs, who was pounding out his own chopped '34 Ford coupe at the time. With similar tastes, the pair became fast friends and soon started their own hot rod business.

Pete's '34 gained its name from a 1973 ABC made-for-TV movie starring Martin Sheen. The movie, along with the motion picture *American Graffiti* from the same year, spurred hot rod enthusiasm and nostalgia, and reminded a generation how a hot rod should look and sound.

Pete bought the car for $250 with the top already chopped. He dropped in the Ford 302-cid V-8, FMX gearbox, and quick-change rear end from a previous rod, and had Manuel Reyes apply the prominent flames. The car originally had a set of Halibrand mags, but they were swapped for red steelies with beauty rings for the movie. The movie producers also had the signature "California Kid" lettering applied to the doors along the belt line.

Today, *The California Kid* resides with Jerry Slover of Peculiar, Missouri, who acquired it in the 1986 purchase of Pete & Jake's business. Jerry was one of P&J's original customers and is a longtime hot rodder. The quick-change is gone in favor of a Ford nine-inch rear end, and several of the chassis parts have been replaced. After all, the car has more than 90,000 miles on it! Now reunited with Jake's coupe (see next spread), *The Kid* has found a good home.

Jake's Coupe

Along with Pete Chapouris' the *California Kid*, Jim Jacobs' 1934 Ford three-window coupe has a secure place as one of history's greatest hot rods. The car simply possesses all the right characteristics. It is owner-built with impeccable craftsmanship. It's made of real Ford steel. It displays a reverence for hot rod traditions while remaining totally original and can't be mistaken for any other rod. It's visually arresting, loud, and fast. And, best of all, it's been driven—a lot.

Jim "Jake" Jacobs started fiddling with old Fords when he wasn't even old enough to drive. He was a founding member of the Early Times Car Club in '64, and in '66 he started working in Ed Roth's shop. He joined the *Rod & Custom* magazine staff in '70 at the request of editor Bud Bryan.

Jake built this car in 1973. Like Pete Chapouris, Jake bucked early '70s resto rod trends by chopping his coupe's top (his first ever chop). The narrowed '37 Ford truck grille was also an unusual addition. He initially installed orange Kelsey-Hayes wire wheels and a torquey 364-cid 1957 Buick nailhead V-8.

That nailhead had been residing in the NieKamp '29 roadster (pp. 42–43) when Jake bought it in 1969.

Soon after the coupe was finished, Jake teamed up with Pete Chapouris to open Pete and Jake's Hot Rod Parts. Pet and Jake's coupes shared unofficial mascot duties for the shop for more than a decade, racking up thousands of miles when the duo attended the NSRA Street Rod Nationals and other events all over the country. What better marketing is there for a rod shop?

While many rods built in the 1970s look dated today, Jake's coupe looks as stylish now as it did when he first finished it. The coupe has seen a couple of engine swaps and several wheel and tire changes over the years. For now, it runs a Chevy 350 that Jake installed in the '80s, as well as 16×10 E.T. III wheels in back and 15×5½ Real Wheels up front.

In 1999, Jerry Slover, the current owner of Pete and Jake's Hot Rod Parts, talked Jake into selling him the coupe so it could be reunited with the *California Kid*. Jerry has no plans of splitting them up again.

Resto Rods

In the hobby's early days, the overriding goal of hot rodders was to make their cars as fast as possible. In the 1940s and '50s, the prewar Fords that hot rodders cut up were simply used cars. Rodders started with the lightest, cheapest body style possible, like a roadster or a coupe, and stripped off any nonessential pieces. Streamlining and weight reduction meant faster speeds, so components like cowl lights, hood ornaments, exterior horns, spare tires, luggage racks, and parking lights were quickly discarded. As a matter of course, this sparse look became common hot rod style.

However, as years went by, prewar Fords became inherently more valuable as "antique" cars. Inevitably, a nice Model A in 1970 was nowhere near as disposable as a nice Model A in 1950. Because of the steadily increasing scarcity and deteriorating condition of hot rodding fodder, a natural tendency toward restoration developed among many hot rodders, and the resto rodding trend emerged.

Improved speed and performance were still the goal, but hot rodders now took pains to preserve the quaint, old-timey geegaws that they used to immediately discard. Chromed wire wheels were a popular choice among resto rodders since they mimicked factory stock wire wheels, and psychedelic paint schemes gave way to stock Ford colors or earth tones with stock two-tone schemes and pinstriping. The late '60s and '70s also saw increased interest among rodders in Ford body styles that they had traditionally shied away from, like phaetons and Victorias.

The black 1934 Ford sedan shown here was originally built by Bob Tinsley and exhibits stock Ford styling traits that belie its modern underpinnings. Underhood, Bob installed a Chevy 350 hooked to a Turbo 350 transmission. He updated the chassis with an independent front suspension and a rear end from a '73 Ford Maverick. Inside, he added stock Ford seats covered in late-model Buick burgundy crushed velour. Air conditioning, power steering, power brakes, a tilt wheel, and cruise control were also added for driving comfort.

Even the most die-hard hot rodders usually have a deep appreciation for bone-stock old Fords, the way that ol' Henry originally envisioned them. The simple, understated elegance of the cars shown here makes it easy to see why.

Fog lights, horns, and stock headlights on a 1934 Ford

Greyhound radiator cap on a 1932 Ford

Rear spare-tire carrier, stock taillights, and stock bumper on a 1934 Ford Tudor sedan

Rear-mounted luggage rack on a 1932 Ford phaeton

Buttera T Sedan

In 1973, John Buttera started building a '26 Ford Model T sedan that would change his career. By now, "Li'l" John (a nickname that refers to his diminutive stature) had made a name for himself as a drag car fabricator, building famous Funny Car, Top Fuel, and Pro Stock cars for the likes of Tom McEwen, Shirley Muldowney, Joe Pisano, Don Prudhomme, Harry Schmidt, Don Schumacher, Barry Setzer, and Mickey Thompson.

Always interested in hot rods, Buttera decided to build the T as a roadworthy resto-style rod, and *Hot Rod* covered the process in a series of 1974 articles. Aiming for a smooth, firm ride, Buttera fell back on his Funny Car experience. He fabricated a two-tier frame, then hung independent suspension at all four corners. Buttera fashioned parts such as the control arms, radius rods, and hub carriers from scratch, and whittled the spindle uprights from a material that would become his medium of choice, billet aluminum. He chose a Jaguar rear end, but modified its uprights.

To make the car as solid as possible, Buttera welded all of the seams in the steel body, then riveted sheet-aluminum roof and floor inserts in place. The result amounted to a unibody design. Those squeaks and rattles Buttera wanted to avoid weren't evident more than 20 years later when Gray Baskerville road tested the car and remarked in *Rod & Custom*, "… now I know what it's like to go for a spin in what just may be the finest street rod ever built."

Inside, Buttera incorporated many creature comforts that have become commonplace today but were unique for a street rod at the time. He added cruise control, digital gauges, power windows, and air conditioning with air ducts routed to the dash.

Buttera had the help of many talented rodders along the way. Metal bender Steve Davis contributed his skills throughout the project, and is responsible for the two 12-gallon aluminum saddle tanks that fit under the side aprons. Art Chrisman rebuilt the 1967 Ford 289-cid V-8, Tony Nancy upholstered the Volvo bucket seats, and "Fat" Jack Robinson applied the metallic-brown paint job.

After his experience with the T, Buttera turned his attention to a 1929 Ford he bought for $50. When he found a pair of stock Model A windshield posts with an asking price of $50, Buttera decided he would rather make his own than pay that price. Thus was born the billet trend that would shape street rod styling so greatly in the 1980s and beyond. After his experience with these two rods, Buttera gave up his drag car business, opting instead to build rods, which were much safer than drag cars.

Buttera drove the T for two years, then gave it to his wife when he decided he "… didn't like it because it was too much like an old man's car." She used it as her daily driver, then sold it in 1982. The car passed through a few owners and was rehabbed once. No matter the owner, ever since Buttera built it, the T has been driven regularly. Isn't that what street rods are for?

Lowriders

The history of lowriding is distinct and separate from the history of hot rods and customs, though the two cultures developed side by side and intersected frequently. Lowered, personalized cars, called "bombacitas" or bombs, first began appearing in Mexican-American neighborhoods in Southern California in the late 1930s. They developed out of the blossoming Chicano youth culture, along with zoot suit-wearing pachucos and a specific slang vernacular.

The emphasis was not speed or performance, but cruising slowly and showing off your fixed-up car. Chevys were vastly preferred, as they were a bit more stylish than the comparable Ford models, yet still affordable. Similar to traditional customs, the first and most important step toward a respectable Chicano cruiser was a lowered suspension. Early lowering methods included cutting or heating coil springs, installing lowering blocks, or simply throwing a few bags of sand or cement in the trunk. Where customizers favored chopped tops and other body modifications, the Chicano cruisers preferred stock bodies adorned with as many factory accessories as possible.

The next major event in the lowrider's evolution was the invention of hydraulic suspension systems, a development that was born out of necessity. Authorities had long frowned upon the severely lowered ride heights of custom cars. In 1959, Southern California police implemented Vehicle Code #24008, which stated that no portion of a vehicle could be lower than the lowest part of the wheel rim. Officers vigorously enforced the law, ticketing cars that violated the minimum ride-height standard. Faced with the new specter of police harassment and expensive citations, cruisers began using World War II-surplus hydraulic parts to create adjustable suspensions that could raise or lower their vehicles at the flip of a switch.

With the advent of hydraulics in the early 1960s, the term "lowrider" was coined, which referred both to the cars and to their owners. Like "Chicano," it was initially a term of derision, though it was soon adopted with pride. Strong club identities formed, with club members proudly displaying metal plaques in their cars' rear windows. By the early '70s, several lowrider-specific trends had developed. Dazzling multicolor paint jobs often wore intricate patterns in candy and metalflake, along with the occasional mural. Wire wheels on tiny thin-stripe whitewall tires became virtually mandatory. Outlandish custom interiors, and even trunk compartments, were lavishly upholstered in crushed velvet. Engines and undercarriages were often obsessively detailed with copious chrome and/or gold plating.

The template for the typical lowrider was pretty well established by the early 1970s, and most modern-day lowriders don't stray far from this classic style. Chevrolets, particularly Impalas, remained the overwhelming favorites, though almost any vehicle became fair game for the lowrider treatment. When mainstream customizing went away in the '60s, lowriders were among the only street-driven customs to soldier on, until the revival of traditional customs in the late '70s and early '80s.

1

2

3

4

5

6

1. In 1962, Oscar Ruelas and his brothers formed the Dukes car club, which focused solely on pre-1955 "bombs." Oscar's '39 Chevy four-door sedan typifies the "bomb" style lowrider. Note the sun visor, fog lights, and bumper guards; all were popular accessories with the lowrider crowd. Unlike customizers, who usually limited themselves to two-door body styles, Chicano lowriders were open to most any body style, four-doors included. The gangster-like styling of the '39 Chevy made it the most popular early model "bomb." **2.** Completed by early 1972, Jesse Valadez's Gypsy Rose '63 Chevy Impala was a landmark lowrider that took custom paintwork to new heights. Painter Walt Prey spent six months adorning Jesse's Chevy with more than 40 hand-painted roses. Tragically, the original Gypsy Rose's paint job was destroyed when jealous cruisers threw bricks at the car. Jesse later built a '64 Impala in the same style. **3.** Prior to the widespread availability of aftermarket wire wheels, five-spoke chrome wheels were a lowrider favorite. This pink pearl '58 Chevy Delray sedan delivery wears Astro Supremes, but Cragar S/S wheels were also popular. Elaborate murals also started appearing in the early '70s. **4.** This hydraulics-equipped 1962 Chevy Impala sits in the "lifted" position. Wire wheels have long been a lowrider staple, though Tru-Spoke cross-laced wire wheels such as these have largely been replaced by straight-laced wire wheels from Dayton and other manufacturers. **5.** Most traditional customizers strip off superfluous trim, but lowriders usually prefer adding as many accessories as possible to their rides. This '52 Chevy DeLuxe hardtop sports headlight visors, bumper and license guards, a sun visor, and fender skirts, as well as subtle pinstriping. **6.** Many lowriders retain factory stock bodywork, but a few wear custom modifications. This '73 Chevy Impala has a reverse-opening trunk and a "targa-top" half convertible treatment. Multi-colored candy paint schemes became more complex as the '70s progressed. **7.** The hydraulic systems originally used strictly to raise lowriders to a legal ride height soon spawned the unusual sport of "car-hopping." This '58 Impala bounces off the ground as its owner works the hydraulic switches inside the car. All modern-day competitive hoppers use remote controls so the owner can stand safely away from the vehicle.

7

Nostalgia Sleeper
In 1974, hot rodding was in the midst of its revival as street rodding. The fifth NSRA Nationals was held in Minneapolis, attracting some 2250 cars, almost four times the number that appeared at the first event just four years earlier. Meanwhile, the traditional custom was at perhaps its lowest point.

Customs weren't forgotten, though. Pat Ganahl was working as *Street Rodder* magazine's technical editor at the time, but he played a significant role in determining the magazine's content. Always a custom fan, Ganahl decided to make the November 1974 *Street Rodder* a "Special Chopped Merc Issue." Without much happening on the custom scene, the only contemporary fully customized Merc to appear in the issue was a '50 coupe built by Charlie Lopez of Midway City, California. The reason was simple: It was the only one the staff could find.

Though he would call the car the *Nostalgia Sleeper*, Charlie, a paint and body man who belonged to the Classics car club of Santa Ana, combined traditional and lowrider themes throughout the project.

In traditional custom style, Charlie treated the car to a considerable amount of bodywork. He shaved the door handles, as well as the hood, trunk, and side trim. Without the benefit of prior experience, Charlie did an excellent job of chopping the top. He also removed the windshield's center post and butted the windshield glass together.

Up front, Charlie modified the fenders to accept deeply tunneled 1966 Olds Cutlass headlights. He molded a complete front pan to house inset bumperettes and a sunken license plate. A '53 Chevy grille bar with seven '54 Chevy grille teeth completed the front end.

At the rear, Charlie tunneled 1962 Olds taillights into the fenders and molded in a rolled pan that picked up the rear fenders' character line. Along the sides, he added triple-tube lakes pipes and dual sunken antennas accented by raised flares in the left front fender.

Inside, Charlie had Unique of Santa Ana lay down shag carpeting and upholster the seats with pink rolls. He also had the dash plated by Rogers Plating. A chromed and detailed stock '65 Chevy 283-cid V-8 provided the power.

Lowrider touches included Cragar SS wheels with bullet center caps on thin-stripe whitewall tires and a hydraulic suspension that let the car sit on the ground, up high, or anywhere in between.

The paint reflected both traditional lowrider themes. Charlie applied a silver metalflake base highlighted with fogged pink scallops. An artist known only as "Steve" did the abundant pinstriping, and "Kinkade" added a mural. While murals were and still are common on lowriders, this one featured traditional rods and customs in a drive-in setting.

The article on the *Nostalgia Sleeper* appeared at a time when customizing needed a boost. It served to carry on the flame of the traditional custom while also embracing lowrider themes. It may have been a rarity at the time, but cars like Charlie's Merc were signs of life during trying times for the custom car hobby.

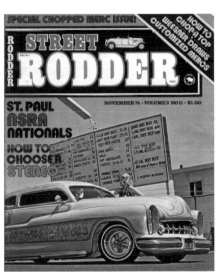

Foose's Ford

By the mid 1970s, fans of '50s-style customs were few and far between, and those that were still interested probably weren't youngsters. Sam Foose was one of the few who liked the old look. In his early 40s, Foose was an accomplished metal man who owned Project Design, a shop in Goleta, California, that built cars to order.

Foose attended high school in the 1950s and had always wanted a custom of his own. In '75, he decided to build one in his off hours. He chose a '48 Ford coupe as the subject matter and built a car that managed to break new ground while paying homage to the '50s custom scene of Foose's high school days.

A unique chop helped give the car a sleek look. Sam chopped the top three Inches at the front and five inches in the rear, reworking the rear quarter windows for better flow. Sam had studied numerous chops prior to the work, but ended up making up his own technique with outstanding results. Sam also removed the windshield center post and butted the glass together.

In fine 1950s tradition, Sam strived for a flowing one-piece appearance for the body. To that end, he molded the front and rear gravel pans into the body; filled the fender seams, parking lights, and fuel-filler door; and shaved the hood, trunk, doors, and side trim. He also dechromed and molded in the trim at the top of the grille, frenched the headlights, and moved the taillights to the rear bumper guards.

Sam installed electric pushbuttons to open the doors, built a new rear seat from scratch, and had John Englehart upholster the interior with white leather and maroon mohair. Sam wired a stereo inside the glovebox, but left the dash stock. He laid down carpeting in the trunk, where he also added a custom fiberglass tool tray.

Underhood, Sam installed a 276-cid Ford flathead V-8 built by Richard Wood. An Evans intake manifold, an Iskendarian racing cam, and two Stromberg 97 carbs helped give the engine a '50s look and 250 horsepower. More striking was the firewall, which Sam painstakingly painted in a black-and-white checkerboard pattern.

To get the right stance, Sam went to work on the chassis and suspension, dropping the car nearly nine inches overall. Up front, he installed a six-inch dropped axle and shortened the spring three inches. At the rear, he Z'ed the frame eight inches and raised the rear spring crossmembers nine inches. Air shocks were installed at all four corners to provide a comfortable ride.

Sam finished the car in a deep-red lacquer color he called Cherry Fizz. Wide whitewalls with smoothie hubcaps completed the '50s theme.

Two years in the works, the completed Ford was the cover car of the August 1977 Argus publication *1001 Custom & Rod Ideas*, which declared "Customs are Back!" Customs may not have been totally back at the time, but throwback cars like Foose's Ford helped bring on a custom car renaissance that continues to this day.

Of course, Foose's Ford wasn't his only contribution to the rod and custom world. He would go on to build several other high-profile cars, and his son, Chip, would become one of the hobby's foremost builders and designers.

Deucari By the late 1970s, some hot rodders had enough money to infuse their cars with truly exotic DNA. In '79, Brian Burnett, the son of '50s and '60s *Hot Rod* magazine cutaway illustrator Rex Burnett, became the first to put a Ferrari powerplant in a traditional hot rod.

Brian, a Ferrari dealer in Los Gatos, California, always wanted to build something different. He jumped at the chance when a Ferrari 365 GT 2+2 engine became available. The all-aluminum overhead cam V-12 had done time in William Harrah's "Jerrari," a Ferrari-powered Jeep Wagoneer. The 320-horsepower 268-cid engine in hand, Brian commissioned Dick "Magoo" Megugorac to build a Deuce roadster.

Installing the Ferrari engine meant Magoo had to extend the front of the frame four inches. The hood of the Wescott fiberglass body required a similar extension. To harness the V-12 power, Magoo chose a Muncie four-speed transmission and a Halibrand quick-change rear end.

He stuck with a Ferrari theme throughout the project, outfitting the car with Borrani wire wheels, a Connolly leather interior, and Ferrari red paint. To maintain a sleek flow from front to rear, Magoo added a DuVall windshield and a lift-off aluminum top with a '37 Cord rear window.

With or without the top, the finished highboy's proportions were well-received. The proof came when the "Deucari" won

the America's Most Beautiful Roadster award at the 1979 Grand National Roadster Show.

The Deucari proved to be more than just a show queen. Brian drove it to the 1980 Street Rod Nationals in Memphis. He also took it for a few passes down the dragstrip, turning a best E.T. of 13.01 seconds at 105 mph.

Current owner Ed Hegarty swapped the Muncie for a Doug Nash five-speed. Like Burnett, he drives the car extensively. While no longer perfect thanks to its road duty, the Deucari is still beautiful. It's also fast, and it's driven, too—like a hot rod should be.

Silver Bullet

Before Boyd Coddington became the biggest name in hot rodding, he was a budding rod builder searching for not only his niche, but his personal style. Boyd's early work was heavily influenced by the work of "Li'l" John Buttera, a former Funny Car builder who had turned to building hot rods in 1974.

Boyd responded to Buttera's first hot rod, a 1926 T sedan, with a similar '26 T sedan of his own. Buttera followed with a '29 Model A roadster and again Boyd responded in kind, this time with the *Silver Bullet* '29 roadster shown here.

Although Boyd took many of his cues from Buttera's '29, he began to find his style with the *Silver Bullet*. Described by *Street Rodder* as "a striking blend of traditional styling, contemporary rodding, and innovation," the car was a precursor to the beautiful, smooth hot rods that would emerge from Boyd's shop in the future.

From the start of his career, Boyd always had the ability to put the right people in the right position to do the right work. Boyd filled the body's seams and smoothed the fenderwells, then had Buttera fabricate a smooth frame to match the contour of the steel '29 roadster body. Boyd also fashioned the suspension, making an independent rear with a Corvette center section and J&J hub carriers.

With a smooth, yet pleasingly traditional body on fabricated frame rails, Boyd opted for a simple and modern interior. Jim Bailey stitched the burgundy upholstery, Steve Borowitz added a woodgrain insert to the dashboard, and Buttera provided the digital gauges.

For motivation, Boyd installed a Chevy 350 with four Weber carbs. In the interest of reliability, the Webers soon gave way to a single four-barrel carb. A beefed-up PowerGlide routed the power to the rear.

The finished car was featured on the cover of the April 1978 *Street Rodder*, drawing the attention of candymaker Vern Luce. Luce soon hired Boyd to build him a '33 Ford coupe, a job that prompted Boyd to quit his day job as a machinist at Disneyland and open his own shop. Hot rodding would never be the same.

Like any good street rod, the *Silver Bullet* did some serious road time over the next 20 years until Joe Ditta of Phoenix, Arizona, found it for sale at a swap meet in 1997. Painted black and in need of repair, Joe bought it, and enlisted the help of several Phoenix-area craftsmen to return it to its former glory. Larry Savi of Westec Customs supervised the restoration, doing justice to the excellent work Boyd and friends did in 1977.

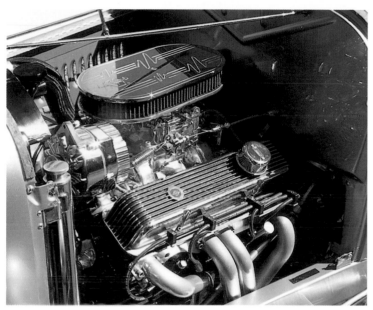

1

Customs of the 1970s

The hot rod and custom explosion of the 1950s was a largely youth-oriented phenomenon. Postwar teens and twentysomethings used the automobile to help define who they were. Cars and car-related activities, like hanging out at drive-ins and street racing, were part of their culture.

By the 1970s, Detroit's muscle cars had displaced rods and customs in the minds of most teens as the latest, hottest cars. There was still a youth automotive culture; traditional rods and customs just weren't a big part of it. In the rodding world, however, things started to turn. Many of those '50s teenagers were now in their 30s and 40s and they still liked the cool cars of their youth. This brought about a hot rod revival that manifested itself in the formation of the National Street Rod Association and the launch of the Street Rod Nationals in 1970.

Customs were slow to follow. The custom scene had always been smaller than the hot rod world and it would take custom fans much longer to organize. Groups like the Kustom Kemps of America, and events such as the KKOA Nationals, Lead East, and the Paso Robles car show would come along in the early 1980s, but the roots of those developments could be traced to the '70s.

Like their hot rod brethren, custom car fans were growing older. Here and there throughout the 1970s, customs were built by and for older enthusiasts. These cars brought back memories for others who fondly recalled the '50s and '60s. Little by little, more custom car fans returned to the hobby of their youth. Eventually, this grassroots enthusiasm would snowball into a custom car revival that continues today.

2

3

1. *John D'Agostino bought a brand-new 1970 Pontiac Grand Prix late in his sophomore year of college, and had Ed Fry customize it. Fry lowered the car, removed much of the trim, and filled the resulting holes. Art Himsl applied the candy gold and tangerine paint. John entered the Grand Prix in the '70 Grand National Roadster Show under the name John Augustine, and won the Outstanding Custom award. He campaigned the car at ISCA shows on the West Coast during the '70 and '71 seasons.* **2.** *John D'Agostino had Ed Fry customize another new car in 1972, this one a Buick Riviera. After working with an artist to flesh out the design, D'Agostino had Fry replace the eggcrate grille with simple horizontal bars, radius and flare the wheel cutouts, and shave off all the trim, including the door handles. The headlights were tunneled six inches, and the taillights were restyled with chrome blades. Art Himsl and Mike Haas painted the Buick in candy-red metalflake, toned to different shades of tangerine with silver scallops. It was named International Class Champion in the Full Custom category in the 1972-73 ISCA season.*

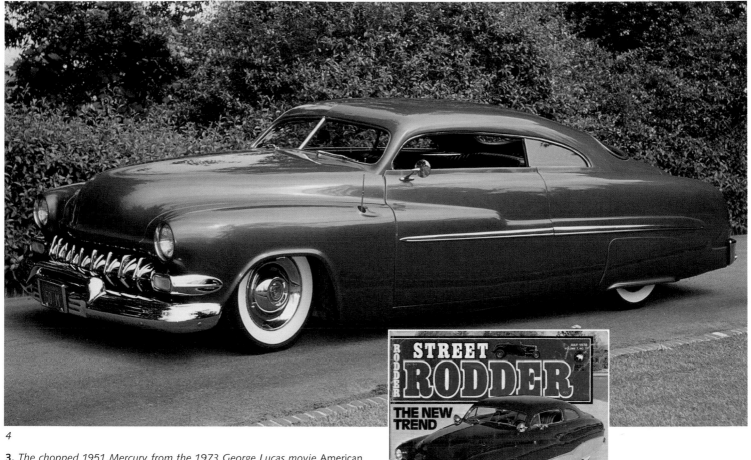

4

5

6

3. The chopped 1951 Mercury from the 1973 George Lucas movie American Graffiti was one of the more influential customs of the '70s, as it inspired a wave of nostalgia. In addition to the top chop, the studio had the chrome trim removed, the headlights frenched, and a custom grille added. It was a rush job and the finished car didn't look very good, but it came off well on film and helped the movie set a nostalgic tone. **4.** Blas Gonzalez of Montebello, California, built this 1950 Merc for his teenage son Steve in the late '70s. Blas incorporated the rear quarters and bumpers from a '51 Merc, a '54 Pontiac bumper guard, and a '54 Chevy grille. He also frenched the headlights and 1952 Lincoln taillights, and flared the wheel openings. Plastic body fillers had come into common use by the '70s, but Blas did most of the bodywork in lead. **5.** In the mid 1970s, Richard Zocchi enlisted Bill Reasoner and others to build his Cool 50 Mercury. The car received a lot of publicity and helped to revive interest in traditional customs. Modifications to the '50 Merc included a 4½-inch top chop, a '52 DeSoto front bumper, '53 DeSoto grille teeth, hood side scoops, '70 Buick Riviera side trim, and a beautiful candy-apple red and silver two-tone paint job. The car appeared on the cover of the July 1978 issue of Street Rodder magazine. **6.** In 1973, artist Robert Williams did a painting for Hot Rod magazine called "A Devil with a Hammer and Hell with a Torch." It depicted legendary customizers George Barris and Ed Roth and a fanciful purple chopped Merc with green flames that Williams called Rudy's Green Flame. The producers of the Happy Days television show decided they wanted this car for the Fonz to drive, and they had Detroit customizers Sam Wade and Jack Kampney build it. Starting with a '50 Merc, the duo gave the top a slight chop, a '54 Pontiac grille, sunken '59 Caddy taillights, and candy-purple paint with darker purple scallops and green flames. The car never appeared on Happy Days, but it did tour extensively on the ISCA custom car show circuit during the late '70s. The car was later refurbished with different paint and a Hemi engine, and now resides in Don Garlits' Museum of Drag Racing in Ocala, Florida. **7.** Loren "Curley" Tremayne, who worked for famous builder and painter Rod Powell, customized his 1950 Mercury in the late 1970s. He had Butch Hurlhey chop the top 3½ inches up front and 5½ inches at the rear, slanting the door posts forward in the process. All the trim, including the door handles, had been removed, so Curley had Paul Lewis make the doors solenoid operated. Curley frenched in a pair of '53 Buick headlight bezels, used wire mesh in the grille, and added a '63 Buick floating bar. Powell applied the candy-tangerine lacquer paint.

7

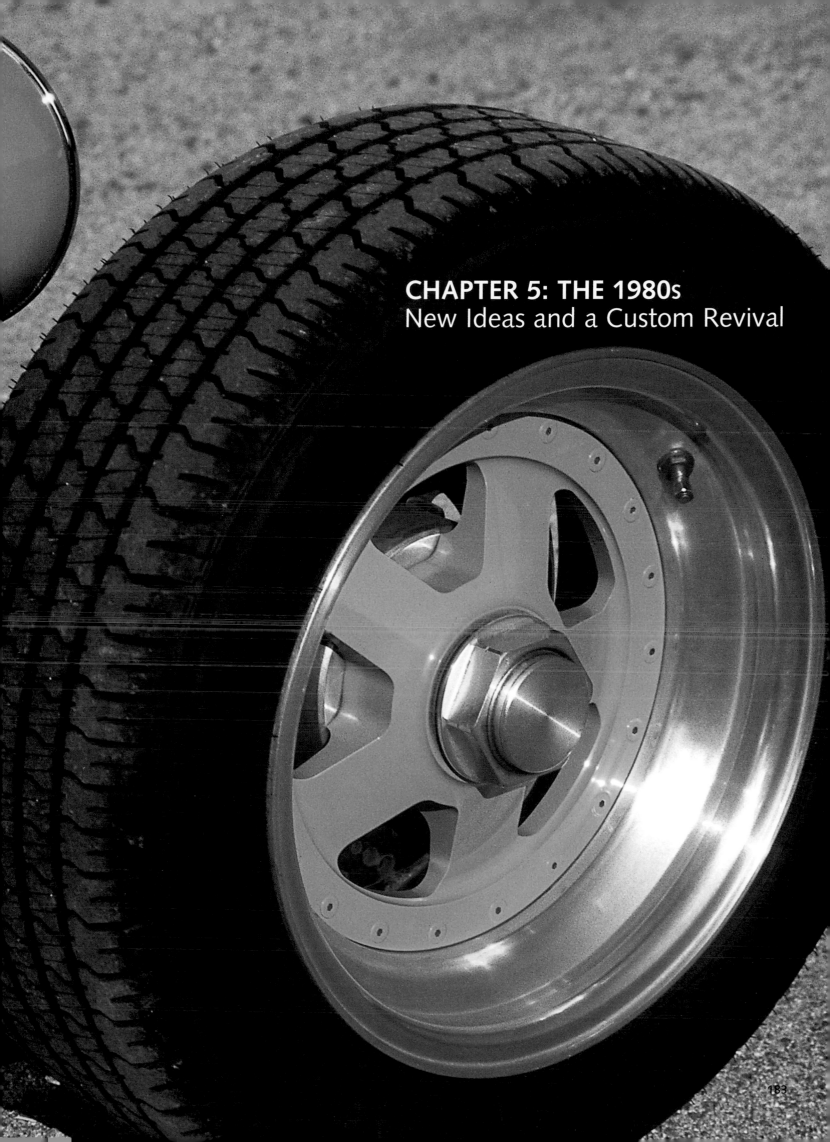

CHAPTER 5: THE 1980s
New Ideas and a Custom Revival

It had always been fairly costly to build a hot rod or custom, but young car enthusiasts had always been able to scrimp and save enough to get their projects done. Beginning in the 1980s, though, more money was flying around than ever before. Those dollars ramped up the level of build quality, components availability, and professional building services. Nearly every aspect of the hot rod and custom scene benefited.

There are several possible reasons for the change. Many of the guys who couldn't have a cool car in high school were now older and had the money to build that car—only better. For the first time, there were shops and aftermarket businesses all over the country that could build great cars and excellent components for those cars. Friendly competition played a part, too. Many wanted to prove "I can build one better than yours." Whatever the reason, it was definitely a new era for hot rods and a renaissance for the '50s custom.

The new design trend in hot rodding could be summarized in one word: billet. Though it was a decidedly 1980s phenomenon, it had its roots in the '70s. In 1976, Funny Car constructor John Buttera built a Model A roadster based on ideas submitted by designer Harry Bradley. It was new and contemporary, and it differed greatly from the way hot rods had been built. The main difference was Buttera's use of machined billet aluminum for some of the suspension components, as well as the windshield posts, rearview and side mirrors, and gauge cluster. Dan Woods had dabbled with machined aluminum in the early '70s with ball-end milled firewalls for T-buckets and Buttera had even made some machined aluminum parts for his own '26 T a couple years earlier. But this was the first time that new machined aluminum components, including exterior parts, were used extensively on a hot rod. John's white roadster was also completely devoid of chrome—another deviation from the norm.

John's friend Boyd Coddington took careful notice. Boyd was a machinist at Disneyland in the 1970s who had built some outstanding hot rods in his garage. In '79, he built a small shop behind his house and went into the business of building cars full time. Boyd and John teamed up to create a couple of billet parts for the car Boyd was finishing, a 1932 Ford Vicky.

The Vicky was really a resto rod with a billet instrument panel, but the next car out of Boyd's shop, Vern Luce's '33 Ford coupe, helped define the new era of billet "smoothie" cars. Smoothie referred to the elimination of all the "barbs" associated with older cars, items such as hinges, door handles, windshield frames, body seams, and in some cases, overlapping body panels (like the doors on a Model A).

Though Buttera's Model A roadster hinted at it, the Luce coupe really cemented the look for the high-tech hot rod of the 1980s. While attending the Art Center College of Design in Pasadena in 1977-78, Boyd commissioned me to design the Luce coupe. The design was a refined amalgamation of Jim Ewing's fenderless orange '34 Ford coupe and Jake Jacobs' '34 highboy coupe. It couldn't have been accomplished without the expertise of people like Boyd, John, and metal master Steve Davis, who, like Buttera, had worked on a few dragsters and Funny Cars.

The Luce coupe came at a time when the landscape was ripe for a new trend, making it extremely influential. Many future rods would follow its design cues.

From there, the billet fad took off, and billet parts are still incorporated into new hot rods today. The difference is that today numerous manufacturers create billet parts that can be purchased with a phone call and a credit card. Billet turned into probably the biggest thing in hot rodding since the tire! And it has even transcended hot rods to become prevalent on custom motorcycles, especially Harley-Davidsons.

For Boyd Coddington, the Luce coupe was only a preliminary step in the billet arena. Again with the help of John Buttera, Boyd came up with a three-piece billet wheel that would start the aftermarket billet-wheel trend. The first billet wheels appeared on a roadster version of the Luce coupe built for Jamie Musselman. That car received a great amount of magazine coverage, and won the first of many America's Most Beautiful Roadster honors at the Grand National Roadster Show for Boyd Coddington.

A form of this type of wheel had previously been manufactured by Center Line Wheel Corporation, but those wheels utilized cast or stamped centers. The billet center allowed Boyd to program a mill to cut an infinite number of different designs. Boyd turned his wheels into a whole separate company.

Interiors got the modern treatment too, with gauge clusters made of billet, integrated instead of screw-on armrests, and elegant designs for the door panels and seats. No tuck and roll could be found in these contemporary "smoothies." The interiors were following the latest styles from Detroit, with instrument panels and window frames painted low gloss colors to match the interior. Interiors were now integrated, instead of making the separate pieces stand out with color or chrome.

Under the skin, electronic fuel injection was finding its way into many hot rods, as were four-speed automatic overdrive transmissions, and elaborate, custom-fabricated independent suspensions. Engine blocks were now ground smooth before being shot with paint to make them as shiny and smooth as the outside of the car. Valve covers, air cleaners, spark plug wiring looms—virtually everything in the engine compartment was available in billet.

While Coddington was changing the way hot rods were built, another hot rod was spreading the word to a new audience. Owned by Billy Gibbons of the rock band ZZ Top, the *Eliminator* coupe was a '33 Ford built in Paramount, California, by Don Thelen in 1983. At the time, a cultural revolution of sorts was taking place on television with the growing influence of MTV. The coupe was incorporated into four ZZ Top videos that saw a lot of airplay. The exposure introduced the hot rod to a new generation.

Two other trends that began in the 1980s on hot rods and customs were pastel colors and the pro street look. Pastels and neon-look colors were popular in mainstream culture and fashion, and these hues spilled over into the automotive world. Pro street cars emulated the Pro Stock class of drag racing. They had huge slicks in the rear, which necessitated moving the rear portion of the frame inward and fabricating huge sheetmetal or aluminum wheelwell "tubs." Skinny tires were run up front, and the cars were lowered as far as was practical, and sometimes further. Big, powerful motors and, in some cases, roll cages completed the look.

In the custom world, a few enthusiasts with a historical perspective began to seek out and restore original customs from the 1940s and '50s. A lot of the custom treasures were lost forever, but a surprising number that had been stuffed into garages for 30 or 40 years began to see the light of day. Kurt McCormick, of Webster Groves, Missouri, who has a bloodhound nose for seeking out original customs, began to find success locating historic cars in the 1980s. But the significant original customs were few and far between. That didn't stop other crafty custom fans who began to build clones of their favorite customs from the past, as Jack Walker did with the Hirohata Mercury.

While the NSRA had given street rodders a national organization and plenty of events to attend in the 1970s, custom car fans felt left out. Street rodding events often cut off participation at the 1948 model year, excluding most customs. That began to change in the '80s thanks to the efforts of a few dedicated custom enthusiasts.

Jerry and Elden Titus formed the Kustom Kemps of America (KKOA) in 1981 and hosted a national car show in Wichita, Kansas. Former *Hot Rod* magazine editor Terry Cook began to produce a yearly custom car gathering and 1950s happening called Lead East in '82. And in California, the West Coast Customs club hosted its inaugural custom car show in Paso Robles in '82. These three events welcomed custom car owners and gave them the opportunity to attend a show without having to drive too far. They may not have rivaled the NSRA Nationals in terms of size, but for the custom car owner, these were "must attend" events. Most of the attendees were older. They were the guys who had either been part of

the custom scene in the 1950s and '60s as young adults or who had admired it as youngsters. Their renewed participation in the '80s represented the revival of the custom car scene.

In 1987, a new organization that welcomed both hot rods and customs was created. Founded by ex-NSRA honcho Gary Meadors, the Goodguys Rod and Custom Association continues to put on events and has since expanded to include cars up to '72. Even with this new association and its events, the NSRA's Street Rod Nationals still grew each year.

As the street rodding scene grew, so too did demand for pre-1935 Fords, which were still the subject matter of choice for hot rodders. But as more pre-

resented major recognition. It effectively said that street rod parts makers had grown to become a major part of the two-billion-dollar-a-year automotive aftermarket industry.

While not a trend *per se*, another development of the 1980s was the use of professional designers to draw plans for hot rods, and eventually customs. Boyd Coddington, John Buttera, Roy Brizio, and others enlisted myself, Steve Stanford, Harry Bradley, "Mr. Hot Wheels" Larry Wood, and eventually, Larry Erickson. These designers, all hot rod enthusiasts, conceived ideas or put down on paper what the customer wanted to help guide ever more involved (and expensive) projects.

'35 cars were built, the prices for original cars or components rose. Suddenly, post-'35 cars seemed like bargains, and their styling began to look appealing as well. Thus began another trend of the 1980s, the acceptance by hot rodders of "fat fendered" cars from the late '30s and '40s.

With this new interest came new products, led by Pete and Jake's in 1985 with a line of fat-fender suspension components. Some of the parts aftermarket companies had been making adapted well to the later cars, while others needed to be newly tooled. The components combined with a seemingly unending supply of available Ford and Chevy sheetmetal to keep interest high in the fat-fendered hot rod.

Also in the mid 1980s, the Specialty Equipment and Marketing Association (SEMA), the organization that supports the automotive aftermarket, set aside a portion of its massive annual trade show in Las Vegas for street rod component manufacturers. Since most were and still are "mom and pop" operations, the new "Street Rod Alley" rep-

Most of these projects involved hot rods (like the Luce coupe at the start of the decade), but later in the decade, Cadillac Design Studio alum Larry Erickson designed a custom called *CadZZilla*™. Commissioned by Billy Gibbons of ZZ Top, and built by the crew at Boyd Coddington's shop in Stanton, California, the car was a contemporary iteration of an "aeroback" or fastback 1948 Cadillac sedanette. It was the first really new type of custom since the heyday of the 1950s. The design language of the top, hood, side window openings, and front and rear ends was completely new and different from anything that had gone before it. *CadZZilla*™ created a stir and was instantly recognized as one of the all-time great customs.

By the end of the decade, custom car show participation had grown considerably, and *CadZZilla's*™ debut pointed the way to new possibilities in custom car design. Meanwhile, hot rodders were busy building new types of cars with new kinds of parts. It was a vibrant time for rod and custom fans. ✂

1

KKOA

In 1978, Jerry and Elden Titus of Wichita, Kansas, felt like they were alone. Both brothers had worked for customizing legend Darryl Starbird, Jerry in the '50s and Elden in the '60s, and they still had a passion for customs. But they could find precious little custom car activity, and like-minded people seemed few and far between.

So, with the blessing of his wife DeVona, Jerry decided to put his life savings, $5000, into producing his own custom car show. Having helped Starbird promote his series of indoor shows, Jerry wanted his to be held outdoors and he would only invite custom 1949-51 Mercurys. But after Starbird told him there might not be 10 chopped Mercs left in the United States, Jerry changed his plans and invited 1932 Fords, too. The first Merc-Deuce Reunion was held the first weekend of August 1979 at Kansas City Dragway. To Jerry's delight, 318 cars showed up, including about 25 chopped Mercs. Like-minded people were out there.

The turnout inspired Jerry to start a custom club. It would be just like the old days. Like the Barris shop in the 1950s, he'd spell custom with a "K." Since anyone with a '35 to '60 custom car or truck would be welcome, he used the word "Kemp," an old jazz term that referred to any automobile. By advertising locally and using his mailing list from the Merc-Deuce Reunion, Jerry got 14 people to show up for the first meeting of the Kustom Kemps of America in Wichita on October 1, 1980.

Within a year, Jerry put on the first official KKOA event, the Lead Sled Spectacular. The show was held in August 1981 in Wichita, and attracted 383 customs. The attendees paid the $18 fee to join the KKOA. For their money, they got $10 off the $15 admission to the event, Jerry's *Leadsled'er* club

newsletter (now called the *Trendsetter*), a subscription card, a window sticker, notifications about other events, and the opportunity to gather with other custom fans.

The Lead Sled Spectacular, as well as two other shows that would spring up within the next couple of years—Terry Cook's Lead East and West Coast Kustoms' Cruisin' Nationals near Paso Robles, California—served notice that a custom car revival was in the works. The participants were, for the most part, the same people that had been involved in the halcyon days of the '50s. "I was about 40 at the time, and so were my members," Jerry noted. "They were the teenagers of the late '50s."

By the early 1990s, membership in the KKOA had grown to 13,000 members. This number remained constant until about '95, when according to Elden and Jerry, some members began dying off or getting too old for the hobby. Elden also noted that the growth of the rat rod and custom movement has helped bring in younger people, though membership is now about 5000.

A total of five Merc-Deuce Reunions were held, each five years apart, with the final event occurring in 2004. The Midwest-based Lead Sled Spectacular has continued annually since that first show in 1981, drawing as many as 2500 cars. The KKOA also expanded to put on as many as six different shows across the country each year. The Spectacular was always the most successful, though, as the East and West Coast guys tended to show better support for events put on by local organizations.

In recent years, the KKOA has waived the 1935-60 restriction. As Jerry put it, "A custom is in the eye of the beholder." He doesn't want to exclude anyone.

2

3

4

5

6

7

8

1. *A wide array of customs showed up at the first KKOA Lead Sled Spectacular, held Aug. 6-9, 1981, at the Kansas Coliseum. Almost 400 customs came from all over the country for the first national customs-only show in years. More than 600 "kemps" would attend in 1982, and by 1985, attendance exceeded 1700.* **2.** *At the first KKOA Lead Sled Spectacular, Elden Titus showed his candy-red Crimson Skull 1949 Buick. Elden did the work himself, molding in the front grille shell, adding 1955 Chevy headlights, flaring the front wheel cutouts, making his own fender skirts, and slanting the B-pillars forward.* **3.** *Wichita native Darryl Starbird had never left the customizing scene. A friend and former employer of the Titus brothers, he gave Jerry advice on how to get the Lead Sled Spectacular off the ground. Starbird showed up at the event with a few cars, including his fully customized 1959 Chevy El Camino shop truck.* **4.** *Conrad Winkler brought his scalloped 1951 Olds convertible. With its candy-stripe tuck-and-roll interior, lakes pipes, '55 Chrysler taillights, and bubble skirts, the car had been featured in custom magazines in 1959, and it was still in pretty decent shape.* **5.** *Lee Pratt built his 1941 Buick to gain acceptance to NSRA-type street rod shows, which usually only allowed '48 and earlier model years. With hydraulic suspension, the frame from a '65 Buick Skylark, tuck-and-roll upholstery, frenched headlights, and metallic lavender and purple paint, the car had street rod, custom, and lowrider characteristics.* **6.** *Doug Reed, one of the first 50 KKOA members, showed off his nosed, decked, and shaved 1949 Oldsmobile fastback. The louvered hood, sunken antenna, and scalloped paint were all traditional custom touches, but the rake gave it the look of an early '60s high school hot rod.* **7.** *Rick Schnell's Misty Blue 1950 Merc was a 1980s take on traditional custom styling. All the old tricks were used: Carson-style top, Caddy wheelcovers, Appleton spots, fender skirts, frenched headlights, and a sunken antenna.* **8.** *Bruce Glascock traveled from California with his freshly restored Dream Truck. Spence Murray had chronicled the original buildup in the pages of Rod & Custom magazine in the 1950s. Bruce brought it back to life in the late 1970s, making it one of the first restorations of a historic custom.*

Wally Welch Merc

It's common among automotive enthusiasts to lust after the cars of their youth. By the 1980s, custom car fans who had been teenagers in the '50s were beginning to remember fondly the cars of their teen years. Older and more financially stable, a few of them gradually began to seek out old, historic cars and restore them.

One of the men who started this trend did so almost by accident. Before we get to his story, however, we should examine the history of one of the first 1949-51 Mercs ever to receive a top chop.

Wally Welch bought a new 1950 Mercury coupe in early 1950 and immediately took it to Gil and Al Ayala's shop in East Los Angeles to be customized. The Ayalas chopped the top about four inches in the front and five in the rear, and removed the drip rails. Up front, they molded in the front pan and grille shell, moved the headlights three inches forward and frenched them in, nosed the hood and rounded its corners, and installed five 1951 DeSoto grille teeth. They also frenched the taillights, rounded the door corners, smoothed the rear deck, shaved the door handles, and set electric pushbuttons into the chrome rub strips. Finished in lime gold paint, the car appeared on the cover of the April 1952 issue of *Hop Up* magazine. Soon thereafter, Wally took the car to the Barris Kustoms shop, where they added two more DeSoto teeth and painted it metallic purple. This version appeared in the December 1952 Trend book *Restyle Your Car*.

Wally sold the car to Joe Contrero of East Los Angeles in 1954 or '55. Joe swapped the stock Mercury flathead for a Ford Y-block V-8, then parked the car in '57 when he joined the Army.

Fast forward to 1985 and enter Joe Eddy of Rosemead,

California. At the time, Joe was a well-known Ford F-100 truck customizer who also appreciated traditional customs. A neighbor kid kept telling him about a '50s custom parked under an avocado tree in East Los Angeles. Finally, after the kid said the car looked like Richard Zocchi's *Cool 50* Merc (pg. 181), Joe decided to investigate. The car was a bit of a mess. It had been sitting for almost 30 years. The top was covered in white housepaint to protect the car from the elements, but everything was there. Joe struck a deal that day.

Joe could tell it was a chopped Merc from the 1950s, but he didn't know that it was one of the first few leadsled Mercs ever chopped. Still unaware of the car's pedigree, Joe began restoring it. He retained the exterior design, but decided to upgrade the mechanicals. He installed a 350-cid Chevy V-8, a Turbo 350 transmission, a Ford nine-inch rear end, and power steering from a '76 Ford half-ton pickup. He lowered the car even further than the Ayalas had by reversing the front spindles and cutting the coil springs. Inside, he added air conditioning, a contemporary stereo, and silver-gray cloth upholstery by Frank's of Whittier, California.

During the restoration process, Joe unearthed the April 1952 issue of *Hop Up* magazine and realized what he had. It was too late to restore the car 100 percent accurately, and besides, perfect restorations weren't so important at the time. Nonetheless, Joe retained the 1950s look and revived a long-lost custom.

Joe kept the car until 2004, when he sold it to collector Justin Mozart. At the time of this writing, Justin had plans for a complete period-correct restoration. He was uncertain if he'd restore it to the Barris or Ayala form. Either way, he'll have an important piece of custom history.

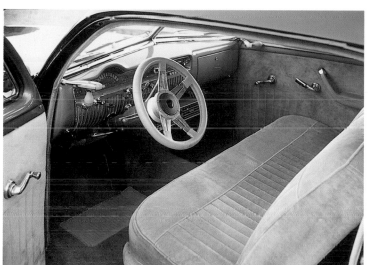

Posies 1936 Ford Cabriolet

Many rod builders in the early 1980s were exploring the possibilities of cutting-edge billet aluminum parts, but others were rediscovering the beauty of long-forgotten rods and customs of the past. Inspired by Jack Calori's famous '36 three-window coupe in the November 1949 issue of Hot Rod (see pp. 30-31), Ken "Posies" Fenical constructed a memorable '36 Ford cabriolet that married the best of the old-style customizing tricks with up-to-date street rod hardware.

Ken was no stranger to street rod construction. He opened his own hot rod and custom shop in 1964 and named it Posies, the nickname he acquired from his family's florist business. By the end of the '70s, the Posies operation had expanded to include a full range of rod building services and a line of street rod chassis parts. The '36 Ford would be the first car to bring Posies nationwide recognition.

For the cabriolet's body modifications, Ken took a page straight out of the Harry Westergard and Jack Calori playbook. The car's nose was reworked to accept a 1939 LaSalle grille. The front fenders lost their horn grilles and stock seams, and were further modified with molded-in parking lights and '40 Ford commercial headlights. The stock two-piece hood top was molded into a single unit and modified to open alligator style, while the stock vented hood sides were replaced with smooth custom pieces.

Ken chopped the windshield posts 3½ inches and relocated the windshield wipers from the top of the windshield to the cowl. He built his own Carson-style top, which was upholstered by Mike Haverstock. The front and rear bumpers came from a '37 DeSoto; the rear bumper was narrowed 6½ inches and fitted with a license guard from a '49 Chevrolet. A pair of new-old-stock '40 Ford fender skirts were tweaked to fit. The taillights were stock '36 Ford, but their mounting posts were smoothed and molded. A covered continental spare was mounted low on the rear deck, slightly sunken into a custom-fabricated rear splash pan.

Despite the extensive body modifications, Ken was careful to retain some stock body details, such as the door hinges and handles, rubber running board covers, and extended chrome running board trim. Genuine Appleton spotlights were added, along with hand-fabricated rearview mirrors. Ken deviated from the dark organic colors typical of the original postwar customs and applied an eye-searing bright-yellow paint job.

While the cabriolet's exterior modifications were straight out of the late 1940s, Ken opted for modern mechanicals underneath. An L81 350-cid Chevrolet small-block V-8 from an '81 Corvette was mildly hot rodded with an aluminum Edelbrock intake manifold and Holley four-barrel carburetor, and mated to a Turbo 350 transmission.

The stock chassis was reworked to achieve a ground-scraping stance while maintaining a comfortable ride. The frame rails were kicked up both front and rear. An independent front suspension was lifted from a 1969 Chevy Nova, which

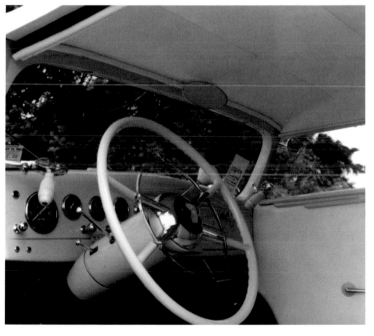

also contributed its power steering and power brakes. The rear suspension utilized a '65 Mustang rear end mounted on Posies' own Super Slide springs. Period-style rolling stock consisted of wide whitewall tires on steel wheels with smooth hubcaps from a '51 Imperial. Ken replaced the hubcaps' stock center crests with Posies medallions.

Nostalgic interior touches included vintage Stewart-Warner gauges and a 1950 Ford Crestliner steering wheel. Ken also added newer conveniences, such as a '69 Chrysler tilt steering column, modern stereo, and Vintage Air air conditioning. A '67 Cadillac bench seat was covered in white leather by Mike Haverstock.

Ken spent a lot of time scrounging swap meets for the proper vintage components, but the car's actual build time was a mere 3½ months. It was finished just in time to appear at the big street rod and custom events of the 1982 season. There, Ken's fresh interpretation of classic custom styling made a tremendous impact, put his shop on the map, and helped fan the flames of the custom car revival.

ZZ Top Eliminator

Rock 'n' roll and hot rodding have a lot in common. Both inject old forms (say, blues music or antique Fords) with horsepower and flamboyance. It's no surprise, then, that many rock stars are also hot rod enthusiasts. ZZ Top frontman Billy F. Gibbons is probably the best-known roddin' rocker.

Heavily influenced by Pete Chapouris' the *California Kid* (pp. 162–163), Billy had Don Thelan's Buffalo Motor Cars shop build him a chopped 1933 Ford in the early '80s that would soon be known as the *Eliminator* coupe. Underneath was a straightforward Pete and Jake's chassis with a dropped tube axle and four-bar suspension up front and a Ford nine-inch out back. Thelan chopped the steel three-window body three inches, Steve Davis made the three-piece hood with unique "scooped" side panels, and Kenny Youngblood designed the "ZZ" graphics. Additional body details included the filled rear splash pan with recessed license plate, '39 Ford teardrop taillights, and lowered '34 Ford headlights.

Finicky hi-po motors have never been Billy's scene, so the emphasis was on reliability. Power was provided by a simple but capable 350-cid Chevy V-8 with a Camaro Z-28 hydraulic cam, a polished intake manifold with a single four-barrel carb, and a Turbo 350 transmission. As a finishing touch, Eric Vaughn milled the ZZ Top logo into the valve covers.

A painting of the coupe was featured on the cover of ZZ Top's multiplatinum 1983 album *Eliminator*, and the real car was immortalized on the small screen in four music videos that were run in heavy rotation on MTV.

Sharp Dressed Man *video shoot*

Each video featured a Cinderella-story vignette in which an earnest but unfairly downtrodden teen is swept away and "saved" by the arrival of beautiful girls in the *Eliminator*. The members of ZZ Top granted the protagonist a magical set of keys with a stylized ZZ key chain, and the hot rod appeared as a magical fantasy object. Gibbons' *Eliminator* gave rodding immeasurable exposure and spurred the interest of an MTV generation of teenagers who hadn't before seen a real hot rod in motion.

Billy had always been a rodder, but the *Eliminator* was his first car to gain international fame. Demand for public appearances was so high that Billy had California Street Rods construct an *Eliminator* clone to go on tour. He still owns both cars today, along with several other high-profile rods and customs. Billy has done almost as much for rodding as he has for rock 'n' roll.

ZZ Top members (left to right) Billy Gibbons, Frank Beard, and Dusty Hill pose with the Eliminator

Kolmos Phaeton

Although this car was built for Chino, California's Bob Kolmos in 1985, the idea started years earlier when he and John Buttera (who grew up together in Kenosha, Wisconsin) attended the 1976 Street Rod Nationals. Bob reflected: "I had a '34 Tudor sedan that I just sold, and John suggested, 'Why don't you do a highboy tub?' "

Bob didn't want a four-door rod, so John recommended using a roadster cowl with a Tudor sedan body minus the roof. Bob liked the idea, but when he couldn't find a sedan body for a reasonable price, he opted for a fiberglass Deuce roadster body. Bob wanted Buttera to build the car, but by the time he had gathered the parts to build the roadster, John was too busy building Indy cars. So, John referred Bob to an up-and-coming rod builder named Boyd Coddington.

Boyd liked the original concept and took it upon himself to make it happen. He found a steel Tudor sedan body, swapped it for the fiberglass roadster body, and had Thom Taylor sketch his vision for a body style Ford had never offered. Boyd and his crew extensively modified the sedan body, cutting new, roadster-style doors. To achieve what has become Boyd's signature smooth, simple look, Scott Knight fabricated a three-piece aluminum hood, a rear rolled pan, a full belly-pan, a bowed aluminum top, and the entire rear body panel.

Boyd mounted the new body on a set of aftermarket frame rails that he pinched in front. Buttera lent his expertise by fabricating an aluminum independent front suspension much like he had for his '26 T sedan (pp. 168–169). A Halibrand quick-change with coil-over shocks was installed out back.

Wisely, Bob chose a reliable driveline, a Chevy 350-cid V-8 hooked to a Turbo 350 automatic transmission. Ronnie Patitucci built the engine, installing three Weber two-barrel carbs. Bob exchanged the Webers for a single four-barrel a few years later because the three twos always ran rich.

Like any Coddington creation, the interior is a work of art. Al Cooper applied butterscotch-colored vinyl and Herculon cloth to a pair of front buckets and a rear seat he made himself. He also covered the aluminum lift-off top in a matching shade of Mercedes-Benz fabric. Inside, Boyd's crew added billet gas and brake pedals, an aluminum dash insert by "Fat" Jack Robinson, VDO gauges, and a Carrera steering wheel.

Any good rod needs cool wheels and smooth paint. Bob chose a bright-yellow Ford commercial-vehicle color for the body and Boyd machined a set of one-off wheels. Simple, yet tasteful and aggressive in stance and performance, Bob's phantom phaeton still looks great today, more than 50,000 miles later.

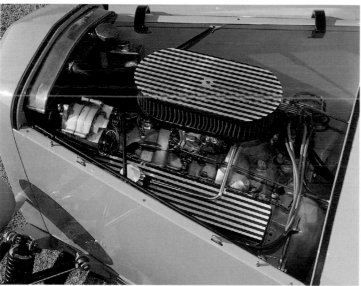

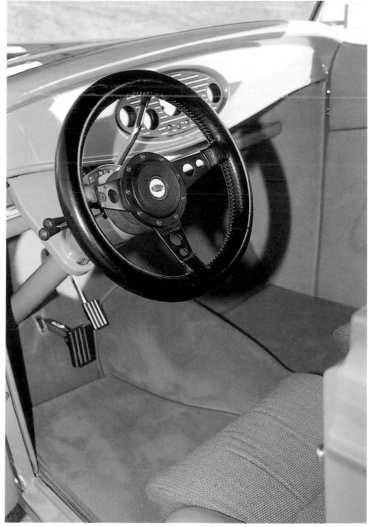

Kolmos Sedan

After Boyd Coddington delivered Bob Kolmos' Deuce phaeton in 1985, wife Sharon realized she needed to replace her car. When Bob asked her if she'd rather have a new car or a hot rod, she replied like any red-blooded American would; she chose the hot rod. She had, after all, fallen in love with the hobby by participating in rod runs with her husband.

Sharon and Bob hired "Fat" Jack Robinson to build her hot rod. From the start, Sharon made all of the stylistic decisions that would shape the car. She chose a chopped, channeled, and fenderless 1932 Ford Tudor body, as well as elements such as the color, wheels, and interior decor.

The body of this fine smoothie sedan was done by Ralph Kirby. It is quite radical and involved, yet subtle. Some of the modifications included chopping the top about three inches, removing the rain gutters, rounding the door edges, and grafting in a Mercedes-Benz roof complete with an electric sunroof. Scott Knight made a three-piece aluminum hood three inches longer than stock. A Dan Fink grille insert fit to the shortened grille shell completed the front end, and six inches were removed from the rear quarter panels to prevent the fenderless car from looking tail heavy. Sharon chose a stylish and understated two-tone paint scheme for the body, combining 1986 Cadillac Firemist Charcoal with dove gray

separated by red and silver stripes.

Sharon tapped friend John Buttera to fabricate the dropped front axle and suspension—a coil-over, four-bar arrangement installed ahead of the frame rather than underneath it. A Ford nine-inch rear end fit with a false quick-change housing and a four-link provided the rear geometry.

Planning to drive her rod regularly like her husband, Sharon also picked a reliable powerplant. Fat Jack dressed up the Chevy 350-cid crate motor with valve covers and a matching air cleaner that he made from billet aluminum. Jack routed the V-8's 300 horsepower through a smooth-shifting Turbo 350 automatic.

Sharon opted for a comfortable interior, too. Jack installed a pair of narrowed Recaro bucket seats stitched in light-gray leather, a gauge insert mounted in front of the driver seat instead of the middle of the dash, and an Emerson Fittipaldi steering wheel of Sharon's choosing. Amenities included air conditioning, a power sunroof, and electric windows. Sharon keeps the windows down and the A/C off to better appreciate the road.

The car was completed in 1987, and Sharon has enjoyed the hot rodding experience ever since. "In a hot rod, it would be good enough to just be a passenger," says Sharon. "But driving is really where it's at."

1950s Revival Leadsled

Though traditional customs had all but disappeared by the end of the 1960s, by the mid '80s they were well on their way back. In the late '70s, mainstream America seemed to rediscover the '50s, and nostalgic TV shows and movies such as *Happy Days* and *Grease* were extremely popular. Ever-growing numbers of car enthusiasts began reviving the styles of the 1950s as well. Some were beginning to seek out the original '50s customs, and '50s-vintage cars were being built in the classic "lead-sled" style.

One of the best examples of the custom revival is this 1950 Chevrolet two-door hardtop, originally built by Doug Thompson for Larry Cochran of Belton, Missouri. Even though it looks like it could have rolled out of the Barris Kustom shop in 1955, this sumptuous Chevy was originally built in '86.

Like any full custom, this Chevy was treated to an extensive list of modifications. The headlights were frenched, and the hood was modified with rounded corners, trim removal, and six rows of louvers. A '50 Mercury grille opening was fit with a grille fashioned from a '59 Imperial center bar mated to '51 Mercury bumper guards. Doug chopped the top a healthy four inches for an extra low profile. Sculpted bodyside character lines were hand-formed in metal to taper into custom rear fender scoops trimmed with '54 Mercury teeth. Rear fins and taillights from a '53 Cadillac were grafted on to the Chevy's rear fenders. Chrome lakes pipes were fully frenched into the rocker panels. Bumper guards from a '52 Pontiac were smoothly molded into the front and rear bumpers. For hubcaps, Doug used the ever-popular Cadillac "Sombreros."

Many custom car enthusiasts lust after the look of the original customs, but only a die-hard few want to relive the relatively crude technology of 1940s and 1950s cars. Like their street rod cousins, most modern-day nostalgic customs take advantage of more up-to-date and reliable automotive mechanicals while maintaining a purely vintage exterior appearance. Thompson replaced the original ball-joint front suspension on this Chevy with componentry from a 1969 Camaro. The engine is a tried-and-true small-block Chevy/Turbo 350 automatic transmission combo, for trouble-free cruising.

After its completion, the Chevy scooped up the prestigious Harry Bradley Design Achievement Award at the 1986 KKOA Street Custom Spectacular. From there, it was rarely seen until custom collector extraordinaire Jack Walker acquired the car in 2000. Jack, who had provided design input when the car was originally being built for his friend Larry, had Doug give it a fresh paint job in custom mixed colors close to the original, and had Bob Sipes stitch up a more traditional white tuck-and-roll interior to replace the '80s-style velour Larry picked. The steering wheel was also swapped out for a more nostalgic 1959 Impala unit. Proving that the appeal of a well-designed custom car is timeless, the Chevy was awarded with a *Custom Rodder* magazine Top Ten Pick at the Goodguys Heartland Rod and Custom Nationals in 2002, 16 years after it was originally built.

Twilight Zone

Like hot rodding and customizing, lowriding began as a street-oriented activity, but it too eventually developed offshoots that drew some lowriders away from street cruising. By the early 1980s, the lowrider scene had grown to the point that it could easily support its own show circuit. Lowriders much too nice and too detailed to be driven on the street were being built strictly for car-show competition. Likewise, hoppers and dancers were now built specifically as competition cars that were no longer street legal, or in some cases, drivable at all.

Lowrider clubs were also maturing and becoming more organized. The Lifestyle car club was formed in 1975, and quickly achieved a sterling reputation for boasting some of the finest competitive show lowriders around.

Lifestyle member Mike Lopez's 1962 Chevy Impala epitomizes the show-only lowrider. Mike first acquired the car around 1980 for a mere $200, and built it into a show car named *Dark Visions*. During the first rebuild, he enlisted Richard Ruiz to apply a dazzling hand-rubbed black lacquer paint job.

Like the customs of the late 1950s and early '60s, competitive show lowriders were redone with ever-increasing levels of finish as their owners strove to remain competitive on the show circuit. In 1983, *Twilight Zone: The Movie* inspired Mike to redo and rename his Impala. In '88, after another successful stint on the show circuit, Mike stripped the car down for yet another redo. That third iteration is shown here.

For the third go-around, Mike took the Impala to the Candy Factory in Palmdale, California, where Mario Gomez laid down an intricate scheme of candy pearl black, candy purple, pearl magenta, and pearl blue fadeaways over Ruiz's original black lacquer paint job. Walt Prey then pinstriped the car in seven colors. The first-class paint and pinstriping were carried throughout the entire car; the frame, wheelwells, even the backsides of the bumpers got the treatment.

Dio Dora and Tony Garcia of Covina Auto Trim were responsible for the jaw-dropping, full-custom interior. The swivel front seats, steering wheel, and rear seats were custom-fabricated. Macabre touches included sword-handle levers on the steering column, numerous skulls, and a spider-web motif on the floor and headliner. The stock Impala rear speaker was relocated to the console, in front of a mirrored turntable. An Alpine stereo and five-inch color TV were mounted into the leading edge of the mirrored console.

The package-shelf area of the interior was left open and the upholstery treatment was carried into the trunk compartment and on to the underside of the hood. The fully upholstered trunk was outfitted with a chromed hydraulics setup installed by A&G Custom Sounds of East L.A.

Mike kept the stock 283-cid V-8, but had most of the engine compartment and chassis drenched in show-quality chrome, including the engine block, heads, exhaust, and even the spark plugs. Three separate plating shops took on the huge workload.

Mike's Impala has a long history of piling up first place trophies at lowrider shows, and serves as an example of the level of detail and finish required to be a lowrider show champion. *Twilight Zone* was also featured in the "Arte Y Estilo: The Lowriding Tradition" exhibition at the Petersen Automotive Museum in 2000. Its inclusion among this select group of lowriders only cemented its status in the upper echelons of lowrider craftsmanship.

CadZZilla™

In the late 1980s, ZZ Top frontman Billy F. Gibbons began dreaming of a vehicle to follow up the success of his *Eliminator* 1933 Ford coupe (pp. 194–195). Billy envisioned a '50s-style custom fused with the extreme proportions of a streamlined Bonneville race car. Fellow Texan Jack Chisenhall of Vintage Air turned Billy on to designer Larry Erickson, and a meeting was arranged between Billy, Larry, and builder Boyd Coddington at the 1988 Street Rod Nationals. The trio hashed out the initial concept for the car, Larry drew up a groundbreaking design, and shortly thereafter a clean '48 Cadillac sedanette was delivered to Boyd's shop so a radical transformation could begin.

Metal man Craig Naff worked from Larry's sketches to form *CadZZilla's*™ body panels in steel. Since Larry was in Detroit working for General Motors and the car was in Boyd's Stanton, California-based shop, many of the details had to be communicated by fax. By the time Craig was finished, a trendsetting new custom shape had emerged.

The focal point of *CadZZilla's*™ design is its hand-fabricated top, which runs in a smooth, unbroken arc from the front to the rear pillars. The curved side window moldings evoke the classic Matranga and Hirohata Mercurys. The gigantic hand-fabricated doors were engineered to open suicide style; original '48 Cadillac bumper guard tips serve double duty as rearview mirrors and door latches. The fastback design flows smoothly into the decklid, terminating in a chrome bumper piece with an inset license plate and exhaust tips. The rear fenders were radically extended and reshaped, with sinister full-length taillights capping off their trailing edges. Larry's idea was to make the rear of the car look as if it had been sliced off.

The simplified grille opening was constructed using the top bar from a 1949 Cadillac. The hand-formed grille bar is fitted with a Moon polished aluminum tank, a nice visual nod to

CadZZilla's™ competition design influence. The reworked front bumper is from a '55 Chevy, with modified Cadillac bumper guards. The headlights were frenched, and the stock hood ornament was attached to a custom trim spear and set into a rounded channel.

Body "cutlines" were kept to a minimum. The hood and front fenders were combined into an enormous tilt-up unit, with the rear cutlines cleverly hidden by Craig Naff's hand-made chrome trim. Likewise, the rear skirt cutlines are disguised by the rear fenders' chrome trim and the curved arc of their leading edges. Painter Greg Morrell sprayed on a gorgeous candy paint job in modern urethane enamel. The color looks almost black until the light hits it right and it shifts to a deep eggplant purple.

Danny Drumm and Bobby Griffey teamed to produce *CadZZilla's*™ interior in tan leather and carpet. Most of the interior was made from scratch, but the stock jukeboxlike instrument cluster was retained and restored. Modern Sony stereo controls were hidden behind the "waterfall" chrome-trimmed glovebox door.

Chassis specialist Larry Sergejeff built *CadZZilla's*™ custom frame from 2 x 4-inch mild steel, then fitted it with a 1985 Corvette front suspension and a nine-inch Ford rear end. A

custom-built auger system was installed to raise and lower the rear end, and a similar electric motor powers the tilt-open front end. Cadillac supplied one of its 500-cid limousine engines, which was tuned by engine building legend Art Chrisman. Sixteen-inch wheels were mounted front and rear, but the fronts wear 22-inch forged aluminum wheel covers that recall the classic Cadillac "sombrero" hubcap design.

The car was finished in an astonishing six months, in time to be featured on the cover of the July 1989 issue of *Hot Rod*. *CadZZilla*™ was instantly recognized as a customizing milestone that set new standards in both design and execution. It was voted onto *Rod & Custom* magazine's All-Time Top 20 Rods and Customs list in the August 1990 issue, the only modern-era custom to be so honored. The ensuing years have done little to lessen its impact.

Fat Fenders, Pastels, and Graphics

As the supply of popular early iron (read: pre-1935 Fords) began to dry up in the mid 1980s, rod builders turned increasingly to "fat fender" cars, namely 1935–48 American iron. One of the earliest cars to define the "fat" scene was a flamed, purple '39 Ford convertible built by Pete and Jake's Hot Rod Shop for Pete Chapouris' wife Carol. The other was a '46 Ford coupe assembled by "Fat" Jack Robinson. Both cars were more than just handsome. They also performed admirably at the dragstrip. Pete's '39 ran 11-second E.T.s. Jack's car was even faster, running in the nines, but it was destroyed in a crash during a run at Fremont Drag Strip.

Pete took the '39 on the newly organized *Hot Rod* Victory Tour in 1985. While on the road, the "Fat Attack" (June) issue of *Hot Rod* hit the stands with these two cars on the cover. When Chapouris' '39 arrived at the *Hot Rod* Super Nationals in Indianapolis, the readers in attendance were blown away. It was the beginning of a surge of popularity for fat-fendered cars as rodders rallied behind the slogan "dare to be different."

Almost simultaneously, paint companies PPG and DuPont discovered hot rods as a potential market and began mixing and promoting pastel colors. Traditional rod colors, such as red, yellow, orange, and black, were no longer the only choices on the hot rodder's palette. Many rodders now opted for pinks, purples, teals, and combinations thereof. Graphics grew more popular, as painters tried to outdo each other with never-before-tried designs. Monochromatic smoothies with painted bumpers and pastel-colored cars with wild graphics dominated hot rod gatherings in the late 1980s and continued to do so into the early '90s.

It was a colorful, but short-lived era. By the mid 1990s, hot rod styling had returned to its roots, and fat fenders, pastels, and wild graphics lost their luster. Like any form of rodding, these cars still have their proponents, but they are no longer nearly as popular as they once were. Some would say that's for the better.

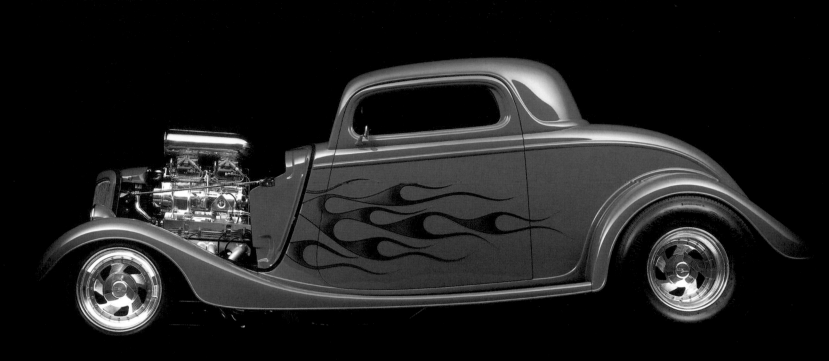

Pro Street '34 Coupe

The pro street trend that began gaining momentum in the early 1980s was not a product of the street rodding scene. Instead, it came from the street machine crowd, who usually built late-model cars. The genre was characterized by narrowed rear ends and tubbed wheelwells to accommodate fat rear tires, narrow front tires, tube chassis, fully equipped interiors with roll cages, and 400-pound gorilla motors. Basically, the cars resembled streetable Pro Stockers.

The cars weren't exactly practical (handling wasn't part of the equation), but the concept was close to the hot rodder's heart. After all, rodders have always longed for speed and horsepower. So, it was not surprising when street rods began adopting the pro street style.

It was that desire for power that led Fontana, California's Gary Gasaway to build this pro street-style 1934 Ford three-window coupe in 1989. Gary, a lifetime hot rodder and the owner of Gary's Montclair Auto Parts, had always wanted to own a supercharged street rod. The project was conceived innocently enough, but resulted in a megahorsepower pro street monster.

Gary's rod was built largely from aftermarket parts by noted rod constructor Don Thelan. Orville Lynes narrowed the Chassis Engineering rails, adding a dropped I-beam front axle and a TCI four-link rear suspension. The Ford nine-inch rear end fit with 4:56 gears gave an indication of what was to come under the hood. Big and little Mickey Thompson tires mounted on Billet Specialties wheels were installed as requisite pro street footwear.

The chopped 1934 Ford body, a Gibbon fiberglass product, received one-piece running boards and a lift-off Terry Hegman louvered hood. Porsche Continental Orange paint covered with pearl purple and aqua-trimmed flames by Little Louie gave the body attitude to match the motor. Inside, Thelan installed Recaro seats upholstered by Mark Stevens and a Billet Specialties steering column.

Bishop & Buehl Race Engines provided the supercharged engine Gary had always desired. The 377-cid Chevy V-8 (a small-block Chevy 406 with a steel 350 crank) was built to the hilt. The combination of a Crane roller cam, Hayes ignition, a Mooneyham 6-71 blower, and two 1040 cfm Holley carbs produced more than 900 horsepower.

As the final bit of attitude for his already bawdy '34, Gary ordered a "TEMP ME" personalized license plate. Should you see this car on the street and choose to tempt it, you had better be packing some serious horsepower. This hot rod sure is.

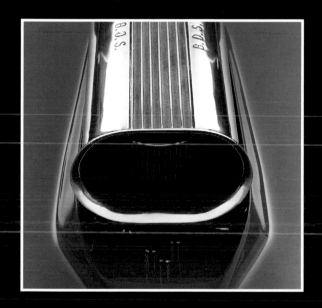

Prufer Deuce

Tom Prufer does it right. When he builds a hot rod, the wheels, tires, paint, details, and stance all add up to a traditional, menacing appearance that captures the very definition of "hot rod."

The 1932 Ford coupe that Tom debuted at the 1989 Grand National Roadster Show is no exception to this rule. A long-time hot rodder, Tom has shown almost 30 different cars at Oakland since 1958, more than any other private hot rodder.

Tom started with a steel 1932 Ford three-window coupe and a genuine '32 frame, and enlisted the help of many talented hot rodders to turn out another in a long line of masterpieces. Pete Eastwood reworked the chassis, while Marcel De Ley and Dan Fink performed their magic on the body. Marcel chopped and filled the top and massaged the once-rough body; Dan fabricated the grille, louvered hood, and rolled rear pan.

Every "100 Pruf" creation requires a monstrous motor. Phil Lukens of Blair's Speed Shop obliged with a big-block Chevy bored to 468 cid and outfitted with Lukens-ported heads, a

Weiand tunnel-ram intake manifold, and a pair of Holley 750 cfm carbs. Eastwood fashioned the beautiful chromed headers, and Tom chose a B&M Turbo 400 transmission and a Championship quick-change rear end. Upholstery by Ken Foster and black paint with Rod Powell-applied flames and pinstriping completed the deal.

Prufer's deft touches can be seen throughout the coupe. These include the 3.5-gallon Moon tank mounted up front, generous bright red-orange accent paint, louvered decklid and rolled pan, and big and little tires with E.T. IIIs out back and Real Wheels up front. Taken altogether, Prufer's Deuce is a timeless hot rod.

In 1994, after completing a red 1932 Ford three-window coupe, Prufer moved from Long Beach, California, to Missouri, declaring he had built his last hot rod. Well, a '29 Ford highboy roadster was the next project to come out of his garage, and he's churned out others since. This hot rodder has it in his blood, and that's good for the rest of us.

Asquith Deuce

Car guys hear it from wannabe speed merchants all the time: "I have a car I drive on the street that runs nines at the dragstrip." More often than not, the braggart is lying. This street rod doesn't run nines at the strip either. It runs eights.

Prior to this yellow roadster, Boyce Asquith, a chrome shop owner from Pomona, California, had a street-driven red Deuce that ran 10.35 at 135 mph. That wasn't fast enough, so he started work on one of the wildest hot rods of all time.

The project began in the late '80s, and Boyce spared no expense finding the right people to build a streetable, and extremely fast, hot rod. Pro Stock builder Gary Hanson fabricated the four-link tube chassis and bolt-in roll bar, while Dick "Magoo" Megugorac assembled the front suspension with an I-beam front axle, Halibrand torsion bars, Chevy Vega steering, inboard shocks, and Wilwood disc brakes. George Cathey set up the Strange rear end.

Mike Brown provided the gennie Deuce body, modifying it with sunken taillights, a sunken license plate, a rolled rear pan, and enlarged wheelwells. Steel rail covers were made to complete the highboy look. To lighten the load, Boyce had Terry Finch fashion a hood and rear deck from aluminum.

Boyce swapped on these panels, as well as a Lexan windshield, to go racing.

The real excitement came under the hood. Boyce had Ray Zeller build him a big-block Chevy V-8 dressed with a B&M MegaBlower supercharger. With that engine, a B&M Pro Stick shifter, and a B&M TH400 transmission, the car ran a 9.30 E.T. at 150 mph in the quarter-mile. Again, that wasn't fast enough, so Boyce installed an intercooler for the blower, a Crane roller cam, and a pair of Holley 1150 Dominator carbs, then went to the dragstrip and turned 8.72 at 158 mph. By now, with 1040 horsepower, the car was no longer streetable, so Boyce built a slightly tamer Chevy 460-cid V-8 for street use. This one featured aluminum heads and the same blower with a pair of Holley 850 cfm carbs. Boyce may have compromised a little, but not much.

Tragically, Boyce succumbed to cancer in 1994. In '98, David Allen of Alamo, California, bought the Deuce. "When I first saw it, I thought: I'm going to own that sucker someday," said David. After spinning out in the rain, David had Roy Brizio Street Rods perform a body-off restoration in 2000. Since then, David has done Boyce proud, driving his wild ride as many as 6000 miles per year.

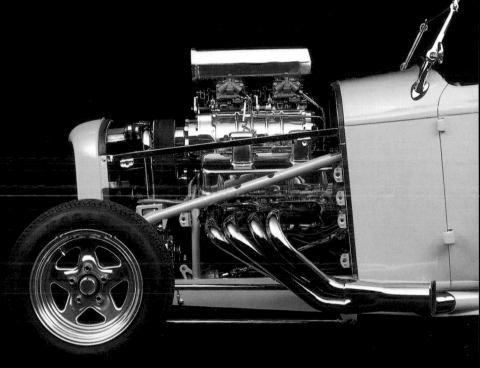
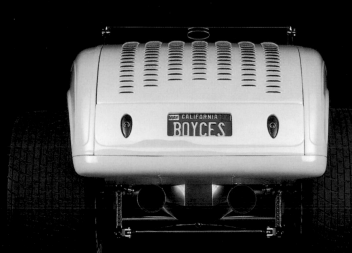

CHAPTER 6: THE 1990s
Hot Rods and Customs Go Mainstream

In popular culture, there is usually a 40- to 50-year lag time from when something was first popular to when it is rediscovered. That held true for what became known in the late 1990s as the "rat rod." Some like the term, some don't, but it has stuck.

While it is hard to classify any type of art form, rat rods take on the rougher look of 1940s and '50s dry-lakes cars. Stripped down and grimy, they look like they were just driven off the dirt and dust of El Mirage. There is usually no paint, just primer. They have minimal interiors, spotty body work, and may or may not have a hood. Exposed welds are quite welcome. The engines are vintage, and they often have rare vintage speed equipment that is probably scarce because it got shelved early on when it didn't work all that well. Fixing, nursing along, and messing with the old iron is part of the deal.

One of the main reasons for the initial growth of rat rods was a series of books containing vintage photography from the personal collections of many early rodders and drag racers. The books were authored by an early rodder and drag racer himself, Don Montgomery. With Don's books, the newer rodders interested in the wheres and what-fors of the early years now had candid shots of the era to reference. Early speed equipment, car configurations, and the general way they did things were all chronicled and accessible.

The rat rod scene soon became a culture, not just a hot rod building style, for a new, younger breed of hot rodder. Go to any rat rod show today, and you'll see it has its own art, music, and fashion, all revolving around 1940s and '50s styles. Tattoos are quite popular with this group; the more the better. Tattoo parlors often display their work at rat rod gatherings. Rockabilly and swing music can be heard from live bands at rat rod shows like Billetproof (no billet aluminum parts allowed) and The Blessing of the Cars—where a priest is on hand to bless cars with holy water!

Rat rods brought about a resurgence of car clubs, too. Some of the earlier clubs, such as the Choppers of Burbank,

California, and the Shifters of Orange County, California, started early in the 1990s and adopted club names inspired by names from the past. Some of these clubs welcomed both rod and custom owners, all in the "rat" style, of course. With the clubs came parties and social gatherings, just like back in the 1950s.

Rat rods also came about as a reaction to the expensive, pro-built cars that were being churned out with ever

higher levels of fit and finish. By the mid 1990s, Boyd Coddington's shop had become a big business, with its hand in many segments of the hot rod and custom worlds. Coddington was no longer the little guy, and to some, his style had become too prevalent. They felt the best way to beat him was to change the rules. Rat rodders were the most obvious and radical shift away from the fiberglass and billet creations that had become street rodding's state of the art.

While the modern street rod was experiencing a bit of a backlash, the modern custom was flourishing. Two Northern California customizers, John D'Agostino and Richard Zocchi, helped spur interest in the custom car scene. The duo began receiving recognition for showing customs built to their designs in the late 1980s. By the early '90s, they had made it a practice to debut their cars each year at Oakland's

Grand National Roadster Show. For custom car enthusiasts, seeing the latest from D'Agostino and Zocchi became an anticipated part of the show.

Both gentlemen's cars are in much the same idiom. They combine vintage custom styling cues with contemporary paint blends, suspensions, interior touches, and wheels. Their efforts have influenced many custom aficionados, carried on the tradition of the 1960s show custom, and boosted interest in customs in general.

While D'Agostino and Zocchi were raising awareness of customs through their beautiful designs and prolific output, another phenomenon gave the custom scene a boost in the 1990s, that of the high-end, high-profile custom. In 1989, CadZZilla™ led off a string of envelope-pushing, highly publicized customs. CheZoom followed in late '92, Frankenstude was finished in '96, and Scrape debuted in '98. All of these cars received publicity beyond the traditional custom car media, introducing a mainstream audience to customs.

At the other end of the spectrum, the youth-oriented rat rod scene inspired a revival of late 1940s/early '50s-style "in-progress" leadsled customs. Builders took pride in leaving the cars in primer or bare metal to better show off the modifications and craftsmanship.

Back in the hot rod world, rodders

also began exploring new/old forms of hot rodding, like lakes modifieds, for the first time in years. Interest in restoring historical cars, presaged by *Rod & Custom* staffer Jim "Jake" Jacobs and the NieKamp roadster back in 1970, was peaking. The prestigious concours at Pebble Beach even got into the act by introducing a hot rod class for the '97 Concours d'Elegance. Reviews have been mixed regarding hot rodders' inclusion in an upscale arena they never dreamed of entering (or perhaps even cared about), but a hot rod or custom class has returned every other year since that first show.

Hot rodding was maturing, too. Companies like Petersen Publishing, Hilborn Fuel Injection, and Edelbrock were celebrating 50 years of service. Some of the icons of hot rodding and custom cars were leaving us as old age crept up. Hot rod events were a mixed bag of young and old, and everything in between. Guys like Rich Guasco, who won the 1961 Grand National Roadster Show and who later piloted the *Pure Hell* Fuel Altered, were restoring their cars and using them in retirement like they had as young adults.

Feeling that they had explored the fringes of modernizing hot rods with the smoothies of the 1980s, many rodders built rods in the '90s that looked and sounded like rods from the past. Flathead engines started showing up more often in newly built roadsters. As a result, speed equipment that hadn't been produced in decades returned to parts catalogs. And new twists on old hot rod staples were becoming more common. For example, electronic fuel injection units were hidden in '60s-style mechanical fuel-injection intake manifolds and '40 Ford-style drum brake backing plates now hid modern discs. Everything old was new again.

Then, a breakthrough product appeared, and it made quite a splash. Brookville Roadsters in Brookville, Ohio, came out with an exact reproduction 1932 Ford roadster body in 1997. While '32 Ford bodies had been available for decades in fiberglass, this body was significant because it was made out of steel, just like the originals. Apparently, a lot of people had been waiting

to find a reasonably priced steel body because hundreds laid out the cash for a Brookville body and made plans to build a '32 roadster.

In addition to the bodies, tires that hadn't been manufactured in decades were now available from specialty tire

suppliers like Coker. Combining the best of the old and the new, Coker offered radial tires with wide white sidewalls. What seemed unimaginable only a few years earlier was now possible. A hot rodder could buy a new version of almost any old speed part!

As more enthusiasts were initiated into the fold in the 1990s, they in turn exposed others to the hobby, and thus even more joined the bandwagon. The Street Rod Nationals grew to 14,000 pre-1949 hot rods, making it one of the largest car shows in the world.

To see just how mainstream the hot rod had become, look no further than Detroit. After Mitsubishi supplied the driveline for Boyd Coddington's *Aluma Coupe* in 1991, Chrysler quietly developed a hot rod-style show car, the Plymouth Prowler, for the '93 auto-show season. The Prowler received a positive response, and Chrysler introduced a production version for the '97 model year. Annual production continued until 2002 at about 3500 units each year. Traditional hot rodders complained that the V-6 wasn't true to the hot rod spirit. Still, the Prowler served as a symbol of how far the hot rod had come in 50 or so years—from stripped down Detroit castoff to limited-production "halo" vehicle.

High-end hot rods caught the interest of Japanese automakers, too. In 1994, the Q29 *Infiniti Flyer* became the first

Oakland Roadster Show America's Most Beautiful Roadster winner with a Japanese engine. Based on a '29 Ford, the car was built by Art and Mike Chrisman for Joe MacPherson. Infiniti didn't pay for the project, but Nissan's luxury division did supply many parts

and much technical support. The yellow roadster utilized the engine and transmission, as well as other components, from an Infiniti Q45. It was quite an engineering feat.

A couple years later, Toyota's luxury arm, Lexus, ventured into the hot rod arena with a one-off highboy roadster show car based on the venerable 1932 Ford. The car incorporated the drivetrain and some suspension components from a Lexus GS400. The marriage of the old and new looked natural.

Hot rods and custom cars had traditionally been preoccupations for young men, but in the 1990s it became obvious that the age of the participants was increasing. Actually, the hot rod and custom fans of the '90s were many of the same participants from the hobbies' earlier incarnations in the '50s and '60s. By now, their children had left the nest, they had ascended to higher income tax brackets, and they had more spare time. They were looking for a hobby that also had a social aspect, and a return to the hot rods and custom cars of their youth fit the bill.

The hot rod and custom hobby was going strong at the end of the millennium, but it had yet to hit full stride. While the rat rod scene had begun to attract a new, younger crowd, another development would soon introduce hot rods and customs to an even wider audience. ➤≫

Aluma Coupe

Aluma Coupe On a flight back to Detroit from Southern California in 1991, then Cadillac designer Larry Erickson sketched a car conceived as a modern midengine combination of the Pierson Brothers' '34 Ford coupe and Art Chrisman's radically chopped '30 Ford Model A coupe. The car that resulted not only pushed the envelope of hot rod design, but also changed the way the automakers thought about hot rods.

Erickson had worked with Boyd Coddington on *CadZZilla*™ in the late 1980s, and this car was the duo's next project. It was originally intended to be a roadster with an American V-8, but plans soon changed. Mitsubishi had been thinking of developing a show car based on its 3000 GT sports car, and when Mitsubishi chief product planner Ron Kusumi met Coddington, he found the man who could build a car to showcase his company's parts.

Erickson built a scale model to flesh out and tweak the concept and Coddington's crew set to work. Dave Willey fabricated the tube chassis, which would later be powder coated in gray, as would the suspension parts. The unique front suspension was built as an independent cantilever unit with inboard coil-over shocks, and the rear received an independent setup as well.

Marcel DeLay fashioned the body, which changed from a roadster to a coupe along the way due to concerns about structural strength. The car received its name, the *Aluma Coupe*, in part because the body panels were fabricated entirely from aluminum.

Mitsubishi parts shaped much of the rest of the car. Russ Collins of Torrance, California's R.C. Engineering tuned the engine—a turbocharged 1991 Mitsubishi Eclipse 2.0-liter four-cylinder—to roughly 320 horsepower. Boyd's crew mounted the engine transversely behind the seats, mating it to a '90 Galant transaxle with billet driveshafts and hub carriers. Erickson also designed the interior, utilizing Mitsubishi Eclipse instruments, custom-made Connolly leather seats, and a Boyd steering wheel.

A glass-smooth yellow-pearl paint job and Boyd's Tri-Fan wheels completed the 11-month project. The *Aluma Coupe* debuted at the 1992 New York Auto Show to extensive press coverage. The car further established Coddington as the premier rod builder of his time, and set the stage for further auto company involvement in hot rods.

Ferrari collector David Sydorick bought the *Aluma Coupe* in 1993. He has since displayed the car at the Petersen Automotive Museum in L.A., as well as at other venues. David drives the car on occasion, shows it at Southern California events, and keeps it at his Beverly Hills home.

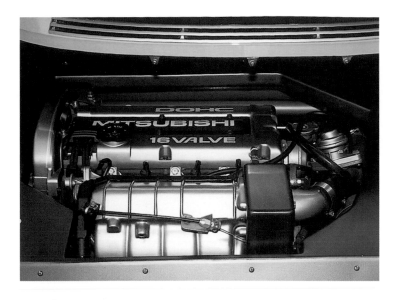

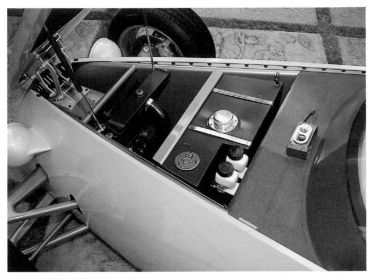

Cole Foster '54

Cole Foster has been doing top-shelf professional customizing, fabrication, and car construction out of his "Salinas Boyz" shop in Salinas, California, since 1989, but being a custom car and bike builder wasn't his first career choice. As a teenager, Cole intended to follow his father, famed drag car fabricator/driver Pat Foster, into a career as a Funny Car driver. Fate nixed those plans, but the beautifully fabricated, purpose-built drag racing machines Cole grew up with would forever influence him. Cole spent the majority of his youth acquiring his own fabrication skills, which he combined with his innate sense of design to create some of the country's best traditionally styled custom cars, motorcycles, and hot rods.

Cole's chopped 1954 Chevy hardtop was the first custom that brought him national acclaim. He pulled the car out of a Northern California junkyard in 1988, then worked on it off and on over the next six years as time and finances permitted.

The chassis was updated with late-model components for reliable cruising. The stock stovebolt six was replaced with a Chevy 350-cid V-8 hooked to a Turbo 350 transmission. A late-model independent front suspension was installed, and the rear suspension was swapped for a '64 Chevy axle on de-arched springs. The frame was altered for clearance and the gas tank raised to allow for the lower stance. Hubcaps from a 1951 DeSoto were modified with bullet center caps.

Cole chopped the top four inches, replacing the entire rear portion of the roof with custom-rolled sheetmetal by Don Fretwell. The new shape eliminated the factory "dog-leg" rear pillar design in favor of an unbroken tapered slope. The stock "wraparound" rear window was replaced with smaller unit from a 1950 Plymouth. A top chop is a difficult and incredibly important modification for a custom because it

dictates the vehicle's overall profile. Cole got this one right.

Cole welded the stock two-piece hood into one piece. He reshaped the grille opening by fashioning a U-shaped grille surround from two 1954 Chevy pieces, cutting down the stock '54 Chevy grille bar to fit within the new opening. In the process, Cole removed the parking-light pods from the grille bar and added four extra teeth. The front gravel pan was molded in and a stock front bumper was mounted in a lower position after its bumper guards were removed.

The headlights were frenched with 1954 Mercury trim rings. The front wheel openings were raised three inches, and the stock front fender body character lines were hammered smooth. All factory trim and handles were removed. Out back, the stock taillights were frenched and bubble lenses from Gene Winfield were added. To match the front, the rear gravel pan was molded in and the rear bumper mounted in a lower position. Note also that the license plate was curved to match the shape of the rear bumper.

The car spent some time in bare metal, then primer, and satin-purple pearl as the work progressed. It was eventually finished with a deep midnight-blue pearl paint job by Jesse Cruz. Later, Mark Dublia applied subtle scallop accents above the head- and taillights.

The interior received pearl-white tuck-and-roll upholstery with blue piping. The steering wheel came from a '53 Merc, and the dash was smoothed and fit with aftermarket gauges in an engine-turned panel next to the factory speedometer.

The finished Chevy illustrates the philosophies that Cole applies to all of his shop's output. He strives to avoid clichéd ideas and flash-in-the-pan trends as he crafts fresh, purposeful design statements that will look as good 30 years from now as they do today.

CheZoom In 1990, Thom Taylor designed *Franken-stude* (pp. 228–229) as a tongue-in-cheek reaction to the Larry Erickson-designed *CadZZilla™*. Thom gave the sketch to Boyd Coddington, hoping Boyd would build the car. Coddington wasn't into the concept, so Thom drew up something a little more mainstream for Boyd. "If you were just going to do the ultimate customized car, the most popular car is a 1957 Chevy. So, let's take one of those and see what we can do with it," Thom explained. Coddington loved the idea, and he shopped it to Joe Hrudka, then president of Mr. Gasket, who gave him the go-ahead to build it.

Thom's concept for *CheZoom* was a modern interpretation of the classic 1957 Chevy. Like *Frankenstude*, the car would be considered a custom because extensive bodywork would be performed. But also like *Frankenstude*, it would be a hot rod too, because modern performance-oriented mechanicals would be used.

To get started, Hot Rods by Boyd acquired a clean 1957 Chevy Bel Air two-door hardtop and gutted it. Chassis man Dave Willey built a new ladder-type frame from rectangular tubing. To the frame, Dave adapted the front and rear clips from a 1985 Corvette, complete with their independent suspensions. No '57 Chevy ever handled like *CheZoom* would. Appropriately, the Chevrolet LT1 V-8 also came from a 'Vette, this one a '92. A GM 700R4 automatic transmission linked to a Hurst shifter completed the drivetrain.

No body panel was left unmolested by Boyd's metal man Roy Schmidt. Thom designed the car to keep the front end

low and to accentuate the rear fins. "I tried to slim up the body and not have it be so heavy, chop the top and not have it be so crowned and heavy, and lighten the front end," Thom noted. Roy formed the front fenders from 18-gauge steel. He kept the stock headlight buckets and wheel openings, but moved the wheel cutouts forward. The grille shell was hand-formed from two-inch tubing, the grille mesh came from a Cadillac, and a custom floating center bar flanked by bullets was added. The hood was fabricated, too, without the characteristic Chevy gunsights.

Roy stretched the doors ten inches. He made the roof by splicing together 1978 Chrysler Cordoba and '68 Plymouth Barracuda roofs. The Cordoba also donated its windshield, which was cut down to fit the chopped opening. For the back glass, Roy used a Ford EXP unit turned upside down.

Like the fronts, the rear wheel cutouts were moved forward to maintain the stock 115-inch wheelbase. To amplify the '57 Chevy rear fins, Roy lengthened the fenders ten inches and rotated them to angle the rear fins upward. The trunk was lengthened ten inches along the top and five inches at the bottom, and a rolled rear pan was fit with a recessed license plate. For trim, Roy used lengthened and slightly curved '56 Chevy lower trim pieces, '57 Chevy upper pieces, and computer-cut chrome appliqués to fill the rear "tail feathers." In the end, only about 10 percent of the original body remained. House of Kolor dark-teal paint applied by Greg Morrell and a set of 17-inch Boyd's Ninja wheels added the final exterior touches.

Thom did not design the interior, which was fit with modified Cerullo seats upholstered in gray leather by Jack Garrison. Hot Rods by Boyd made the billet steering wheel, smoothed the dash, installed VDO gauges, and moved the glovebox to the center of the dash to hide controls for a trunkful of Kenwood stereo components.

CheZoom was finished in about a year and appeared in the January 1993 issue of *Hot Rod* magazine. Plastic kits, diecast models, and other magazine stories followed as *CheZoom* became one of the best-known customs ever built. Hrudka sold *CheZoom* at a Barrett-Jackson auction in 2002, where it commanded $183,600. After a series of upgrades to the interior, wheels, and various other components, it was sold at another Barrett-Jackson auction in 2004 for $345,000.

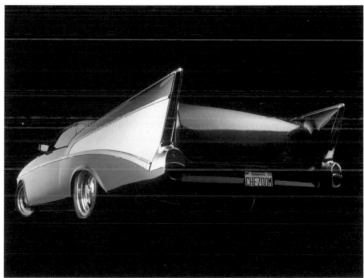

Nadean The tremendous impact of *CadZZilla*™ spawned several other new-wave style customs in the early 1990s. Owner Pat Hurley and body man Jim Bailie, both of Windsor, Ontario, Canada, collaborated with *CadZZilla*™ designer Larry Erickson to bring to life a wild 1953 Buick-based custom named *Nadean*.

Following Larry's design sketches, Jim and Pat set to work on Pat's $200 1953 Buick in 1992. By the time they were finished almost two years later, very little '53 Buick would be left. The entire roof from a '65 Chevy Impala two-door hardtop, including the windshield and rear window, was grafted onto the Buick's body in a lowered position. The rest of the body was extensively reshaped with panels handcrafted from 18-gauge steel to complement the new profile. The Buick's doors were sectioned three inches, and the ice cream cone-shaped rearview mirrors were handmade.

Up front, the front fenders were extended four inches and their wheel openings were enlarged and reshaped. The headlights were frenched into custom-formed teardrop-shaped coves that echo the stock Buick headlight bezel design. A simple grille bar crafted from a 1968 Mustang front bumper was mounted in a hand-formed grille opening. Jim also formed a crisply shaped rolled pan with an inset channel that neatly terminates into custom-made turn signal lenses. The front-hinged hood was created by melding together '49 Mercury and '53 Buick pieces.

At the rear, the fenders were extended five inches and the wheel openings were lowered. The rear fascia was formed by hand to include stainless steel exhaust outlets and an inset license plate well. The plate flips down for filler access to the gas tank. Full-length vertical taillights were handmade to mimic the attractive shape of early '90s production Cadillac lenses; not surprising, since Larry Erickson was employed as a

Cadillac designer when he penned *Nadean*.

The reconfigured body was set on a frame and modified floorpan from a 1976 Cadillac Eldorado that was shortened six inches and stepped up five inches at the rear. Some of the Eldo's chassis components were carried over intact, including the front-wheel drive transaxle and four-wheel disc brakes. The stock 500-cid Cadillac engine was treated to a wild custom-fabricated flip-forward air cleaner and body-color-matched valve covers with hand-painted "Nadean" lettering.

A full hydraulic system was hidden at the forward edge of the trunk, and is accessible via a lift-off panel. With the suspension in the "dropped" position, *Nadean*'s overall height is just 46 inches. One-off billet aluminum 16-inch wheels were designed by Erickson and machined by Budnik; they feature a modern interpretation of the Buick tri-bar shield.

After the extensive bodywork was completed, Todd Hillman coated *Nadean*'s voluptuous contours with an understated silver-lavender metallic paint job. John Wilke then handled the upholstery chores. The chassis-donor 1976 Eldorado also gave up its power front seats, which were covered in tweed-like mauve-colored cloth along with the rest of the interior. The 1965 Chevy dashboard was narrowed four inches and fitted with a custom billet-aluminum panel filled with VDO gauges. Creature comforts include Vintage Air heating and air conditioning and an Alpine six-speaker CD stereo.

Nadean made her debut at the 1994 Detroit Autorama, arriving at the peak of the forward-thinking, high-tech, billet-aluminum phase of custom history. In the ensuing years, customizing trends gravitated back to a more traditional style, with fewer wholesale changes to an old car's design. *Nadean* remains incredibly ambitious restyling effort. It's a virtual clean-sheet redesign that retains only faint elements of the original vehicle and makes a very modern design statement.

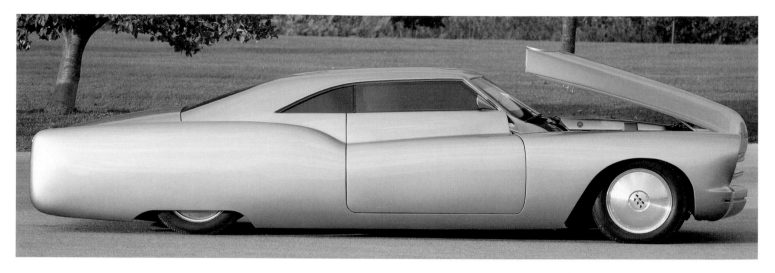

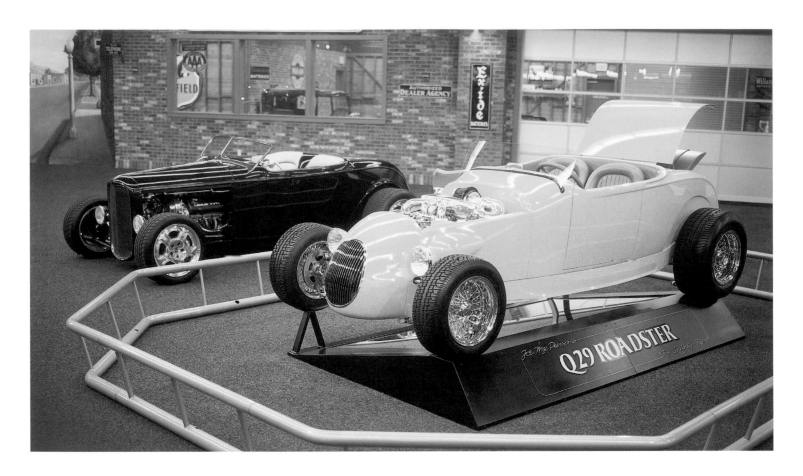

Corporate Rods

In the 1990s, several automakers recognized that hot rod-inspired show cars could draw attention to their brands. The phenomenon began with the Boyd Coddington-built/Mitsubishi-backed *Aluma Coupe* (pp. 216–217), and spread among a number of automakers.

The car that would become known as the Q29 *Infiniti Flyer* didn't begin as a factory project. Instead, it started when Tustin, California's Joe MacPherson decided he wanted a hot rod roadster. After considering his options, Joe opted to build a tracknose 1929 Ford as a modern interpretation of the NieKamp '29 that won the inaugural Oakland Grand National Roadster Show in 1950. A successful auto dealer, Joe asked Chevrolet for a four-cam Corvette engine. When he was turned down, his Infiniti representative offered to provide the running gear from a damaged 1992 Q45 sedan. Determined to make history, Joe set out to build the first rod to win the Grand National Roadster Show's America's Most Beautiful Roadster trophy with a Japanese engine.

Joe tapped some of the best names in hot rodding to build the Q29. Art and Mike Chrisman headed up the project, fabricating the chassis, optimizing the Infiniti 4.5-liter V-8, and chrome-plating virtually every exterior and undercarriage component. The bodywork was done by Steve Davis, upholstery by Tony Nancy, and paint by Junior Conway. The Q29 debuted at the 45th Grand National Roadster show in 1994 and won the AMBR trophy that Joe had so coveted.

A few years later, when Toyota was looking for a vehicle to draw attention to the technology in the new Lexus GS400, a 1932 Ford roadster provided the ideal show car. The idea came about when Keith Crain, publisher of *AutoWeek*, showed Yale Gieszl, then executive vice president of Toyota Motor Sales, his hot rod collection.

Yale commissioned Hot Wheels designer Larry Wood to provide the concept, then gathered Chuck Lombardo of California Street Rods and representatives from Rod Millen Motorsport and Toyota Racing Development to lay plans for a Lexus-drivetrain-equipped hot rod. TRD tuned the Lexus 4.0-liter V-8 to 400 horsepower. CSR stretched a set of Just-A-Hobby frame rails to a wheelbase of 112 inches and turned the frame over to RMM, which installed a custom-built IFS and a modified Lexus IRS.

Completed in just 12 weeks, the candy-red hot rod featured a Brookville steel body, Coach leather upholstery, King Bee headlights, and Budnik aluminum wheels. The finished car was sent on the 1998 new-car show circuit where it got rave reviews for its appearance and Lexus received kudos for taking on such an enthusiast-driven project.

Plymouth went one step further by introducing the Prowler, a production hot rod for the 1997 model year. Though it never sold in high volume, it was offered through the 2002 model year and it demonstrated a commitment by Chrysler to the enthusiast crowd. No matter how deep their involvement, though, the fact that automakers built and backed these cars during the '90s is a testament to the allure of the hot rod.

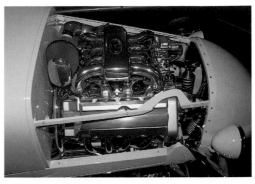

Burk Roadster

One of the most impressive traits shared by hot rodders is the ability to build their cars themselves. "Checkbook rodders" certainly do exist, but the do-it-yourself-attitude that permeated the hobby in its early days continues. This car, built by Dave Burk of Glen Ellyn, Illinois, is proof that the self-sufficient rodder is alive and well.

Dave acquired fabrication skills during the ten years he worked as a mold maker for a now-defunct die manufacturer. There, he learned how to operate lathes, mills, and eventually a CNC machine. With access to these tools, Dave set out to build this '28 Ford Model A roadster in 1993. He completed the project in only four months.

Dave had been a hot rod fanatic since childhood, when he saw a Model A filled with nitroglycerine blow up the monster in the 1959 movie *The Giant Gila Monster*. Inspired by that car, he set out to build a rod with the stripped-down look of a dual-purpose '50s drag/street car.

The project couldn't begin until Dave had the right parts. After acquiring a $100 1950 Ford pickup flathead and a gennie Latham Axial Flow supercharger (the culmination of a 12-year search), Dave started by rebuilding the engine. He installed an Isky cam, a Vertex magneto, and several parts he machined from billet aluminum, including the intake manifold and all of the pulleys and brackets.

A boxed aftermarket Model A frame accepted the flathead, which Dave hooked to a 1937 Ford transmission. Again, Dave fabricated most of the suspension parts. To lower the car, he mounted the rear axle on top of the frame instead of below it and the front leaf spring behind the axle, not above it. Channeling the steel '28 Ford body dropped it another

four inches. With Sprint Car rear wheels on vintage-style slicks, the car sits so low that Dave welded the doors shut; he just hops in. In keeping with the bare-bones look, Dave moved the radiator to the trunk, which required routing all four hoses underneath the car, next to the frame.

A sparse interior completed the project. Dave outfitted it with pressboard door and dash panels covered with pleated vinyl, a three-foot-long shift rod replete with a hand-carved skull, and a pair of boat seats that he had a friend cover with vinyl. Rubber mats cover the floor, the transmission and torque tube are exposed between the seats, and the only two gauges (oil and temperature) reside below the simple, smooth dash panel.

Dave has made a few changes since he put the car on the road in 1993. The primered body gave way to a 1959 Chevy Crown Sapphire paint job in '94, and the beautiful, one-off heads were added in '95 after Dave had learned how to use a CNC machine. Dave designed the heads for a 7.5:1 compression ratio, perfect for the Latham blower. He programmed the CNC machine to cut them from billet aluminum, adding his name to the surface. Dave says the flattie puts out 275–300 horsepower.

Today, Dave works to make sure a future generation of rodders will know how to build rods too, as an admissions representative for Wyoming Technical Institute. Located in Laramie, Wyoming, the Institute offers 9–12 month programs that teach rod, custom, and high-performance engine and chassis construction techniques. If the students he recruits can build anything approaching his Model A, the future of hot rodding is in excellent hands.

Frankenstude

In 1990, Thom Taylor drew a bullet-nose Studebaker design dubbed *Frankenstude* as a tongue-in-cheek response to the Larry Erickson-designed *CadZZilla*™. "I was pushing the bulletnose Studebaker thing because it was the most outrageous, ridiculous car," said Thom. "I wanted to see it done radically and seriously, like *CadZZilla*™."

Thom shopped his design to friend and noted rod builder Boyd Coddington, but Boyd took a pass. Later, Thom mentioned it to Prior Lake, Minnesota-based race car and rod constructor Greg Fleury. Fleury floated the idea to Minneapolis fine art printer Steve Anderson, who was looking to have a radical car built, and a deal was struck. Thom's drawings were published, and the project began.

Working alone, Greg built the body. He started with 1948 Starlight coupe, adding a '51 nose and hood, '50 front fenders, and '47 rear fenders. Every panel was massaged to match Thom's drawing, and the door skins, doorjambs, roof, and rocker panels were fabricated from scratch. The bare-steel body was shown in 1992, but it would take almost another five years to complete the car.

Much of the delay was caused by engineering problems that had to be solved. Greg welded the nose into a flip-front-end unit, and engineered it to raise up, move forward, then tilt open with the push of a button. To make the doors open scissor-style, he designed them to first move out away from the body, then turn vertically.

Other body components consisted of Harley-Davidson mirrors, handmade taillights, and custom glass. Town & Country Glass cut down a Pontiac Grand Am windshield to fit and cut the door glass from Ford van windshields. Thom's design called for the Starlight coupe's characteristic four-piece wrap-around rear window to slant forward. The glass was custom-made in two pieces by Glass Pro of Santa Fe Springs, California. A bulletnose was cast in brass to mimic the '50's design, but it replaced the stock "Studebaker" relief with "Frankenstude" lettering.

Though *Frankenstude* exhibited the radical bodywork of a custom, it would have the engine and chassis of a hot rod. Greg completely fabricated a race car-like 115-inch-wheelbase tube chassis with an integrated roll cage. He designed the tube frame to double as the exhaust system, and installed a Chevrolet L-98 V-8 crate motor. Cotrell Racing Engines of Chaska, Minnesota, tuned the tuned-port-injected 350-cid engine to 400 horsepower. Greg mated it to a GM 700R4 automatic transmission, and as well as headers, exhaust pipes, and a driveshaft that he fabricated.

Thom envisioned all-wheel drive, and Greg made it work by using a GMC Syclone all-wheel-drive center section up front, an early Corvette center section in the rear, and a GM all-wheel-drive transfer case. Four-wheel independent suspension and disc brakes were added.

Inside, Greg scratchbuilt the dash, and had it upholstered in bone-colored leather by Bobby Griffey, who also did the seats. Keith Nybo upholstered the door panels, and installed the headliner and carpeting. Vintage Air air conditioning, gauges by Classic Instruments, and a one-off Boyds steering wheel on an ididit steering column completed the interior.

The final touches included custom-mixed House of Kolor Frankenstude Purple paint sprayed by Rand Bailey and a set of 17-inch billet wheels custom-made by Boyd Coddington.

Six-and-a-half years in the works, several scale replicas made it to market before the full-size project was complete!

The finished *Frankenstude* made its debut in an exhibit at the Minneapolis Institute of Art. Within the car community, its unique design, complex engineering, and robust performance potential made it a hit. *Frankenstude*, like *CadZZilla*™, helped launch a new wave of customs conceived as a modern take on '50s cars.

Steve Anderson kept the car until 2000, when he sold it to Steve and Mary Barton of Las Vegas. The Bartons switched out the rear suspension for air suspension by Air Ride Technologies. As Steve put it, he and his wife wanted the car because "it's a magnificent custom with a perfect design."

1

Jimmie Vaughan Customs

Like most custom car fans of his generation, Jimmie Vaughan got into cars at an early age. Born in 1951, he grew up in Oak Cliff, Texas, near Dallas. He was reading custom car magazines as soon as he could make out the words, and he began building model cars as a kid. At the age of 13, he found another passion, the guitar. He's been playing ever since, and has become one of the most respected blues/rock guitarists in the business.

As a cofounder of the Fabulous Thunderbirds, occasional collaborator with late brother and legendary guitarist Stevie Ray Vaughan, and a successful solo artist, Jimmie has had a varied and successful musical career. He moved to Austin, Texas, to be close to that city's thriving music scene, but he's always kept cars close to his heart, designing a series of early '60s-style customs. Jimmie doesn't like the word "design," though. He says the automakers designed the cars; he prefers to refer to his efforts as restyling. Jimmie summarizes his philosophy of customs on his website, jimmievaughan.com: "It's not like transportation. It's art you can drive to the store."

1. 1951 Chevrolet. *Always a fan of late-1950s/early '60s customs, Jimmie designed his first major custom, a '51 Chevy Fleetline, in the late '80s. When it was first featured in the December 1988 issue of Rod & Custom, the car had frenched '54 Ford headlights, hood louvers, shaved door handles, smoothed bumpers, '55 Buick side trim, '59 Chevy rear wheel openings, sidepipes, a Chevy 350-cid V-8 with tri-carbs, and a Chevy Nova subframe with C'd rear rails and lowering blocks. Inside, it featured a '63 Buick steering wheel and white and purple tuck-and-roll upholstery by "Bruce" of San Marcos. It was finished in purple and lavender primer. Jimmie hooked up with Gary Howard of Georgetown, Texas, to revamp the car in 1990. Howard reworked the front and rear wheel openings using '56 Chevy lips, removed the hood louvers and sidepipes, rounded the rear hood corners, added '54 Chevy rocker moldings, and added a one-piece '50 Olds windshield. Howard also reshaped the grille opening and inserted 31 Corvette teeth, installed a set of custom taillights by Rod Powell out back, and painted the car a lavender color that Jimmie calls "Violet Vision."* **2. 1963 Buick Riviera.** *After the Chevy, Jimmie and Gary Howard teamed up again on a 1963 Buick Riviera. The changes are subtle, but they're there. Howard shaved the body, gave the top a sneaky two-inch chop, dechromed and smoothed the center of the hood, extended the front fenders 1½ inches, added '68 Imperial headlights, placed '65 Corvette taillights in the rear bumper, and made the grille using sheet aluminum and '59 Cadillac bullets. He also lowered the car around a set of '54 Buick wire wheels and topped it off with an organic candy-lime-gold paint job that has elements of metallic, metalflake, and pearl. Jimmie talked noted upholsterer Vernon McKean out of retirement to stitch the pearl-white tuck-and-roll in one-inch pleats. Jimmie won the Harry Bradley Design Achievement award at the 1992 KKOA Nationals with the Buick.*

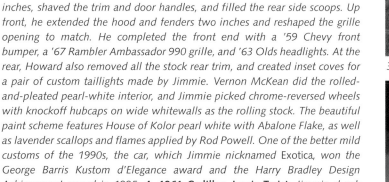

2

3. 1960 Chevrolet, Exotica. *Jimmie's third project wasn't even his car. Looking for a cruising partner, Jimmie talked friend Mike Young into letting him restyle a 1960 Chevy that Mike had owned for several years. Jimmie even promised that Mike could have the Riviera if he didn't like the finished Chevy. Mike handed over the reins and let Jimmie work with Gary Howard to turn the Chevy into a beautiful custom. Howard chopped the top a modest 2⅞ inches, shaved the trim and door handles, and filled the rear side scoops. Up front, he extended the hood and fenders two inches and reshaped the grille opening to match. He completed the front end with a '59 Chevy front bumper, a '67 Rambler Ambassador 990 grille, and '63 Olds headlights. At the rear, Howard also removed all the stock rear trim, and created inset coves for a pair of custom taillights made by Jimmie. Vernon McKean did the rolled-and-pleated pearl-white interior, and Jimmie picked chrome-reversed wheels with knockoff hubcaps on wide whitewalls as the rolling stock. The beautiful paint scheme features House of Kolor pearl white with Abalone Flake, as well as lavender scallops and flames applied by Rod Powell. One of the better mild customs of the 1990s, the car, which Jimmie nicknamed* Exotica, *won the George Barris Kustom d'Elegance award and the Harry Bradley Design Achievement award in 1995.* **4. 1961 Cadillac, Ironic Twist.** *Jimmie shook things up a little more with his fourth project. What was originally going to be a mildly customized 1961 Cadillac Coupe de Ville turned into a custom Caddy with show car, drag car, and hot rod influences. For this project, Jimmie teamed up with Craig Willits, Lee Pratt, "Roach," and Gary Howard. Willits stitched the black leather upholstery, while Pratt did the initial mild custom body modifications and helped with final assembly. Jimmie ordered the engine, a stroked 526-cid V-8, from C.M.D. in Lakeland, Florida, and Roach, a local mechanic, built it and installed the Latham supercharger. Howard performed the major customizing work. His contributions included a two-inch top chop that incorporated the rear portion of the roof from a '61 Cadillac four-door sedan, extending the trunk to the rear bumper, pancaking the hood and hinging it at the front, installing Lucas headlamps, and applying the bright-green pearl/candy paint. Airbags were installed to get the right stance, and a set of '54 Buick wires were mounted on B.F. Goodrich Silvertowns with the rears recapped as slicks. Jimmie named the car* Ironic Twist *and recorded an instrumental of the same name.*

3

4

Kopperhed®

Hot rodders and customizers have always looked for a way to stand out from the crowd. In the early 1980s, street rodders began turning to "phantoms." A phantom is a rod or custom modified to mimic a factory-stock body style that the factory never actually produced. Though many phantom street rods had been done, Billy Gibbons' *Kopperhed®* 1950 Ford three-window coupe, built in 1996, was one of the first post-'48 phantoms.

Kopperhed® started as a 1950 Ford business coupe that Gibbons intended to have mildly customized by Pete Chapouris' PC3group (later known as the SoCal Speed Shop). That changed, however, when Billy saw a Steve Stanford "Sketchpad" drawing of a phantom '50 Ford three-window coupe in the June 1992 issue of *Rod & Custom* magazine. Thereafter, the plan was to have Chapouris' crew realize Stanford's drawing in metal.

The most impressive aspect of *Kopperhed®* is the beautifully realized three-window coupe body style. The design involved considerable changes to the top and doors. The guys at PC3g chopped the top 3½ inches in front and 3¼ inches in back. The business coupe was a five window, but PC3g changed it to a three-window design by filling in and smoothing over the rear side windows. The rear window was left stock but moved down and angled forward.

To make the top design work, the doors had to be lengthened ten inches. The rear of each window frame was angled to match the front, and the wind wings were reshaped to fit the top's new shape. Six '50 Ford door skins and four win-dow frames were needed to accomplish these tasks. Stainless-steel trim was fabricated for the windows. All told, 500 hours went into the top and door modifications.

Since the 1940s, customs have been shaved of their trim. *Kopperhed®* instead made use of all that trim. To drive home the illusion that this was a factory body style, Billy left on the hood, trunk, headlight, and side trim, as well as the door handles. Only the front and rear bumper guards were removed. As Pete Chapouris told *Rod & Custom* magazine, "This is the first radical custom that hasn't been nosed, decked, or frenched."

The rolling stock represented another bit of trickery. Pete's shop cut the centers out of stock Ford wheels and welded them into modern 16-inch steel rims. Stock center caps and BFGoodrich radials with add-on Coker whitewalls provided a vintage look with modern performance.

Kopperhed® was also given updated mechanicals. To lower the car and modernize the front end, PC3g replaced the front frame rails with a Fat Man Fabrications front clip that allowed for a four-inch drop. Dropped front spindles, Mustang II suspension components, ECI disc brakes, and cut-down front coil springs completed the front end. At the rear, PC3g installed a Ford nine-inch rear end with de-arched springs.

Underhood, Billy had Pete's group install a vintage 1957 Ford 312-cid Y-block bored .030 over and outfitted with an Offenhauser tri-carb manifold and Ford F600 truck exhaust manifolds. They mated the engine to a Ford three-speed manual transmission with overdrive.

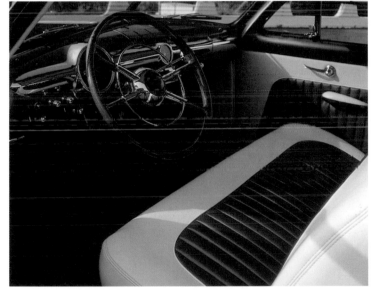

Ron Mangus stitched the tuck-and-roll upholstery in copper and white vinyl. Other interior details included engine-turned step plates, a Crestliner steering wheel, a Kenwood stereo, power windows, and air conditioning.

Painted black with copper wheels and interior trim, the car's colors reminded Billy of the copperhead snake from his native Texas—thus the name.

After making custom history in 1989 with *CadZZilla*™, a car that gave set the custom scene in a new direction, Gibbons did it again in '96 with *Kopperhed*®. With its phantom three-window body style, modern versions of vintage components, and use of stock trim, *Kopperhed*® was unlike any custom ever built. Isn't that what customizing is all about?

The Dick Williams 1927 Ford Model T, entered by Blackie Gejeian

Hot Rods at Pebble Beach Since 1950,

the Pebble Beach Concours d'Elegance has been the ultimate car show. Steeped in tradition, it is an exclusive and elegant celebration of the history of the automobile. To be invited to display a car at Pebble Beach is an incredible honor. To win your class is an affirmation that your car is the best of its breed.

Held each August at the Lodge on the 18th green at Pebble Beach, which overlooks Monterey Bay, only 175 cars are invited to participate each year. Anyone willing to pay the triple-digit admission fee is welcome to attend.

Known primarily as the purview of blue bloods and their vintage Ferraris, Duesenbergs, and coachbuilt classics, hot rods had never appeared "on the lawn" prior to 1997. In fact, the rebellious hot rod spirit was somewhat at odds with the staid atmosphere of such an elite car show.

Initiated by longtime Pebble Beach competitor Bruce Meyer, a group of crossover automotive enthusiasts changed all that. Meyer, along with Pebble Beach judges Ken Gross, Gordon Apker, and Glenn Mounger, as well as regular competitors Kirk White and Dennis Varni, appealed to event organizers Jules Heumann and the late Lorin Tryon to include a class for hot rods. After years of asking, their wish was finally granted with the introduction of the Historic Hot Rod class in 1997.

Gross established the class criteria and invited the first hot rod competitors. He chose nine fenderless roadsters from the 1940s and '50s, all of which had pedigrees as either street/show or street/lakes race cars. Gross, Ray Brock, Alex Xydias, and Don Montgomery were the judges at that first event. The winner was Bruce Meyer with his restored Doane Spencer Deuce (pp. 24–25), which also won the Ford-sponsored Dean Batchelor award for the most historically significant hot rod. Kirk White took second with his '32 Ford lakes racer originally owned by Ray Brown, and third place went to Don Orosco for his Tony LaMasa Deuce roadster. When the winners drove across the ramp to accept their awards, the standing ovation they received confirmed that hot rods belonged at Pebble Beach. The pictures shown here are from that show.

A hot rod or custom class has been part of the Concours every other year since the 1997 event. Don Orosco won in '99 with his Dick Flint '29 Model A roadster, then took first in 2001 with the Alex Xydias So-Cal Coupe (pp. 52–53). Brock Yates won in 2003 with the ex-Duffy Livingston *Eliminator* track roadster/sports racing car. The 2005 event marked the first-ever custom car class (pp. 282–283). Given the number of legendary rods and customs being restored today, they should be well-represented at Pebble Beach for years to come.

Kirk White (right) and Ray Brown in the Ray Brown '32 Ford lakes racer

Judges Ray Brock, Ken Gross, Alex Xydias, and Don Montgomery (l to r)

Don Orosco accepts the third-place award in his Tony LaMasa Deuce roadster

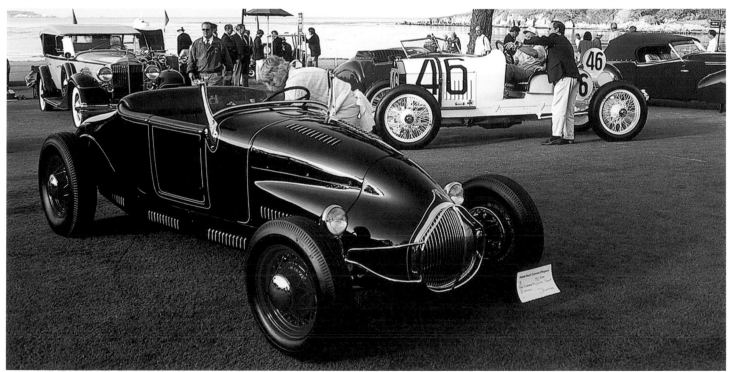

The Jack Thompson 1927 Ford Model T, entered by Gary Schroeder

Scrape A longtime hot rod and custom show producer and former magazine editor at *Hot Rod* and *Car Craft*, Terry Cook had always appreciated the flowing design of the 1930s and early '40s Lincoln Zephyrs. The cars had a stunning forward motion and fluidity that sparked Terry's imagination.

Terry knew no classic car collector would sell a stock Zephyr to a customizer, so he joined a Zephyr club and posed as a restorer when he went to investigate a Zephyr coupe that had been stored for 23 years in Farmington, Maine. Terry purchased the car in January 1993 for $3300. Over the course of the next 4½ years and 4500 man hours, the car was transformed into one of the most noteworthy customs of the 1990s: *Scrape*.

Scrape's frame and running gear came from a 1978 Chevy Caprice station wagon that Terry bought for $350. Terry had Dave Cronk of Wayne, New Jersey, do much of the chassis work. Dave lengthened the Chevy frame to match the Zephyr's 116-inch wheelbase, and Z'd it in the area of the flywheel. Dave then lifted the Zephyr body from its frame, and channeled and welded the Lincoln body over the Chevy frame rails.

Terry shipped the car to bodyman Ramsey Mosher's Ram's Rod Shop in Dover, Delaware, for the metalwork. There, the car was given a '41 Zephyr nose and grille, and the top was chopped a dramatic eight inches. Mosher made the sharply raked A-pillars from sheetmetal following the shape of a Chrysler Cirrus windshield, then installed a cut-down '90-93 Honda Accord windscreen. Mosher also cut away the door window frames. Suicide doors with hidden hinges added a distinct custom feel.

To match the Chevy frame's width, the front and rear fenders were widened 2½ inches. Up front, frenched 1939 Ford headlights were added. The hood was lengthened by an inch, and the front pan was rolled under the grillework.

The rear fenders were extended six inches, making the car 16½ feet long. Mosher filled the back window, then cut another smaller window opening that mimicked the stock appearance. The steel body is as close to a single, seamless piece as possible. The rear bumper, adapted from a '52-53 Kaiser front bumper guard, was smoothly frenched into the tail. Despite the considerable alterations, the car remains recognizably a Zephyr.

Cronk installed a mild 1974 Chevy 350-cid small-block V-8 under the hood. Eddie Denkenberger applied the House of Kolor Passion Pearl Purple paint. For rolling stock, Terry chose 14-inch Coker wide whitewalls with Moon "ripple-disc" wheel covers, though he occasionally displayed the car with a modern 17-inch chrome wheel on one side to demonstrate that the car blends the old with the new.

To make the car drivable, Terry had Hydro Toys of Dover, New Jersey, install a twin-pump hydraulic suspension. When fully lowered, *Scrape* stands just 48⅜ inches high, its frame rails kissing the pavement. Skid plates prevent damage to the nose, tail, and rocker panels.

Inside, Mosher modified the stock gauge cluster to include a vaguely art deco television screen. The screen projects an image from a rearview camera to aid rear visibility. Terry replaced the stock seats with a Cadillac split bench. Bobby Sapp did the tuck-and-roll upholstery in black and white leather and Naugahyde. Sapp also added a dropped section to the headliner to hide indirect purple neon lighting.

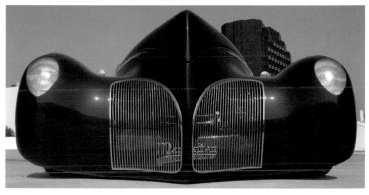

The finished car appeared in numerous magazines, and it was even replicated by Mattel as a ⅛-scale diecast model. During the building process, Cook and Mosher did some replicating of their own. They made molds off the body and subsequently sold more than 50 fiberglass coupe and ragtop bodies through Terry's Deco Rides company. Later, turnkey cars, starting at about $85,000, were made available through Speedster Motorcars of Clearwater, Florida.

In August 2000, *Scrape* was sold at auction to the Petersen Automotive Museum for $275,000. The Petersen purchase was a rare honor for a newly constructed custom, and it cemented *Scrape* as a landmark example of the customizing art.

50th Anniversary Hot Rod

As *Hot Rod* magazine's 50th anniversary approached, the editorial staff considered building a Deuce roadster as its anniversary car. Illustrator Chip Foose had a better idea: They should build a modern version of the tracknose '27 T that appeared on the first cover. Once Chip provided a design sketch, the wheels were in motion.

That first cover car, Regg Schlemmer's 136-mph dry-lakes racer, featured a flathead, yellow and black paint, and a race-ready aerodynamic look. *Hot Rod* planned to build its car a bit differently; it would have state-of-the-art parts and be a thoroughly modern, domesticated street rod.

To bring the vision to life, the *Hot Rod* staff enlisted the expertise of Roy Brizio Street Rods of San Francisco. Brizio dove into the project by acquiring a Wescott fiberglass body and a Speedway Motors dirt-car nose that was modified to fit. The yellow-and-black paint scheme of the original gave way to *Hot Rod* magazine colors—red and white—applied by Art Himsl.

Schlemmer's car had a specially built tubular frame, a 1937 Ford tube axle, and a quick-change rear end. Brizio followed suit with a tapered steel-channel frame, a custom-bent tube axle modeled after a '37 Ford unit, and a Halibrand quick-change. The front suspension changed considerably, though, as Brizio's shop installed a pair of inboard-mounted coil-over shock absorbers. A Chevy Vega steering box, four-wheel disc brakes, and set of Boyds aluminum wheels on BFGoodrich radial tires rounded out the rolling chassis.

An engine builder by trade, Schlemmer installed a Mercury flathead V-8 equipped with Navarro heads, an Evans manifold, and a Smith cam in the original car. The *Hot Rod* staff opted for a more modern and reliable powerplant. Edelbrock's Curt Hooker built a dual-quad-equipped Ford 302-cid V-8 hooked to a T5 five-speed manual transmission. With 304 horsepower in a 2200-lb car, Schlemmer would be proud.

Like Schlemmer's original race car, this hot rod has a spartan interior. Oxblood leather upholstery, a Bell-type midget steering wheel, Stewart-Warner gauges, and three pedals were the only items needed.

Appropriately, the T roadster appeared in the January 1998 issue of *Hot Rod*, 50 years after that important first issue. A modern take on a historic hot rod, the anniversary car is much more civilized than the seminal hot rod that inspired it. The idea is the same, though: power, speed, style, and open-air excitement.

So-Cal Roadster
In 1997, Pete Chapouris, a rod builder of considerable accomplishment, approached Alex Xydias to license the So-Cal Speed Shop name. Alex agreed, and thus one of hot rodding's legendary names was resurrected. Under Chapouris' direction, the new So-Cal Speed Shop has flourished. So-Cal has six licensed stores in addition to its Pomona, California, headquarters, and they all sell traditional hot rod and restoration parts, as well as T-shirts, posters, and lots of other So-Cal merchandise.

The So-Cal Speed Shop will also build you a hot rod much like the one featured here. This particular car is quite special, though. Much like the *California Kid* represented Chapouris' first rod shop, Pete and Jake's Hot Rod Repair, the So-Cal Roadsters are flagship cars for the various So-Cal Speed Shop locations. Each licensee has a So-Cal Roadster to help attract customers and show off the company's products. Plus, they're great fun to drive.

So-Cal Roadster no. 001 (note the Xydias and Chapouris signatures on the firewall) resides where all So-Cal roadsters originate, at the Pomona shop. Like the So-Cal Speed Shop itself, this roadster rings of tradition but is actually quite modern. Styled after Clyde Sturdy's Class B Modified that ran

142 mph at Bonneville in 1951, the car is built from state-of-the-art parts, from the blown Chevy 355-cid small-block V-8 to the So-Cal step-boxed chassis to the handcrafted Brookville Roadster steel '32 Ford body.

The car originally featured a potent (390 horsepower) 355-cid Chevy V-8. However, always looking to put more hot in its rods, the So-Cal gang swapped out that engine for a Chevy 355 equipped with a Holley 420 MegaBlower supercharger, dual Holley 600-cfm carbs, Holley aluminum heads, and a hydraulic roller cam. The mill routes its 540 horsepower through a B&M four-speed automatic transmission to a Ford nine-inch rear end. An I-beam front axle with hairpin radius rods and a rear transverse spring with ladder bars work to keep the car on the pavement. Meanwhile, the 31-inch-tall, 16-inch-diameter bias-ply Firestone tires provide far too little grip for all that horsepower. But, with their Halibrand-style wheels, they do look right.

The price for all this four-wheeled nostalgia is in the ballpark of $125,000, and that's with a lesser, yet still-potent, engine. You can see one in person at your friendly neighborhood So-Cal Speed Shop. Or, if you have the means, you can order one of your own.

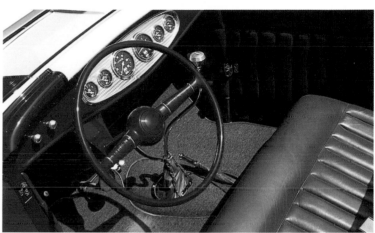

Choppers

Choppers Much like punk rock music was a reaction to the overly corporate mainstream rock 'n' roll of the late 1970s, the "rat rod" revolution of the '90s was partly a response to the excessively finished, ultra-expensive street rods and customs of the day. Just like punk brought back the raucousness and rebelliousness of real '50s rock 'n' roll, the outbreak of these "low-fi" cars dislodged the billet-and-fiberglass establishment by recalling rodding's primal past. It was a new counterculture uprising within an aging counterculture.

The Choppers were among the first and most prominent clubs of young enthusiasts to begin creating and popularizing this new/old type of rod and custom. The club actually has its roots in the late '80s. The core members kept seeing each other at the same swap meets and car shows, and eventually developed friendships rooted in their similar interests and tastes. The first iteration of the club was called the Chislers, but in 1998, the most active members broke off to start anew, christening themselves the Choppers.

All six Choppers members reside in Burbank, a Los Angeles suburb. Many inherited their passion for hot rodding and customizing at an early age, from their hot rodding fathers. Though most of the club brought out their hot rods for this photo shoot, several members also own accurate '40s- and '50s-style customs.

Since the club's beginnings, their philosophy has stayed the same. The Choppers don't refer to their projects as "rat rods" or "crude customs." Their cars are works in progress; they're rough around the edges, but also fastidiously researched and carefully pieced together from authentic vintage parts. The Choppers have a deep appreciation for rodding and custom-

izing's colorful history, and feel obliged to preserve the traditional bits and pieces that others have cast off. The worn patina is part of the appeal. They strive for total era correctness so they can re-create what it was like to drive a real hot rod or custom in the late '40s and early '50s. That means no "cheating" by using modern advances such as alternators, radial tires, or modern aftermarket components.

As the 1990s came to a close, it became clear that the influx of young, retro-obsessed builders would be a trendsetting force in the hobby in the years to come. The proliferation of active, dedicated clubs like the Choppers was heartening evidence that traditional hot rodding and customizing had a bright future.

1

1. Keith Weesner started collecting parts for his 1929 Ford Model A roadster in 1993, then put it all together over a four-month span in '95. Inspiration was provided by old Hot Rod magazines and the vintage photos in Don Montgomery's series of hot rod history books. Keith installed a Hallock windshield and adapted a '40 Ford DeLuxe dash to fit the cowl. A dual-carbed 1953 Ford flathead supplies the power. The taillights are actually '47-48 Ford parking lights with red lenses. Here, Keith displays the 2nd Place Elapsed Time trophy he received at the 2005 Pasadena Roadster Club Reliability Run. 2. Sandy Wachs' 1956 Ford F-100 pickup has a four-inch top chop, '61 Chrysler headlights and grille (which is decorated with chrome drawer knobs), Dodge Lancer hubcaps, and satin metallic-blue paint. The hoodsides are adorned with '56 Buick "porthole" trim pieces. Front and rear bumpers from a '57 Chevy truck were cut down to fit. The chromed running boards are topped with white tuck-and-roll upholstery to match the blue and white tuck-and-roll interior. Homemade custom taillights were frenched into the rear fenders to match the angle of the canted headlights.

2

3

4

5

3. Verne Hammond sold a roadster project car to buy his 1934 Ford coupe. He chopped the top a healthy six inches, laying back the front roof and door posts in the process. Being a stickler for era-correct detail, Verne had the decklid louvers punched on Eric Vaughn's vintage louver press. **4.** Jon Fisher's 1929 Model A roadster was an original '40s race car that he found and bought sans engine. The chromed and drilled Ford brakes, Auburn dash, and '48 Lincoln Zephyr steering wheel were on the car when he got it. Jon installed a flathead with Belond headers and two Stromberg 97 carbs on a Tattersfield high-rise manifold. **5.** With its magnesium American Racing Torq-Thrust wheels on blackwall tires and front-mounted Moon gas tank, Deron Wright's 1932 Ford three-window coupe has more of an early '60s vibe than the Choppers' other rods. The '58 Chevy 283 was enlarged to 292 cid, then topped with six two-barrel carbs on a Weiand intake. The three-inch top chop was originally performed in the '60s. **6.** The buildup of Aaron Kahan's Bad News 1927 Model T Coupe was filmed for an episode of The Learning Channel TV show Rides. Aaron had the body since his grandfather gave it to him in 1971, when he was just five. Power comes from a '51 Olds Rocket V-8 hooked to a '37 LaSalle three-speed transmission. The canted taillights came from a 1946-48 Buick. Pinstriping and lettering were applied by artist Van.

6

Rob Fortier '29 Roadster

Most hot rod and custom car journalists are hands-on enthusiasts, and Rob Fortier is no exception. Rob put together this well-proportioned 1929 Ford in 1999, when he was a staffer at both *Custom Rodder* and *Street Rodder* magazines. While the roadster has a rat rod-inspired patina, Rob also used a few more-modern mechanical components for improved reliability.

Rob worked with Gary Dagel to build a repro frame consisting of American Stamping 1932 Ford frame rails and Deuce Frame Co. crossmembers. He placed a genuine '29 Ford roadster body atop the frame. The front suspension consisted of a dropped I-beam axle on a Model A leaf spring and tube shocks. At the rear, a '57 Ford nine-inch rear end was suspended by a Model A spring and tube shocks on '48 Ford truck mounts. Custom-made stainless hairpin radius rods by Carl Fjastad were used front and rear. Simple steel wheels on reproduction bias-ply Firestones were trimmed with '47-48 Mercury hubcaps and trim rings.

The 425-cid nailhead V-8 from a 1966 Buick Riviera was bored .030 over but otherwise left basically stock internally. The Sanderson "Limefire" headers had no provisions for a full exhaust system, but modified Bugpack stinger baffles were installed to serve as makeshift mufflers. The weather-beaten body was left mostly stock, but a reproduction Hallock windshield was adapted to the Model A cowl and a Deuce grille shell was fitted in place.

The interior was outfitted with a 1946 Lincoln red-lucite

steering wheel on a '40 Ford DeLuxe column. Jimmy White and Rob modified a '40 Mercury dashboard to fit the tighter confines of the Model A interior and accept a So-Cal Speed Shop gauge panel filled with vintage Stewart-Warner gauges. Rob covered the door panels in teak wood and the floor with '40s Ford running board rubber material. The seat was custom-made by Van Butler and upholstered with an antique Pendleton wool blanket that Rob got from his grandmother!

Rob sold the roadster in 2000 to move on to other projects, but it remains a perfect example of the vintage-style aesthetic that made a strong comeback in the late '90s. It's easy to see the appeal of this bare-bones, back-to-basics approach.

Ken Gross Roadster

Although it's built in the late-1940s style, Ken Gross' 1932 Ford roadster transcends many eras. Gross, an automotive writer by trade, dreamed of this Deuce roadster all of his adult life. He first sketched it out when he was in high school, influenced by the beautiful hot rods he saw in the many magazines he collected. He didn't get to build his dream rod until he was well into middle age. Ken likes to quote Bruce Meyer who says, "it's never too late to have a happy childhood."

Ken didn't copy any one particular car. Instead, he selected elements from several different cars and went to great lengths to collect pieces true to the 1940s era. From the polished, SCoT-supercharged, 304-cid flathead V-8 equipped with Eddie Meyer high-compression heads, to the "Culver City" Halibrand quick-change rear, to the vintage SCTA and NHRA badges, and the drilled-and-filled handmade dropped axle— all the parts spell "hot rod" the way Ken sees it. The steel-bodied highboy is set off by a Carson-style padded top and handmade lakes pipes. The windshield is chopped 3 ¼ inches, and the posts are slanted to achieve the slight rake that was popular in the 1940s.

One look into the interior and you are mesmerized by the genuine 1933 Auburn dash with its period winged Stewart-Warner curved-glass gauges. Other components, such as the Bell hand-pressure pump, vintage heater, and handsome '39 Ford banjo steering wheel, give it a period-correct feel.

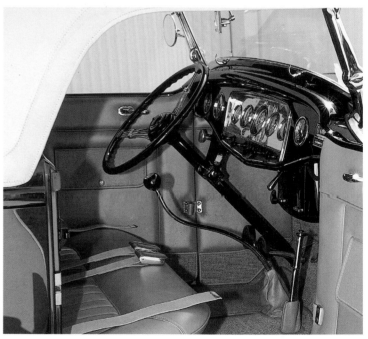

Ken's roadster made its debut at the 50th Grand National Roadster Show in January 1999. Although it wasn't entered in any class, it won the coveted Bruce Meyer Preservation Award for the most authentic representation of a period hot rod. It's a most appropriate trophy that Ken shares with builder Dave Simard, upholsterer Steve Pierce, painters Kevin Olson and Phil Austin, and flathead-builder Mark Kirby. Those men turned Ken's dream into a magnificent car that many would consider the quintessential hot rod.

KEN GROSS ON HIS DEUCE ROADSTER

My heroes in the late 1940s (and today) were hot rodders like Walker Morrison, Doane Spencer, Hank Negley, Nelson Taylor, Ray Brown, Dean Batchelor, Ed Stewart, Joe Nitti, Pete Henderson, and John Ryan—guys who drove their '32 Ford roadsters on the street and raced 'em on weekends at the dry lakes. Early on, they figured out what constituted a primo Deuce—the proportions, the rake, the speed equipment, and a few subtle body modifications. They set the standards and we're all still copying them. I'd like to think my roadster combines the best features of all the great '32 roadsters, done with respect for the guys who built these cars.

Dave Simard's philosophy is that you have to accurately restore a steel roadster body before you can hot rod it. If you work on a body that's aged, rusted, and probably not true, you'll never have a straight car. So he and his talented crew repaired, restored, and metal-finished every panel on my car. We decided not to use any filler. Meticulous welding, patch-

ing, filing, and sanding ensured this body was better than any Ford ever built. It had to be; black lacquer doesn't lie.

I wanted to be able to drive this car, so it had to be as practical as a roadster can be. I know now it's possible to build a car that looks old but incorporates tricks that make it livable and drivable. Here are a few from my '32.

Dave Simard specified chip-resistant urethane paint for the frame and any running gear that wasn't already painted. We installed a Carson-type Haartz-cloth-covered top and side windows, a period accessory hot-water heater (found in *Hemmings Motor News*), and a big Walker finned tube-core radiator, so it idles happily in traffic.

I don't mind stretching the metaphor in a few practical places. I wince when someone tells me they have a period-perfect car and they're running an alternator and disc brakes. Here's the deal. If you can see it, it has to be consistent with the era. If you can't see it, you can take a little license.

For example, this roadster has a hidden electric fuel pump and fuel-pressure regulator; the firewall-mounted Filcoolator A-4 oil cooler is functional, but it incorporates a modern screw-on Ford filter. The Harman & Collins 8R-101 magneto was converted to solid-state operation by Ollie Morris, former chief engineer of Offenhauser Equipment Co. The mag is preset for five degrees of advance with an Offy lead plate. An MSD 6A ignition control, which replaces the points and is hidden under the dash, allows about 18 more degrees of ignition advance. The rheostat is actually one of the dash knobs.

Wherever possible, we used old-style or genuine Ford nuts, rivets, bolts, and fasteners. If they were good enough for Dick Flint and Doane Spencer, they were right for this project. Thankfully, the contents of Dave's barn, plus a spare frame and engine, were there when we needed to cannibalize parts. Hot rodding is all about clever reengineering. You can have your old cake and eat it, too. Trust me—and Dave Simard.

1

John D'Agostino
Anyone who follows the custom car magazines knows the name John D'Agostino. At least once a year, another D'Agostino custom is featured. The cars usually aren't traditional subjects, like leadsled Mercs or shoebox Fords. Rather, they tend to be 1950s and '60s luxury behemoths, often Cadillacs and Lincolns.

D'Agostino, who works full-time at a steel company, doesn't do the customizing work himself. Instead, he's one of a handful of custom car "project managers" who turn to professionals to realize their ideas. His method is unique. He finds a car he wants to restyle, then sketches how he would build it, including the front, rear, top, trim, and wheel treatments. He sends those drawings to professional artists such as Steve Stanford or M.K. John, who further flesh out the design and add color. Sometimes this involves a little back and forth, but once he's happy with the design, D'Agostino farms out the project to one of his favorite builders.

The building process itself starts with lowering. "When I lower a car, I go for the ride height and the ride itself. I like my cars to have a factory ride," John said. "Lowering affects the silhouette. It can make or break a car. I like my cars front and back about even." From there, John has his builders give each car an appropriate chop. "I like the back to be a little lower than the front, so it has that real pretty flow to it," John noted. Next, John moves to the front and finally the rear treatments. "I try to balance the back like the front, bringing elements of the front into the rear end," John said. "It's not how much you do to a car, it's what you do. I really like balanced cars."

John makes use of many of the best craftsmen in the cus-

2

tomizing business. While in progress, his cars are often used as the subject of how-to articles in the various custom magazines. When finished, the look is 1960s traditional, often employing Winfield-style fades (sometimes sprayed by Gene Winfield himself), wire wheels, whitewalls, and a beautiful long, low stance.

John is a member of the KKOA, Kustoms of America, and West Coast Kustoms. A few of his cars have been replicated in scale as Hot Wheels, and still more have appeared in various museums across the country. For his great contribution to the hobby, John was inducted into the Grand National Roadster Show Hall of Fame in 1995, and has been inducted into five other halls.

Born in 1950 in the Northern California town of Pittsburg, D'Agostino was too young to own a car during customizing's golden age of the '50s. But he was hooked on cars early, building models and admiring the work of local builders Joe Bailon, Gene Winfield, and George and Sam Barris. When he was old enough, he bought a 1956 Chevy that he had mildly

3

customized by local builder Frank DeRosa.

D'Agostino drove a customized 1963 Pontiac Grand Prix in college, then had seven different customs built in the lean times of the 1970s, many of them earning major awards. He had another four cars built in the '80s, but it was in the '90s, when he started customizing luxury cars, that D'Agostino really made his mark. John commissioned nine cars to be built in the decade, each of them garnering numerous awards and showing up in the newly revived custom magazines. Like his friend and compatriot Richard Zocchi, John made it a point to unveil his cars early each year at the Grand National Roadster Show. Custom enthusiasts caught on to this practice, and began looking forward to the event as a chance to see the latest from D'Agostino and Zocchi.

But D'Agostino didn't stop there. Since the turn of the century, he has picked up the pace, completing two cars each year. Though he is known for large '50s iron, D'Agostino has also helped break down traditional barriers by customizing out-of-the-ordinary '60s cars and taking on rare subjects that would make him unpopular with classic car collectors.

Each D'Agostino car is shown on the West and East coasts, in Canada, and even in Europe. When they return to the United States, they are put on display at the Petersen Automotive Museum in Los Angeles. From there, some go to other museums, such as the Darryl Starbird National Rod & Custom Car Hall of Fame Museum and others are auctioned off. *Gable*, his custom 1941 Packard, sold for an amazing $450,000 at the Petersen Museum's Cars & Stars Gala in 2004. But it's not the money that keeps D'Agostino interested. It's the whole custom scene. "I'm going to do this as long as I can," said John. "I really like restyling the cars, meeting the people, and making people happy."

1. 1940 Mercury, Stardust. *John had Bill Reasoner build* Stardust *as a tribute to the Barris-built Matranga Merc from the late '40s (see pp. 34–35), starting in 1986. Reasoner chopped the top four inches in front and five in the rear, formed the Matranga-like curved window channeling, installed smoothed '46 Ford bumpers, channeled the body three inches over the frame, and molded the fenders into the body. Unlike the Matranga car, John's Merc was painted a dark-black-cherry color, featured sculpted molded-in running boards, and used an oval '46 Ford rear window. Jerry Sahagon did the white-pearl and maroon mohair interior, and Sam Foose fashioned the custom taillights which were set into the rear bumper guards. The car made its debut at the 1988 Grand National Roadster Show, where it won its class.* **2. 1956 Lincoln, Royal Empress.** *D'Agostino's first luxury custom was the* Royal Empress, *a 1956 Lincoln Premiere that made a splash at the 1991 Grand National Roadster Show. Bill Reasoner started the project, shaving the trim, extending the headlight hoods, peaking the front fenders, and reshaping the tailfins. Gene Winfield completed the bodywork, chopping the top four inches, fashioning the unique full-length taillight lens, smoothing the bumpers, and setting 268 bullets into the front grille. Sid Chavers did the interior in a European luxury style, installing a full-length console and four bucket seats upholstered in silver and lavender mohair. Winfield finished it all off with a signature fade paint job using purple and lavender hues.* **3. 1957 Lincoln, Royal Emperor.** *A Thom Taylor drawing inspired John to restyle a 1957 Lincoln Premiere for the 1995 show season. The front half of the radical new top was fabricated from the rear half of a second '57 Lincoln hardtop. John Aiello, working at Sahagon's Custom Car Concepts at the time, did the bodywork. Other modifications included frenching the headlights, extending the hood and front fenders to match the new grille opening, and using '59 Mercury grille material front and rear. Jerry Sahagon fabricated a full-length center console for the interior, which he upholstered with mint-green leatherette, English tweed, and jade-green velvet. Customizing legend Gene Winfield applied the Jade Idol-inspired mint-green and candy-green fade paint.*

4

5

6

7

4. 1961 Oldsmobile, Golden Starfire. *John picked an unlikely subject, a 1961 Olds, to mildly customize as second of his two cars for the '95 season. Sahagon's Custom Car Concepts did the work. John Aiello installed a modified 1960 Mercury grille with Lucas headlights, added custom taillights, stripped off the chrome trim, and moved the fuel filler to the trunk. He also C'd the frame in the rear and cut down the coil springs to lower the car. Jerry Sahagon installed a pair of '63 Buick Riviera front bucket seats upholstered in pearl-white V-shaped tuck-and-roll in the interior, which was also outfitted with a small television screen and a 45-rpm record player. Darryl Hollenbeck applied the Candy Pagan Gold paint.* **5. 1961 Ford Thunderbird, Fire Star.** *John had the Lucky 7 Custom Shop in Antioch, California, do the bodywork on his custom '61 T-Bird. Lucky 7 chopped the top 3½ inches at the front and 4½ inches at the rear. A total of 178 Gene Winfield chrome bullets were used for the grille. Air suspension gave it the proper low-down stance, and John used Kelsey-Hayes wire wheels on wide whitewalls as the rolling stock. Lucky 7 also sprayed on the Watson-style deep-candy-red paint scheme with gold scallops. The car made its debut in 1997 and a tour of Europe followed. It was displayed at the Petersen Automotive Museum's "Kustoms With a K" exhibit in 2002, and it eventually became part of Jack Walker's collection of historic customs.* **6. 1957 Chrysler Imperial, Imperial Royale.** *John Aiello and Darryl Hollenbeck opened their own shop, Acme Auto Body of Antioch, California, in 1996, and D'Agostino gave them a '57 Imperial to customize right away. John conferred with Steve Stanford to design the Imperial Royale. Acme grafted on a chopped stainless steel top from a '59 Imperial, pie-sectioned the front fenders at their leading edge, used '57 Mercury Turnpike Cruiser headlight assemblies, and modified the rear fenders to slant at a steeper angle. Gene Winfield applied his trademark fade paint in candy-pearl-copper, gold, and cinnamon over a cream base. The car was first shown at the 1997 Grand National Roadster Show and went on to win the coveted Harry Bradley Design Achievement Award at that year's Sacramento Autorama.* **7. 1953 Cadillac convertible, Marilyn.** *John worked with a silent partner to turn a '53 Cadillac convertible done into a tribute to Marilyn Monroe. John Aiello of Acme Auto Body performed the custom work, which was aimed at creating a phantom Eldorado Biarritz. Modifications included adding an Eldorado-style beltline dip, fashioning a removable Carson-style top, modifying the side scoops, and lengthening the fins. Craig Willits upholstered the interior in champagne leather and accented it with gold brocade inserts and blonde-maple woodwork. Darryl Hollenbeck applied the light-yellow pearl paint with gold highlights. The car was named the World's Most Beautiful Custom at the 1998 Sacramento Autorama, and was sold in August '99 at Christie's Pebble Beach auction.* **8. 1957 Cadillac Eldorado Biarritz, Cool 57.** *Much of the customizing on Cool 57 was originally done in the '70s by Gene Winfield and Rod Powell for a Hollywood producer. John bought the car and had Acme Auto complete it in 87 days for the '98 show season. John Aiello did the work, which included fashioning a custom grille, adding wraparound front-fender trim, and tunneling the custom taillights. Greg Philbrick and Ken Whisler stitched the pearl-white Swedish Elmo leather interior and Darryl Hollenbeck applied the House of Kolor candy magenta paint. Imperial Royale, Marilyn, and Cool 57 were all purchased by Hollywood Classics, an Australian company that rents out cars for the movie industry and special occasions.*

8

9. 1954 Cadillac Coupe DeVille, Cad Star. *D'Agostino introduced two customized Cadillacs at the 2000 Grand National Roadster Show. John Aiello, by then at Lucky 7 Customs in Antioch, California, built Cad Star, a '54 Coupe DeVille. Aiello chopped the top three inches, shaved all the chrome, fabricated the custom bar grille, and modified the rear tailfins to make them flow better. Gene Winfield painted the car with his signature fades in House of Kolor lime-gold candy. Travis Barker of the rock band Blink 182 bought Cad Star in 2002.* **10. 1959 Cadillac Coupe DeVille, Cadster.** *The most radical custom John ever did was Cadster. Built as a joint venture with A&A Auto in Brentwood, California, the car was designed to recall GM styling studies of the '50s. Carl Slawinski of A&A turned a 1959 Cadillac Coupe DeVille into a two-seat roadster by shortening the car some 30 inches, fabricating a new windshield frame, removing the roof, sectioning the body six inches, and thoroughly reworking every body panel. Art Himsl applied the Lilac pearlescent paint.* **11. 1956 Packard Caribbean, Caribbean.** *The 1956 models were considered the last real Packards, making them highly collectible today. That didn't stop John from customizing a '56 Packard Caribbean for the 2002 show season. John had Oz Welch at Oz's Kustoms of Oroville, California, chop the windshield frame four inches, build a liftoff Carson-style top, section the body four inches (essentially removing the car's characteristic side trim), and perform a multitude of other tweaks. Modified '53 Packard side trim was used, and Marcos Garcia of Lucky 7 Customs sprayed on the House of Kolor pink-pearl fade paint with magenta scallops. Bob Divine of Divine's Custom Interiors upholstered the interior in Italian leather.* **12. 1941 Packard, Gable.** *The second in John's evolving series of Hollywood glamour customs was Gable, a heavily modified 1941 Packard for the 2004 show season. Built as a tribute to actor Clark Gable, the car started as a model One Twenty two-door sedan. Oz Welch at Oz's Kustoms turned it into a two-seat roadster by removing 16 inches from the cockpit, cutting down the doors and making them open suicide style, lengthening the dashboard and cowl area nine inches, building a Carson-style top, and completely reworking the rear deck. To make the beautiful front end sleeker and more visible, Oz angled the top of the grille back two inches, lowered and molded in the gravel pan, and installed a model One Eighty Packard front bumper set lower than stock.*

9

10

11

12

1

Richard Zocchi
Walnut Creek, California's Richard Zocchi was just a child during the initial heyday of the custom car in the 1940s and early '50s. He caught the bug early, though, and he's been involved ever since he was old enough to drive a car. Over the years, Zocchi's numerous custom creations have been at the forefront of the custom car hobby.

Like friend and contemporary John D'Agostino, Zocchi is essentially a custom car project manager. He works with numerous Northern California customizers to realize his ideas, but his method is much different than D'Agostino's. Zocchi, a self-professed fan of late 1950s and early '60s Chrysler products, doesn't sketch his ideas before committing them to metal. Instead, he picks a car he wants to restyle, then thinks about what he'd like to incorporate in terms of headlights, grille, taillights, stance, and trim. It's all done in his head and he doesn't confer with designers. Once his ideas are fully formed, he buys the necessary parts and takes them to a shop to begin the building process. Zocchi explained his philosophy: "Customizing is an expression of what I think a car should look like. I take off the bad components and replace them with parts from other cars and still make them look like they came from the factory."

Though no two Zocchi customs look alike, he does have a signature style. Rocker panels are often extended downward to make a car look lower, chopped roofs are widened to make them proportional to their bodies, '56 Olds headlights are often used, and so are pastel paint schemes.

Zocchi had his first custom in the late 1950s, during his high school days. It was a '53 Ford with a '54 Chevy grille, a C'd frame, and '56 Olds flipper hubcaps. By 1961, Zocchi

had commissioned his first show car. It was a Gene Winfield-built '57 Oldsmobile hardtop with a '58 Buick grille and candy-gold paint. Zocchi's next car, a brand-new '62 Pontiac Grand Prix, was built by Winfield as well. With its bullet grille, extended and finned rear fenders, and metalflake paint, the Pontiac won the Custom Car d'Elegance award at Oakland's 1962 Grand National Roadster Show. It was Zocchi's first major recognition, and it put him on the map as one of the

2

nation's top custom enthusiasts at a time when the custom show car scene was still going strong.

As the custom scene waned in the late 1960s and early '70s, Zocchi didn't lose interest. He had six different customs built between the Grand Prix and his next landmark car, a 1950 Mercury. The Merc, dubbed *Cool '50*, was built by Bill Reasoner, Art Himsl, and Ken Foster as a traditional '50s-style custom. When it debuted in 1976, *Cool '50* struck a chord. It appeared on the covers of *Street Rodder* (see pg. 181) and *Custom Rodder*, sparked the interest of custom fans that remembered cars like it, and caught the attention of show promoter Bob Larivee. Larivee bought *Cool '50* and used it as a feature attraction at his shows. By the end of the '70s, Zocchi had built two other '50s-style customs that further aided the growing traditional custom car revival.

Zocchi had three cars built during the 1980s, then became much more prolific in the '90s, churning out nine cars. He was inducted into the Grand National Roadster Show Hall of Fame in '91 for his already considerable efforts, and helped boost interest in the Roadster Show by unveiling his cars there throughout the decade.

Today, Zocchi is semiretired from his full-time job as a building contractor, but he continues to turn out at least one finished car each year. He doesn't build them for customers or to be auctioned to the highest bidder. Instead, he keeps most of his creations in his personal warehouse, though he can occasionally be talked into selling one.

1. 1956 Dodge Royal Lancer D500. *Zocchi won his third Grand National Roadster Show George Barris Kustom d'Elegance Award in 2000 with this 1956 Dodge Royal Lancer two-door hardtop. John Aiello did the bodywork, which included chopping the top four inches, lengthening front and rear fenders four inches, smoothing the front and rear bumpers, flaring the wheel cutouts, and modifying the front grille. The headlights came from a 1956 Olds, '57 Pontiac side trim was added and modified at the rear, and an airbag suspension was installed. Lucky 7 Customs in Antioch applied the PPG violet and white paint custom-mixed with gold pearl.* **2. 1956 Lincoln Premiere.** *Zocchi's seventh project with John Aiello was this 1956 Lincoln two-door hardtop. Working out of his Acme Auto Body shop in Antioch, John chopped the top five inches, extended the hood 2½ inches, and raised the front wheel openings one inch. For more visual interest along the sides, he filled the tops of the rear fenders along the body's character line to create scoops. John designed the front end around a '58 Cadillac front bumper, incorporating '56 Olds headlight bezels and a handcrafted grille made from 22 pieces of ¼-inch round rod. Bob Divine at Divine's Custom Interiors of Martinez, California, created the four-place bucket-seat interior with a full-length center console. Darryl Hollenbeck, also of Acme, sprayed the yellow and cream-white paint, then covered it with gold pearl. The pinstriping was performed by Art Himsl. The car debuted at the 1999 Sacramento Autorama and took home the prestigious Harry Bradley Award. It was also on hand at the 50th anniversary of the Grand National Roadster Show in '99.*

3

3. 1957 Ford Fairlane. *Zocchi and Lucky 7 Customs collaborated on a 1957 Ford Fairlane for the 2003 show season. John Aiello chopped the top three inches, extended the fenders two inches over the headlights, extended the front pan over the top of the bumper, lowered the wheel openings ¾ inch, and installed a bar grille made by Glory Grilles. At the back, the taillights were frenched and perforated metal was formed over red plastic to make the lenses. The license plate was frenched into the body, the gas filler was moved to the trunk, and the rear pan was handformed. Lucky 7 owner Marcos Garcia sprayed on the blue-green PPG paint and fogged around the edges of the stainless steel side trim and body contours with a darker shade of the same color. For rolling stock, Richard chose Diamondback Classics 195/75R15 tires with modified '56 Lincoln Premier hubcaps.*

4

4. 1959 Plymouth Fury. *John Aiello, by now at Lucky 7 Customs of Antioch, California, and Zocchi teamed up on this 1959 Plymouth Fury two-door hardtop for the 2002 season. Aiello chopped the top a modest two inches, retaining the rear window but sinking it into the body. Up front, the look was completely changed through the use of a widened '57 Chevy bumper, a '57 Buick grille surround, and frenched '60 Buick headlights. The hood was given a scoop and lengthened to match the new front end. Frank DeRosa & Son of Pittsburg, California, flared all four wheel openings, reworked the rocker panels, and extended the tops of the rear fins to flow into the doors. The rear bumper came from a '60 Buick, a 1955 Chrysler New Yorker rear bumper overrider bar was used for the taillight assembly, and the lenses originated on a '50 Ford. Bob Divine of Martinez, California, made the interior's custom headliner and upholstered the seats, trunk, and console in white vinyl with chartreuse piping. Like most Zocchi customs, the Fury received a modern stereo, this one with a Pioneer cassette deck. Art Himsl applied the custom-mixed chartreuse and off-white paint, and added side graphics to mimic the trim of a '57 DeSoto. Zocchi unveiled the car in 2002, and won his fourth Sam Barris Memorial Award at the Sacramento Autorama. Later, the car went on display at Darryl Starbird's National Rod & Custom Car Hall of Fame Museum in Oklahoma.* **5. 1962 Pontiac Grand Prix.** *In 1962, Gene Winfield modified a brand-new Pontiac Grand Prix that turned out to be Zocchi's first major award winner. In 2003, John Aiello built a replica of that car. Up front, Aiello added grille bullets fashioned after 50-caliber machine gun ammunition, extended the outside headlights a couple inches, and frenched all four headlights. At the rear, Aiello added fender fins, filled the stock taillight openings, and installed custom taillights in the Pontiac's characteristic concave rear fascia. Each taillight pod was made by adding '62 Imperial lights to either side of a tubular chrome bezel. Though the original car wasn't chopped, Zocchi had Aiello take 2½ inches out of the new version. The original car was first painted metallic-lime-gold and green, but after about a year it was repainted orange and white pearl by Gene Winfield in his trademark fade style. Lucky 7 owner Marcus Garcia replicated the second paint job.*

5

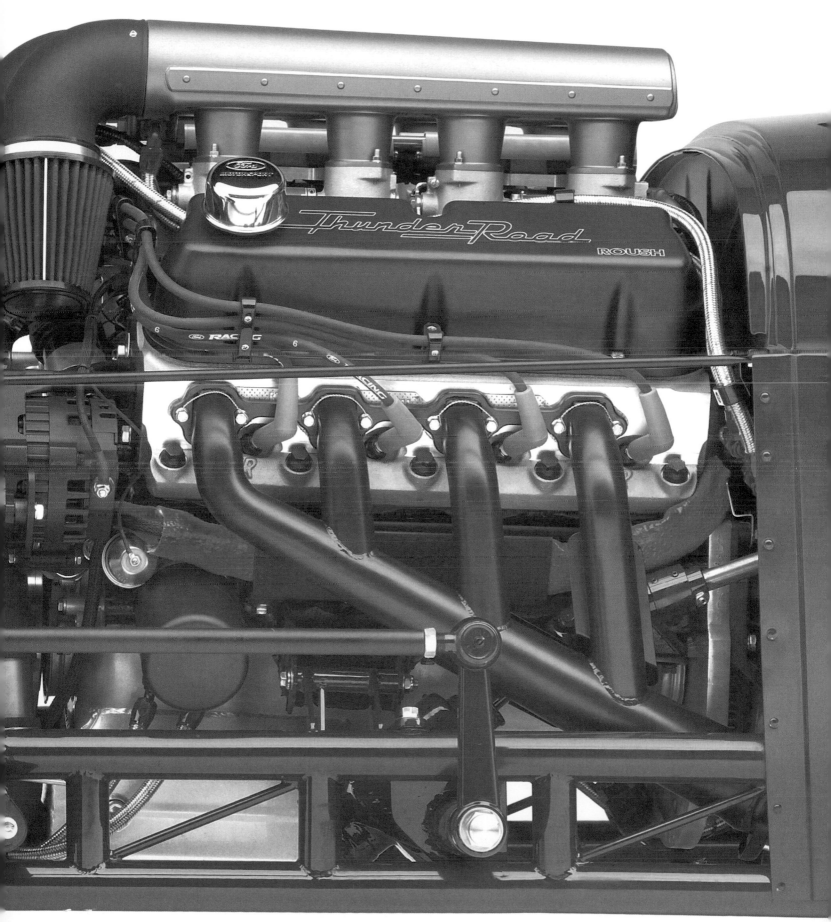

Throughout this book you've seen the evolution of the hot rod and custom car over the last 75 or so years. Besides the physical evolution, you've read about its growth and steady increase in popularity. So, by the start of the new millennium you might imagine that its image was set in the hearts and minds of America and that exposure was at its peak.

Not so.

Television, that vapid wasteland of sitcoms and teleprompter news readers, can popularize a pastime faster than you can say "nitro-burning Funny Car." In 2001, the Discovery Channel documentary *Motorcycle Mania* took viewers into the world of Long Beach, California, chopper builder (and former Boyd Coddington employee) Jesse James. The documentary spiked ratings, and a second documentary on Jesse and his shop followed. That program saw excellent ratings as well, and the success begat *Monster Garage* in 2002. *Monster Garage* was conceived as a weekly program about building a crazy car or truck in five days. Several automotive personalities have been guests

custom car. In 2004, Discovery launched *American Hot Rod*, a show that follows the workings of Boyd Coddington's shop. Also in 2004, The Learning Channel (TLC), a sister to Discovery, introduced *Overhaulin'*. Starring hot rod and custom designer/fabricator (and another former Coddington employee) Chip Foose, the show follows the building process at Chip's shop as he turns guests' project cars into modern rods and customs.

Hot rods and customs also began appearing in the TV documentaries that had formerly been devoted to classic or exotic cars. With the popularity of these and other television shows, it's a sure-fire bet that hot rods and custom cars have found new recruits eager to build or just own something like they have seen on TV. While television has not changed hot rod and custom styling trends, it could very well affect their popularity for years to come.

As for those trends, building styles continue to evolve. Today, anything can be seen at a rod run or custom car show. Many of the more-contemporary components and equipment developed

been abandoned for a more traditional look. Many of today's hot rods are highly detailed and look like they may have come from any era.

The difference between the rods and customs of the past and those that emulate them today is detail. From fabrication to execution, these new nostalgic cars are rolling art. Today's builders have taken the construction of hot rods and custom cars to heights that the builders of the 1950s couldn't have fathomed. Heck, they've taken them to heights that builders of the '80s couldn't have imagined! The flathead Ford engine has experienced a resurgence in popularity, but the cars they end up in today are usually more detailed and better built than those of the past.

Some of this interest in vintage styling has come from rat rods, but it also came about as a backlash against the ever more computer-controlled engines and drivelines in today's new cars. The use of modern drivetrains in hot rods and customs complicates construction and maintenance. As a result, a lot of builders are going back to simpler ways to build cars to keep the fun factor in their projects. If a project requires an engineer to package the engine, transmission, computers, and electronics, and another one to keep it all running, the fun's gone.

The rat rod genre continues to add more recruits. These cars often incorporate more-radical customizing and hot rodding elements. Severely chopped tops, drastically channeled bodies, and radically equipped vintage engines all provide striking looks. And there is no segregation of the rods and customs—if it's cool and primered, it's welcome.

on the show, including myself. Concurrent to *Monster Garage*, *American Chopper*, a show about a dysfunctional family building choppers in New York, also garnered excellent ratings for the Discovery Channel.

Following the success of these shows, Discovery looked for the next big thing, and that honor fell to the hot rod and

since the mid '70s—by companies such as Pete & Jake's, Super Bell, TCI, and the Deuce Factory, and later Magnum Axle, Chassis Engineering, and the So-Cal Speed Shop—can be seen on hot rods and custom cars today. Some of those parts have fallen out of favor, though, as a few of the styling trends of the 1970s, '80s, and even '90s have

From the looks of things, the participants seem to be having fun, which is what it is all about. Rat rods are often stripped down without a lot of detailing and finish, making them quick to build and worry-free. In some ways, owners of highly detailed rods and customs must be envious. I doubt that many high-tech hot rod owners can park their cars and walk away without worrying about what may befall their cars in parking lots or on city streets. Rat rodders don't have that problem.

As we dig back into the past for inspiration, many are finding that their past may not be the same as their friends' or contemporaries'. The older fellows might like '40s and '50s styles, while younger guys might relate better to the '60s. As a result, we are now seeing interest in the '60s styles—things such as bubble-tops and exotic fiberglass rods like those from Ed "Big Daddy" Roth. These types of cars appear from time to time at car shows and rod runs. There may only be a handful due to the expertise required to make a body from scratch, but their inclusion points to styles from the past coming back, seemingly in chronological order.

Along these same chronological lines is the new interest in the Gasser look. Gassers were the stock-bodied hot rods of drag racing's golden days of the mid 1960s. To aid weight transfer, they were jacked up in front with big slicks in back. The Gasser look is finding its way back into hot rodding in increasing numbers. It had to happen: As cars got lower, there would inevitably be an opposing trend.

So we see that styles from the 1940s, '50s, and '60s have returned. It hasn't happened yet, but we may soon see a groundswell of interest in resto rods of the '70s, and then who knows, maybe even the smoothie style of the '80s. You may not want to think about saving that hard-edged billet mirror for the nostalgic smoothie rod you might be building in 2020, but things could be heading that way. With the number of magazines and events that existed in the '80s, a lot of youth were exposed to rods and customs at the time. In the future, adults who remember those cool billet windshield wipers or independent front suspensions may strive to create something similar for themselves.

Most of these trends affect rods more than customs. While the custom car will certainly never go away, it may become a shadow in the midst of hot rods, as well as other enthusiast subjects such as muscle cars, Volkswagens, tuner cars, pickups, you name it. As stock automobiles from the 1940s and '50s become increasingly rare and more expensive, it

becomes a little harder to take a torch to one. And for those who do, there is no turning back. It's best to be versed in the intricacies of custom metal fabrication or face the task of saving it if that chopped top goes awry.

In recent years, many good-looking newly built customs have appeared at events throughout the country. That's a good sign, but their numbers are only a fraction of the hot rods touching asphalt for the first time. Currently, brand-new Model A roadster and 1932 Ford roadster and three-window coupe bodies are produced in metal—and just about any body style and year of Ford is available in fiberglass. There are also reproduction metal 1969 Chevrolet Camaro and 1947–54 Chevy pickup bodies, with '67–68 Ford Mustangs not far behind. No shoebox Ford or 1949–51 Mercury body has been produced in metal, though, which speaks to their demand. Though fiberglass Mercury bodies are available from longtime customizer Gene Winfield, they don't seem

to be making it onto the street.

As hot rodders and custom car enthusiasts act and react to current and past trends in building styles and components, one thing is for sure: Hot rods and customs are an American phenomenon—one that participants are proud to carry on. The cars are creative, interesting, and just plain cool. They are a celebration of the last 75 or so years of innovative backyard efforts, some of which have turned into multimillion-dollar industries. Many rodders and customizers have become heroes or icons to other enthusiasts. In all cases, the cars have thrilled owners and onlookers.

It takes vision, determination, and the skill of a metal virtuoso to take on the challenge of making an old car handle, run, ride, and look better. These qualities seem to be innate in many American men and women, and they have been for years.

Though its roots were with the postwar youth, those original participants are aging to the extent that one might expect the whole phenomenon to fade with their memories. But the state of the hot rod and custom car hobby is as strong and vibrant as it has ever been. It appears that this marvel of American ingenuity and imagination will remain for future generations to prize and admire—possibly forever.

Jimmy Shine's '34 Ford Pickup

In the 70 or so years since Ford released its 1934 models, hot rodders have reinterpreted those designs in a multitude of ways. Jimmy "Shine" Falschlehner has found a new and creative way to combine old parts with this "unfinished" '34 Ford pickup.

Jimmy is a rod builder of the highest degree. Employed as a metal man and fabricator by the So-Cal Speed Shop, Jimmy used the facilities there to build this car after hours. Starting in 1997 with a '34 Ford pickup cab and bed, he bobbed a set of '34 Ford frame rails front and rear, adding an 18-degree kick-up at the back. Jimmy set up a suicide-style front suspension, and added handmade steering arms, So-Cal hairpin radius rods, and customized tube shocks.

In keeping with the pickup's retro flavor, Jimmy opted for a 1949 Ford flathead engine bored to 254 cid. Engine builder Mike Gilbert assembled the flathead, installing a pair of Stromberg 97 carbs and a set of uncorked zoomie headers fashioned by Jimmy. The flattie routes its power through a '39 Ford transmission and a modified '41 torque tube to a '40 Ford banjo rear end with 3.25:1 Richmond gears and '37 Ford wishbones. Jimmy originally mounted a set of wire wheels, but then opted for something totally unique. Shown

here is a set of Firestone bias plies with spoked wheels that Jimmy made by welding 1932 Studebaker President spokes to custom-made outer rims and '35 Ford wire wheel centers.

The true beauty of this pickup is in the raw metalwork. Jimmy refurbished the stock pickup body, modifying it along the way, and incorporated reproduction and hand-fabricated components. The grille shell is a modified '34 Ford truck unit. The top sports a five-inch chop and the cab has been channeled six inches. Thus far, Jimmy has opted to forego paint, sticking with bare metal that may be more appealing than any paint color. He fights nature by applying WD-40 with a ScotchBrite pad frequently.

The bare-metal theme continues in the bed and interior. The pickup bed houses a B-52 hydraulic tank that acts as the fuel tank and a battery cover pirated from a '50 Ford pickup. Inside, the modified '40 Ford dash is accompanied by early aircraft seats and more handmade panels that sport the same bare-metal look.

A tribute to the past, this '34 pickup is also an affirmation of the present. Still unfinished (Jimmy may or may not ever add paint), the pickup shows that today's rodders have a reverence for the past, the ability to build great cars, and an eye for unique and inspiring design.

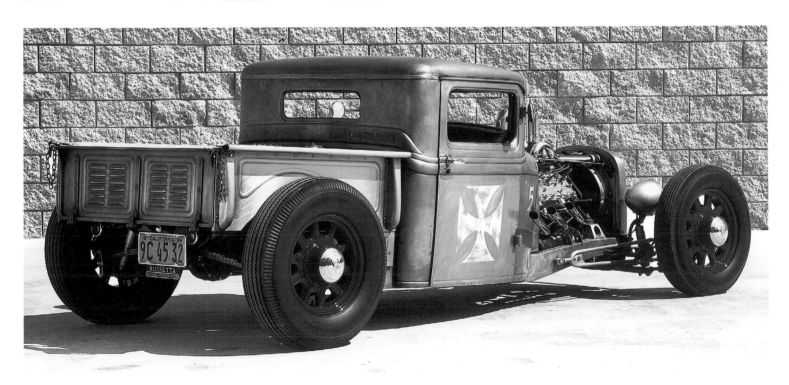

Muroc Roadsters

For almost 30 years, Jerry Kugel provided the means for rodders to ride in comfort. Now he helps them ride in style.

Kugel started selling Jaguar independent rear suspension kits for hot rods in 1969 through his La Habra, California, company Kugel Komponents. He developed numerous other hot rod-specific parts over the years, always testing them thoroughly on his own '32 Ford roadster first. Kugel took the development process one step further in the early 1990s, when he began offering complete Deuce roadsters based on stretched-wheelbase Zipper fiberglass bodies.

In 2001, Kugel upped the ante even further with his line of full-fendered and fenderless Muroc roadsters. From the out-set, the plan was to build ten of each body style. As of early 2006, the fenderless cars were sold out and five of the full-fendered cars remained.

Muroc roadster buyers get steel-bodied rollers with independent suspensions; the customer chooses his own engine, paint, and upholstery. The steel bodies aren't just stock reproductions. Kugel sought out noted hot rod illustrators Thom Taylor and Chip Foose to help design a stylized body, then commissioned Marcel DeLay at Marcel's Custom Metal in Corona, California, to fabricate the bodies. Marcel and his sons, Luc and Marc, made a square steel-tubing buck for use as a template while bending the body panels, then put more than 500 hours of work into each body. All of the panels are steel, except the hoods, which are aluminum. Dan Fink Metalworks stainless steel grille inserts complete the look.

Chip Foose also helped design the frames. Kugel Kompo-nents builds each 112-inch-wheelbase frame from a set of SAC Hot Rod Products rails. Kugel parts can be found throughout each car. Kugel independent front and rear suspensions provide a smooth ride, and the DuVall-style windshield frames were developed in-house. All this skilled hand fabrication doesn't come cheap. The highboys ran $75,000 each, and customers pay $110,000 for a full-fendered car.

The two cars featured here are the property of Nick Barron of Irwindale, California. Nick owns Hallett Boats, a high-performance boat manufacturer. Forty years building ultraluxury boats has helped him develop an eye for design. Accordingly, Nick made every decision along the way to completing both cars, and enlisted the help of several people to realize his vision. His industry connections landed him a pair of Corvette 350-cid LS1 engines and 4L60E automatic transmissions. Mike's Street Rods of Hesperia, California, completed the bodywork and applied the custom-mixed bright-red paint. Gabe's Custom Interiors of San Bernadino stitched the beige leather interiors. Boyd Coddington wheels were used on the fendered car, and a set of Budniks was chosen for the highboy. Unique headlights were chosen for both cars, both from motorcycle-light manufacturers. Headwinds of Monrovia, California, provided the fendered car's lights, while Joker Machine made the highboy's lights.

After six months of hard and exacting work, both cars turned out to be jaw-droppingly beautiful. The full-fendered car has the hardware to prove it, too. It won the America's Most Beautiful Street Rod award at the Pleasanton, California, West Coast Nationals in August 2001.

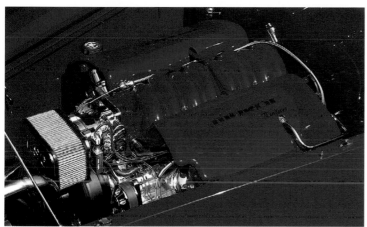

1

Rick Dore
Like John D'Agostino and Richard Zocchi, Glendale, Arizona's Rick Dore is an incredibly prolific custom designer/owner with an uncanny ability to crank out award-winning cars on a regular basis. Rick works up his own design concepts, sometimes collaborating with artists such as Steve Stanford to visualize and fine-tune his ideas. Dore then enlists some of the country's best custom shops to bring his styling visions to life, carefully overseeing his vehicles through the buildup process.

While all of Dore's rides draw styling inspiration from the historic customs of the past, they take advantage of modern, reliable powertrains and chassis components. Rick doesn't limit himself to strictly vintage-look exterior details either. Many of his cars are sprinkled with modern design elements, such as tastefully styled billet wheels and contemporary upholstery patterns, which are carefully blended with the nostalgic overall theme. Another Dore trademark is an eye-popping candy/pearl paint job. Rick works closely with some of the world's best painters, painstakingly testing custom-mixed colors for a truly outstanding finish.

Both Rick and his vehicles have received plenty of deserved recognition in the rod and custom world, and beyond. In 2001, he was inducted into Darryl Starbird's Rod and Custom Car Hall of Fame, and in 2002 he was named Trendsetter of the Year at the Oakland Rod, Custom, and Motorcycle Show. In '05, Jada Toys came out with line of "Road Rats" diecast toys that replicate Rick's full-size customs. Rick shows no signs of slowing down the pace anytime soon. Pictured here are a handful of his most famous cars.

2

1. 1953 Buick Riviera, Breathless. *Rick completed his '53 Riviera in 1995. Dick Dean chopped the windshield and built the Carson-style top. Bill Reasoner handled the rest of the body modifications and the deep candy-purple paint job. The attractive Buick grille was retained, but augmented with Packard bullets. The headlights were frenched, with custom aluminum bezels replacing the stock units. A reworked front bumper from a 1957 Plymouth was frenched in at the rear, along with custom wraparound taillight lenses. The stock '53 decklid was replaced with a '51 Buick unit for a sleeker profile.*

2. 1936 Ford, Tangerine Dream. *Rick put his own contemporary spin on the classic Westergard style with this pearl-tangerine '36 Ford. The car actually started as a coupe, but the top was cut off and replaced with a Carson-style top and a chopped '47 Chevy windshield molding. John Aiello and Darryl Hollenbeck handled the bodywork, which also included incorporating a '40 Packard grille, molding in '37 Buick headlights, and widening a set of '39 Lincoln Zephyr rear fenders. Marcos Garcia shot the custom-mixed House of Kolor paint. Tangerine Dream won several awards in 1998.* **3. 1963 Ford Thunderbird, Tango.** *This stunning '63 T-Bird was Rick's contender for the 2000 show season. Major bodywork was performed by John Harvey in Los Lunas, New Mexico, and finished up by Squeeg Jerger at Squeeg's Kustoms in Mesa, Arizona. Squeeg's son, Doug, laid on the amazing Tequila Sunrise finish with a custom mix of House of Kolor paint. The three-inch top chop is the most noticeable modification, but the T-Bird also features shaved trim, front and rear rolled pans, reshaped rear wheel openings, custom head- and taillights, and a '59 Cadillac-style grille.* **4. 1952 Cadillac, Kashmere.** *Rick rolled out Kashmere in early 2004. The car started out as a two-door hardtop, but the top was removed to turn it into a two-seat roadster. Brian Cline made the windshield frame, which was filled with custom-formed Swedish safety glass by Timo Taskanen. Floyd Oldewurtel tackled the rest of the bodywork, which included frenched lights, custom hood and bodyside scoops, and an overall smoothing. Erin Ruddy fashioned the removable tonneau cover in fiberglass. Marcos Garcia of Lucky 7 Customs handled the subtly blended candy/pearl-blue paint job.* **5. 1940 Pontiac, Decadence.** *Rick acquired this 1940 Pontiac as an in-progress project in 2001, and had it finished by early 2002. The car was a coupe, but John Aiello cut off the top and chopped the windshield three inches. The distinctive Pontiac grille was retained, but the rest of the body was smoothed and shaved. The smooth running boards came from a Lincoln Zephyr. Marcos Garcia at Lucky 7 coated the whole works with a custom-mixed House of Kolor Candy Emerald Green paint job.*

3

4

5

Grand Master

The son of well-known rod and custom builder Sam Foose, Chip Foose has made a name for himself with his TLC network television show *Overhaulin'*. But it wasn't just the name that got him his own show. Foose did a lot of great design and construction work to get there.

Foose graduated from Pasadena, California's Art Center and worked as a designer for Boyd Coddington before opening his own design and fabrication company called Foose Design in 1998. Through his company, he designed and built several high-profile rods and customs, including a series of America's Most Beautiful Roadster winners.

Perhaps the best rod Chip had a hand in, though, was one his company did not build. The *Grand Master*, a 1935 Chevy built by owner Wes Rydell's team in Grand Forks, North Dakota, pushed the envelope for hot rod fabrication.

Foose designed the car as a cohesive modern rod, rendering each component individually to become part of an integrated whole. Both he and Rydell also wanted a car that would set a new standard for craftsmanship. Foose's design called for a swoopy look with every possible wire, bolt, fastener, and handle hidden beneath a smooth exterior. Even under the surface, each component would take on a jewellike quality.

The project began with Foose's drawings, but the fabrication work started when Rydell, owner of more than 30 Chevrolet dealerships, delivered a 1935 Chevy Master two-door sedan to his Rydell's Toy Shop crew in January 1996. For the next six years, and some 13,000 to 15,000 man hours, the Toy Shop, led by metal man Doug Peterson, strived to turn Foose's sketches into a piece of automotive jewelry.

More than 1000 modifications were made to the body to give the car a smooth, flowing look. They are too numerous to list, but some of the changes included incorporating elements from a '35 Chevy coupe roof at the rear, installing a curved windshield, sweeping back the fenders, raking the B-pillars, and adding a grille custom-made by Dan Fink.

Rydell's team cold-rolled the frame from ¼-inch plate, and fit it with Dodge Omni rack-and-pinion steering, front and rear independent suspension, and Wilwood discs all-around. The frame also accepted a 5.7-liter LT-4 V-8 and four-speed automatic from a 1996 Corvette Grand Sport. The rear differential came from an '84 'Vette. Every exterior surface of the engine and chassis was ground smooth, polished, and painted or chromed as if it were an exterior piece. To top it off, Rydell's crew fabricated an engine cover that Foose had designed to double as a ram air system. Underbody panels were also fashioned to give the chassis a finished look.

Jim Griffin of Bend, Oregon, helped bring Foose's interior design to life. The seat backs and bottoms were sculpted in carbon fiber and the seats were upholstered in smoke-colored leather. Foose fashioned the steering wheel himself, cutting down an 18-inch diameter 1956 Chevy Bel Air wheel to 15 inches and reworking it. The dash panel was hand-formed from steel and fit with vintage-style instruments.

Jason Mortenson and Tom Marcotte applied the tasteful paint, spraying Millennium Jade on the upper body and Chip Silver on the lower body, separated by a pearl-orange stripe. Simple chrome trim spears and 17- and 18-inch Foose Thrustar wheels added the final touches. When all was said and done, only portions of the fenders and roof remained from the original car. Everything else was handmade. The project's estimated cost was $700,000.

The car, dubbed the *Grand Master*, was unveiled at the 50th Detroit Autorama in 2002, where it won the coveted Ridler Award. Pitted against numerous well-built cars, the competition wasn't even close. Foose, Rydell, and their team had indeed set a new standard for craftsmanship.

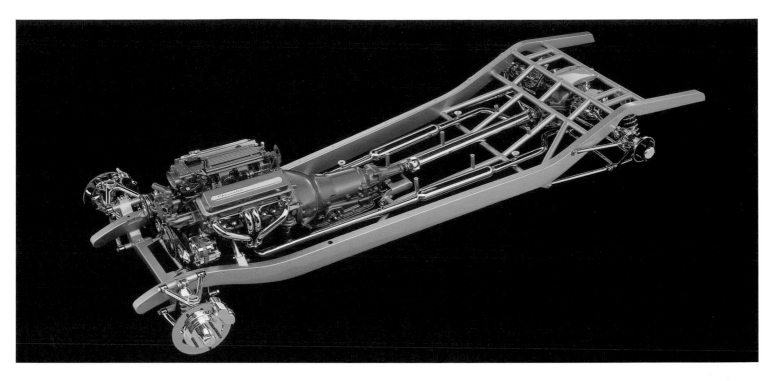

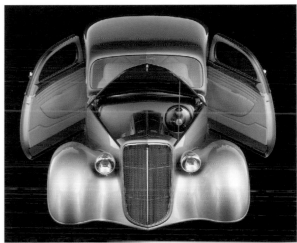

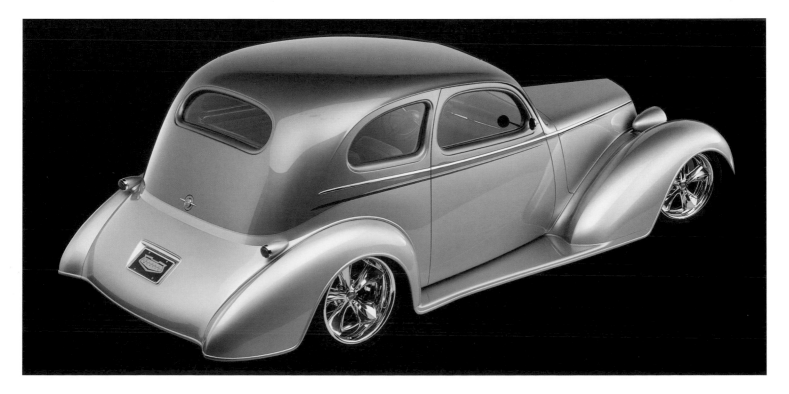

Pratt's Impala

Lee Pratt grew up in Des Moines, Iowa, but has since moved out to live in an art colony in Los Angeles and work as a sculptor. But that can't keep him from numerous automotive projects, which have ranged over the years from mild to radical customs and hot rods of various vintages. While his rods and customs have been of divergent styles, there is one micro custom car era he admits is his strong favorite.

Car customizing was largely pushed to the background in the mid-to-late 1960s. In fact, it splintered, with one off-shoot morphing into lowriders and another, larger segment disappearing altogether. But one strain, though it didn't flour-ish, at least survived in a small area along Bellflower and Hawthorne boulevards just south of Los Angeles. Led by impresario Larry Watson and others, such as Bill Hines and Joe Anderson, it somehow infected others across the country, including Pratt in Iowa and impressionable artist-to-be Steve Stanford in Utah. Stanford characterized this custom mini era as "metalflake, pompadours, and Astro Supremes." Include sculptured pearl-white tuck-and-roll, lace painting, Buick Rivieras, '58–66 Chevy Impalas, the first hydraulic suspen-sions, and '53–54 Buick Skylark wire wheels, and you have the full picture.

With its sculpted design, the 1958 Impala begged for this type of mild customizing. It didn't need much more than cus-tom paint and upholstery, wheels, and lowering. The factory did the rest for you. And having built one back in the day, Lee had a nostalgic itch to do one again. After much search-ing, he found a 48,000-mile, two-owner example in Georgia. It had a good black paint job and a rebuilt four-barrel 348-cid

V-8 (Chevy's first "big block") with an automatic. Lee bought the car and drove it home. His initial plan was simply to lower it, do some '60s-era custom paint magic on the roof, and have the interior done in a mini-pleat, white-pearl design.

Though it looks intricate and complicated, painting the roof in old-school lacquers was the easiest part for Lee. He painted it purple metalflake, then taped off the roof and sprayed on a darker design over real lace material. Locating the interior fabrics and someone who knew how to stitch them was harder, but Lee found old-timer Frank Gonzales, who was working out of his garage in San Diego. Lee supplied Frank with silver-white pearl Naugahyde, purple cut-pile carpet, and sketches of how he wanted the upholstery to look. Frank was up to the task, stitching an excellent late-'60s-style interior.

Lee cut the coil springs to lower the car, and the reproduc-tion Buick wire wheels came from the aftermarket.

But then Lee went a little further than he had originally planned. He thought he would just shave the hood, trunk, and door handles, fill in the resulting holes, and cover those areas with touch-up paint. Next thing he knew, he was filling in the "gun sights" and faux louvers on the front fenders, the chrome "thingies" on the lower rear fenders, and the rocker moldings. All this work meant Lee had to fully block-sand the body and repaint it in black lacquer.

Lee completed the car by summer 2003 and drove it extensively, including three cross-country trips. The subtle, mild '60s-style Impala appeared in a series of magazines, representing the best of a little-known yet stylish era in custom history.

–Pat Ganahl

Ritzow Deuce

Troy Trepanier is well-known among car enthusiasts for his cutting-edge street machines. As proprietor of Rad Rods by Troy of Manteno, Illinois, Troy has never placed tradition high on his list of priorities. That is, until Roger Ritzow of Franklin, Wisconsin, asked Troy to build him, "a nice little Deuce roadster."

The project started with a Pete & Jake's reproduction Deuce frame. To get the right stance, Troy and project manager Levi Green modified the frame to lower the car front and rear. At the back, they incorporated three-inch kickups and notched the frame rails to allow the frame to sit lower on the axle. They also installed a Model A rear crossmember, a Posies Super-Slide spring, a Dutchman quick-change rear end, and '36 Ford pickup rear radius rods. Up front, Rad Rods thinned the frame rails one inch and gave them a two-inch kickup. They installed a custom crossmember, another Posies spring, a modified Super Bell axle, and '40 Ford wishbones. It was all pretty traditional, really.

The brakes and rolling stock were also given a traditional look, but they're far from it. Rad Rods installed Wilwood disc brakes up front and hid them behind custom-made Buick-style finned "drums" by Billet Specialties. Billet Specialties also carved 16x5-inch front and 19x7 rear wheels from billet aluminum. The wheels mimic vintage Ford steel wheels and accept stock Ford hubcaps. The "trim rings" are not separate at all. Rather, they were machined into the wheels' edges. Rad Rods painted the wheels tan and mounted them on vintage-style Firestone bias-ply tires by Coker.

Troy and Levi cut and raised the Brookville steel body's rear

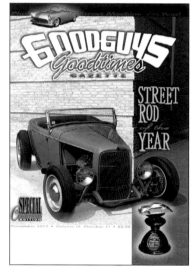

fender reveals two inches so they would outline the tires. Up front, they chopped the windshield two inches, smoothed the firewall, fabricated a stretched hood, and installed commercial headlights with sectioned buckets on custom-made stainless steel headlight stands/shock mounts. A lot of subtle work was done to make the back flow better. In addition to recessing the license plate and frenching the '39 Ford taillights, Rad Rods modified the body to wrap around the gas tank, which was also reshaped. The body was finished in subtle gray-green Glasurit paint.

Rad Rides teamed up with Bob Sweeney of FX Engines to build the 1949 Mercury 260-cid flathead V-8. Performance parts included Edelbrock heads, JE pistons, and an Isky cam. The vintage Hilborn injector stacks kept their functional butterflies, but modern electronic injectors and fuel rails were hidden below the injector stack mounting plate. John Meaney built a modern EFI control system to make it all work. Rad Rides made the headers, and linked the engine to a Tremec five-speed manual transmission. Any engine or chassis component that would typically be chromed was instead given a nickel-plated satin finish. When possible, the wiring and

plumbing was hidden, and the modern spark plug wires were wrapped in fabric for a vintage look.

Jim Griffin Interiors stitched the green-dyed buffalo-leather interior. The instrument cluster came from a 1933 Plymouth. A So-Cal Speed Shop steering column was topped with a '40 Ford-style billet steering wheel by Giovanni. And as the final nod to both the past and the present, a vintage auxiliary heater was fitted with modern speakers and a pull-on ignition switch, then installed under the dash.

Though it had subdued paint and subtle details, Ritzow's Deuce still managed to stand out from the crowd. Goodguys named it Street Rod of the Year for 2004. The little roadster set new standards for melding the old with the new. Best described as "high-tech traditional," the car's look is rooted in the 1940s, but it utilizes modern construction techniques and benefits from state-of-the-art technology.

Afterglow At its core, customizing is modifying a car to improve its looks. Removing parts can make a design flow better, and no changes should be made unless they enhance the overall aesthetic. The best customizers have always followed these simple rules.

One of the first to practice customizing in this manner was Jimmy Summers, who operated out of Los Angeles as far back as the 1930s. In 1947, Summers built a '40 Mercury convertible that helped define the genre. Summers made a Carson-style top with a three-inch chop, removed the running boards and fabricated frame covers, raised the front and rear fenders to make the car look lower, sectioned the hood, fashioned a grille that mimicked a '39 Buick's, and added smoothed Lincoln Zephyr bumpers. The car was a beautiful example of early customizing.

In 1993, noted designer Harry Bradley produced sketches of a modern tribute to the Jimmy Summers Mercury. Bradley teamed up with Donn Lowe of Oregon City, Oregon, to build the car, and in '94 John Babcock of Palatine, Illinois, came on as the project's financier and owner.

Lowe worked with Dave Crook to realize Bradley's vision, modifying every body panel along the way. While he left the firewall in its stock position, Lowe moved the windshield posts, cowl, and passenger compartment rearward three inches. He lengthened the largely handmade hood accordingly, flaring it at the bottom to meet the custom-made Buick-shaped grille. Lowe also chopped the windshield posts three inches and angled them inward 15 degrees. He sectioned the upper por-

tion of the windshield frame ½ inch to visually lighten it, and made a removable Carson-style top to fit the reworked body.

The incredible grille was first designed in clay, then made into a plaster mold. A fiberglass rendition of the grille was pulled from the mold and Gilbertson Machine used the resulting shape information to cut each of the 23 grille bars from aluminum with a CNC mill. The finished unit weighs 80 pounds! Lowe finished the front end with thin handmade bumpers, a hand-formed front pan, and headlights custom-made to Bradley's design by Prototype Source in Santa Barbara. The taillights and rear pan were also custom-made.

Along the sides, Lowe angled the tops of the doors upward to sweep into the A-pillars. He lengthened the front fenders three inches, then moved the wheel openings upward 1½ inches and radiused them to match the 205/75R15 Coker Classic tires that would be used. Lowe molded the front and rear fenders into the body, and fit the rears with handmade fender skirts. Like Summers did on his Merc, Lowe removed the running boards and fabricated new rocker panels. The original had no trim, but Bradley designed tapered trim to complete the profile.

While the Summers car was channeled six inches over the frame, Bradley had Lowe channel the modern version only 1½ inches and lower the car with Air Ride Technologies airbags and a six-inch kickup at the rear of the frame.

Lowe used contemporary driveline and suspension components. Heidt's tubular independent suspension and Wilwood disc brakes were installed up front. The 4.6-liter V-8, trans-

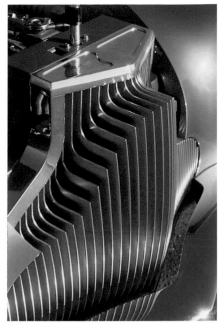

mission, and rear suspension came from a mid-1990s Lincoln.

Little John's Interior Concepts of Fountain Valley, California, stitched the leather upholstery, adapting a late-model Ford Ranger bench seat to fit. Lowe completed the interior with a modified a 1947 Studebaker dash, a '63 Buick Riviera steering wheel, Vintage Air air conditioning, a $7000 Alpine stereo with a GPS display, and a steel tonneau to cover the rear seating area.

The Summers car was painted maroon, then dark green, but Bradley's wife chose a honey gold color for the modern interpretation. Dale Withers applied the custom-mixed PPG urethane. The paint turned out so bright and eye-catching that it inspired the car's nickname, *Afterglow*.

Afterglow made its competitive debut at the 2004 Grand National Roadster Show in Pomona, California, where it won the Outstanding Custom, Chip Foose Design Excellence, and George Barris Kustom d'Elegance awards. The flowing proportions, inspired by a car built by a custom pioneer more than 50 years ago, teamed with quality execution and modern building techniques to produce a winner.

The original Jimmy Summers 1940 Mercury

Posies ThunderRoad

Ken "Posies" Fenical, of Posies Rods and Customs in Hummelstown, Pennsylvania, has a history of designing and building cars that shake up street rodding's status quo. Posies' genre-blurring vehicles virtually demand attention and usually inspire intense discussion about how they're stylistically "right" and "wrong." Tellingly, Posies calls his shop's cars "statements."

Inspired by the intense popularity of the modern-day "rat rod" scene, Posies built *ThunderRoad*, a 1929 Ford pickup, in 2004. *ThunderRoad* fuses the exaggerated proportions and radical stance of traditionally inspired rat rods with brand-new parts and fully finished, pro-shop style craftsmanship. Just as rat rods were a reaction to the high-buck, billet-laden street rods, *ThunderRoad* is a reaction to rat rods.

Most rat rods are comprised primarily of scrounged old parts, but the only vintage part of *ThunderRoad* is the body, which started out on a 1929 Model A Tudor sedan. The top was chopped 5¾ inches and shortened 1½ feet behind the doors to create an extended-cab pickuplike unit. Despite the extreme modifications, the Posies crew took care to retain stock Ford design details, such as door hinges and handles, the cowl's body seams, and the fabric top insert. Most high-tech-style street rods eliminate these elements. The bed is hand-fabricated from .080-inch sheet aluminum, but also retains a vintage-Ford design. Smoothly beveled holes on the bed and grille shell put a modern spin on racing hot rods of the past, which sported drilled holes in various components for weight savings. The deep maroon color is a 2004 Ford Taurus hue, for easy color matching and repair.

The Posies crew channeled the body nine inches over a custom-built double-tube-frame chassis. A highly unconventional suspension setup uses quarter-elliptical leaf springs over full leaf springs at the rear. The suicide-style front tube axle is suspended by quarter-elliptical springs and adjustable diagonal rods. Colorado Custom billet wheels measure 20 inches and recall the look of vintage Halibrand mag wheels. The wheels mount motorcycle tires up front.

The powerplant is a 402-cid Ford engine built by Roush Performance. It puts out around 500 horsepower and 500 pound-feet of torque through a GM 700R4 transmission. An Accel DFI fuel-management system was used as a decidedly modern take on a vintage-style mechanical-injection system.

The art deco-styled interior features plenty of far-out design ideas. Pep Boys 1962 Ford Falcon seat covers are used as upholstery inserts on the seats and door panels. A wild, hand-fabricated aluminum dashboard carries Haneline gauges, art deco-look speaker grilles, and bird's-eye maple trim. Unusual details include a bud vase behind the passenger quarter window and a pull-down rear-window blind.

Not everyone likes this car, and in a way, that's the point. Hot rods aren't supposed to be safe and nonconfrontational, even within the hot rod community. Though hot rod building trends are in a continual state of flux, occasionally the largely unspoken rules and mores of the hot rod culture threaten to take precedence over pure creativity. Then a vehicle like *ThunderRoad* stirs the pot and folds the whole thing back on itself.

Paso Robles

To the custom car cognoscenti, one word says it all: "Paso." Located halfway between Los Angeles and San Francisco, the small California wine-country town of Paso Robles hosts what is widely viewed as the best custom car show in the world each Memorial Day weekend.

The Cruisin' Nationals, as the event is officially titled, was conceived by Rich Pichette in 1982. Pichette had recently founded the West Coast Kustoms car club as an outlet for fans of 1950s customs in Southern California. Though there were plenty of street rod shows at the time, Pichette decided custom fans deserved a get-together of their own. The news of an upcoming event spread quickly to Northern California car guys, who said they wanted to be included, too. So, Pichette and West Coast Kustoms looked for a spot between Los Angeles and San Francisco to host the inaugural event. The town of Paso Robles was amenable, and the first Cruisin' Nationals was held on Sept. 18–19, 1982, at Lake Nacimiento, just outside Paso Robles. A total of 82 cars showed up for the initial gathering, including just one hot rod.

Over the years, the annual Cruisin' Nationals has become a mecca of sorts for more than just California custom fans. Hot rod and custom car lovers from all parts of the country and abroad make it a point to travel to California for this annual celebration of the artistic side of the car culture. For the 2005 event, two Japanese custom enthusiasts shipped their cars all the way across the Pacific to take part in the fun. Registration is limited to 850 cars, but more than 1000 show up consistently, and many more attend without a car to show.

The highlights of the three-day event are the Friday-night cruise and the Saturday car show, which is centered on the lawn at City Park but spills out onto the surrounding streets. The event offers plenty of other activities as well: a Friday-night dance, a model car show, a Hall of Fame induction ceremony, a Saturday-night concert, the Sunday awards ceremony, and a bustling vendor market rife with airbrush artists, pinstripers, T-shirt and magazine sellers, and plenty of rockabilly kitsch. All of these elements mix with the cars themselves to make Paso Robles a full-blown experience. The car show takes over the town. For the rod and custom fan, it borders on sensory overload.

The Friday-night cruise features rods and customs of every stripe cruising up and down Spring Street to the delight of the crowds that pack the sidewalks. Custom car legends cruise with little-known newcomers. Historic customs mix with ground-scraping lowriders, vintage hot rods follow modern street machines, and billet beauties share the spotlight with grungy rat rods. Everyone is welcome.

A walk through the park on Saturday afternoon reveals a who's who of custom heroes. At any point, you might see a magazine cover car, stumble across a legendary builder, or venture into the stable of a dedicated custom car club. All of those experiences are great, but the cars displayed by average Joes are often just as exciting. Unknowns do some great work, too, and Paso Robles is where many rod and custom movers and shakers are discovered.

Look deeper and you'll see the true allure of the Cruisin'

Nationals. Each car is, in its own way, a work of art. Every panel that has been cut, color chosen, part used, and detail added represents a choice by the owner and/or builder. The customs at Paso are among the most creative cars in the world, and each depicts the vision of its creator.

To attend Paso Robles is to reset your parameters for what a custom can be. It is also proof positive that automotive creativity and the rod and custom scene are alive and well. Shown here is just a smattering of the types of cars that can be seen each year at the Crusin' Nationals.

"Rod"riguez

As hot rodding and customizing advanced into the new millennium, the hobby's international following became stronger and more visible, particularly in Japan. Interest in American rods and customs among the Japanese had been growing steadily since the mid 1980s. Japanese enthusiasts began importing vintage American cars and parts, and soon they were building hot rods and customs of their own. By the early 2000s, Japan boasted a distinctive and thriving hot rod and custom scene.

In February 1987, Junichi Shimodaira started a business in Nagoya, Japan, called Paradise Road. In addition to importing American cars and parts, Paradise Road became a full-service hot rod, custom, and lowrider shop capable of a variety of construction tasks. In 2002, Junichi turned a 1930 Ford Model A Tudor sedan into a wild show rod which he named "Rod"riguez.

"Rod"riguez blended hot rod, custom, and lowrider styling cues in a completely original way. The startling, show-rod-inspired nose was made by cutting off the ends of a 1959 Cadillac front bumper and welding them to a hand-fabricated center grille section. The grille opening was filled with expanded metal mesh and hardware-store coat hooks.

The body was radically channeled over the frame, and the leading edge of the cowl was reshaped to complement the outlandish grille shell. Inverted 1958 Chevrolet parking-light bezels were frenched into sculpted pods to serve as taillights. The frame itself was boxed and Z'd four inches up front and

six inches in the rear. Traditional hot rod suspension components consisted of a TCI dropped-axle kit up front and a Chevy 10-bolt rear end with tube shocks and a TCI spring out back.

A 303-cid Rocket V-8 and Hydra-Matic transmission from a 1949 Oldsmobile was installed. The mill was essentially stock, but got a far-out show rod look via a '60s-style fogged paint job, a custom dual-inlet carburetor scoop, custom-made rippled headers, and plenty of chrome. A radiator from a '68 Mustang was mounted behind the wild nose.

In this form, "Rod"riguez was featured in the February 2003 issue of Cruisin', a Japanese hot rod and custom magazine. Junichi still had more ideas, and tore "Rod"riguez down for a redo. The top was chopped in a unique wedge fashion. The rear of the top was left at stock height, but the A- and B-pillars were cut four and two inches, respectively, to bring the top down at a rakish new angle. The original grille insert was replaced with a new one fabricated from square tubing, complete with a stylized gold "R" in the center.

Junichi also added wildly sculpted fenders, crafted in metal. Spiderweb-shaped supports were fashioned from chromed rebar rod to hold the forward sections in place. Cragar Star Wire wheels with bullet center caps were mounted on '60s-style whitewall tires. For the second go-around, the body was finished in Tequila Gold metallic paint, with impressive pinstriping by multitalented Japanese artist Makoto Kobayashi of M&K Custom Signs.

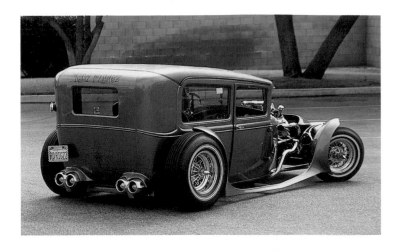

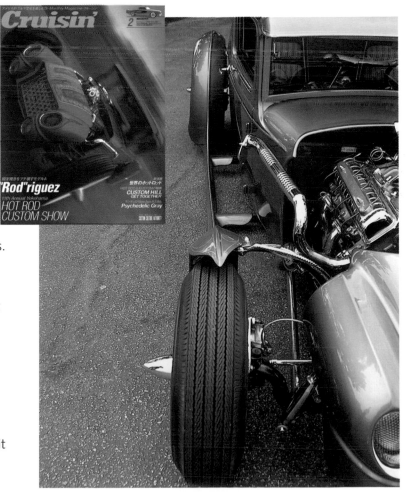

"Rod"riguez's interior matched the genre-bending style of its exterior. The dash and gauge panel were left mostly stock. Custom-made seats with segmented cushions in between outer tube frames were mounted flat on the floor. The gas tank and battery were hidden behind the seats, underneath furry, '60s show rod-style carpet. An early '60s Ford steering wheel was cut down into an aircraft style yoke, yet another '60s show rod-inspired trick.

Junichi shipped his prize to the U.S., where he entered it in the 2005 Grand National Roadster Show in Pomona, California. He and his car were also on hand for the 2005 West Coast Customs Cruisin' Nationals in Paso Robles.

Junichi is prominent among a new wave of Japanese car enthusiasts that brought a fresh perspective and groundbreaking ideas to the world of hot rodding and customizing in the early 2000s. Concurrently, several American hot rodding celebrities made the long trek over to Japan to be honored guests at the Mooneyes Yokohama Hot Rod and Custom Show. This cross-continental cross-pollination of building ideas and cultures provided an exciting shot in the arm for hot rod and custom building trends. Best of all, the blossoming Japanese scene served as evidence that the spirit of hot rodding and customizing transcends cultural, geographic, and linguistic barriers.

The winning cars line up for their awards in 2005. It was the first appearance of custom cars at Pebble Beach.

Customs at Pebble Beach

Pebble Beach, a gated, forested community along the California coastline, is probably the most expensive and exclusive piece of real estate in the western United States. Don't even think about buying a house there unless you're a multimillionaire. They'll let you play on their fabled golf course, but it will cost you $450 a round. If you'd like to stay at the adjoining The Lodge at Pebble Beach hotel, with a view of the bay, that's $685 a night more.

Back in 1950, officials at The Lodge decided it would be high fun to stage a sports car race on the narrow roads winding through the cypress and eucalyptus trees, and to invite some classic cars to gather on Sunday on the 18th green of the golf course for a small Concours D'Elegance. With the emphasis on Elegance.

The road races lasted only six years, but the classic car show developed quickly into the most respected, renowned, and prestigious concours in the world. Especially in the 1950s, the last thing the locals would have wanted there were scruffy, Neanderthal hot rods, or their only slightly more-refined custom car cousins.

As the name denotes, classic cars are vehicles of the highest order—a "class" completely set apart from mundane passenger transportation. If Pebble Beach Concours organizers members gave hot rod and custom owners a thought at all, they considered them butchers and miscreants. Of course, hot rodders and customizers couldn't have cared less. They didn't build their cars to pose and be judged on any golf course. They built them to out-drag the hot wheels at the local burger drive-in. Or, if they weren't built for speed, they were sleek, smooth, and lowered to look like higher-class vehicles. They were built to impress their peers at the same burger stand—especially those of the female persuasion.

But things can certainly change with time. Nearly 50 years later, hot rods—stripped-down, fenderless, loud, early V-8 Fords—were parked on the Pebble Beach lawn right along with the Duesenbergs, Delages, Pierce-Arrows, and Ferraris. The seemingly impenetrable barrier was broken in 1997, and they were so well-received by the softening-upper-lip classic crowd that they were invited back again in '99, 2001, and '03. They were a smashing success.

Custom cars took quite a bit longer to achieve acceptance—until 2005, in fact. Customs are much harder for the public to understand, which has always been a part of their *raison d'être*. Customs are often built to trick the onlooker; to make him ask "what is that?"; to be a bit sinister. On the weekend of August 18–21, 2005, those sinister cars appeared and competed at Pebble Beach in a class called Early Custom Cars 1935–1948 (Class T).

Perhaps inadvertently, the mysterious nature of early customs posed a couple of minor problems for the pioneering group shown at Pebble Beach. These early customs—though they were chopped, channeled, and sectioned, richly lacquered and upholstered, and fitted with parts like grilles, lights, and wheel covers from more expensive cars—were not originally built to win car shows. Though custom car shows proliferated in the '50s, there weren't any before 1950. Those early customs were built to be classy, yes, but they were modified to be more subtle and deceptive than showy.

Second, customs were much more difficult (and expensive)

1939 Ford convertible sedan built by Harry Westergard. Displayed by the National Automotive Museum of Reno, Nevada.

1940 Mercury sedan built by Harry Westergard and Dick Bertolucci for Buddy Ohanesian. Entered by Ed Hegarty.

1940 Ford coupe built by owner Bob Creasman and the Brand Brothers Body Shop. Entered by Mark Drews.

Second-place 1940 Mercury built by Valley Custom for Ralph Jilek. Entered by Tom Gloy.

to build than hot rods, so relatively few were built. And even fewer of those originals exist now, especially in restored, show-quality condition. Not surprisingly, a couple cars the organizers hoped would make it to Pebble Beach didn't.

Of the eight custom cars that did make it, three were for show only, not for competition. The competitors included three Harry Westergard cars (perhaps the only remaining examples of this legend's work), one from Barris Kustoms, and one from Valley Custom. All but two were 1939–40 Fords or Mercs, and the majority were black. Only two were expressly restored for, and debuted at, Pebble Beach. These two, the Jack Calori '36 Ford coupe (pp. 30–31) owned by Jorge Zaragoza and the 1940 Ford Valley Custom convertible owned by Tom Gloy, as you might expect, placed first and second. The Calori coupe, which was painstakingly restored by Roy Brizio Street Rods, also won the Dean Batchelor Award, which was given by Ford Motor Co. for the most historically significant custom.

While the early customs might have taken a bit of a back seat to the 220 (reputedly $300-million-worth) classic Alfa Romeos, Bentleys, Bugattis, and so on, they were an impressive, historic lineup in their own right.

With a foot in the door at Pebble Beach, the future looks bright for more customs to grace the lawn of the country's most prestigious car show. And there are a slew of historic 1949–51 custom Mercs just waiting for their day on the lawn by the ocean.

–Pat Ganahl

Third-place 1940 Mercury convertible built by Bill Hines for Jerry Yatch. Entered by Beth Myers.

First-place 1936 Ford three-window coupe built by owner Jack Calori and Herb Reneau. Entered by Jorge Zaragoza.

HOT ROD & CUSTOM GLOSSARY

aftermarket: Source of parts made by companies other than the original manufacturer. In the hot rod and custom world, the term is used to refer to the many companies that manufacture parts specifically for hot rods and custom cars.

baby moons: Small, smooth, dished chrome hubcaps that cover only the center bolt circle area of a wheel.

banjo steering wheel: A 1935–39 Ford accessory steering wheel, named for its banjo-stringlike spokes.

bellytanker: A dry-lakes/salt-flats competition-only car made from a surplus WWII aircraft belly tank. Belly tanks were used for their aerodynamic shape, and fitted to custom-fabricated, midengined chassis.

big block: The larger of a manufacturer's V-8 engines with a block that is physically more massive (as opposed to just having more displacement) than the manufacturer's smaller V-8. Big blocks usually have a displacement of more than 370 cubic inches.

bigs 'n' littles: The typical hot rod or dragster front and rear tire combination; big tires in back (for increased traction in drag racing and higher effective gearing in dry-lakes racing), little tires up front (for reduced rolling resistance and lighter weight).

billet: Solid blocks of aluminum that are machined to create custom parts for hot rods. The term "billet" also refers to the parts themselves. Billet can be used as a noun, as in, "there is too much billet on that car," or as an adjective, as in, "I just got a new billet steering wheel."

bobbed: Shortened or abbreviated, usually refers to fenders or frame rails.

bomb: A pre-1955 model-year lowrider. Bombs are built to appear stock, but they are lowered and often use numerous add-on factory and vintage aftermarket accessories.

bore: As a noun: The diameter of an engine's cylinder opening, usually measured in inches. As a verb: To increase the diameter of an engine's cylinders.

Buick wires: (also Skylark wires) A style of wire wheel that was factory equipment on 1953–54 Skylarks. They were also offered as Buick factory accessories in the 1950s. Extremely popular with customizers.

bullets: Chromed grille, hubcap, or other trim pieces with a pointed cylindrical shape that looks like a bullet. Also 1959 Cadillac taillights, so-named because of their shape.

C'ing: Removing a C-shaped section from the frame of a car over the front or rear axle to gain additional clearance for axle travel with a lowered suspension. A frame with this modification is called a "C'd" frame.

candy: A type of paint finish achieved by spraying a transparent color coat over a metallic or pearl base coat. The top coat allows the base coat to show through for a rich, deep effect.

Carson top: A padded, nonfolding style of custom convertible top named for the top/upholstery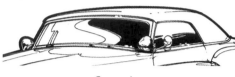

Carson top

shop where it originated. Carson tops are smoothly contoured and can usually be lifted off the vehicle.

channel: To lower the body of a car over its frame, usually by removing the floorpan and welding it to the body at a higher location so body drops down over the frame rails.

chop: To lower the roof of a car by cutting a vertical section out of the top and welding it back together. Can be used as a noun, as in, "Nice chop on that Deuce five window," or as a verb, as in, "Are you going to chop your Deuce?" Top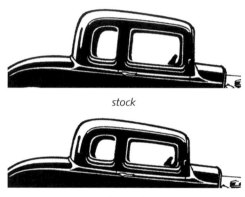

stock

chopped

chopping on hot rods started because rodders were looking for ways to make their cars more aerodynamic, but now the appeal is aesthetic as well. On customs, the appeal is completely aesthetic, as customizers strive to reproportion the sometimes tall, chunky stock automobiles.

chrome-reversed wheels: Stamped steel wheels that have had their center hub sections removed, reversed, and rewelded to the rims to gain a deeper offset. The reworked wheels are then chrome-plated.

cid: An abbreviation for cubic inch displacement, a measurement of the size of an engine.

cutouts: An exhaust system that allows for exhaust gases to run through the mufflers, or straight out the headers or unmuffled pipes. "Uncorking" the headers (opening up the exhaust block-off plates) allows the exhaust gases to flow out of the headers.

deck: To modify a trunklid by removing any stock trim and handles. The resulting holes are filled in.

Deuce: Any Ford made in 1932.

DuVall windshield:
A V-shaped after-market windshield popular on hot rods and named for its creator, George DuVall.

DuVall windshield

fadeaways: On 1939–48 model-year cars, denotes front fenders that flow all the way into the rears. On 1949–51 Mercurys, describes bodysides with the characteristic hump removed from the front doors, creating a clean, unbroken line from the front of the car to the back.

Fad T: Another term for a T-bucket. T-buckets are sometimes called Fad Ts because their sudden explosion in popularity and relative ease of construction made them ubiquitous in the 1960s and '70s, and they spread like a fad.

fat fender: A term coined in the 1980s to refer to a car manufactured between 1935 and 1948, because of the relatively bulbous shape of their fenders. The National Street Rod Association uses the 1948 model year as its cutoff date, so post-'48 automobiles are generally not considered street rods.

Fiestas: A three-bar hubcap so-named because it came as original factory equipment on 1953 Oldsmobile Fiesta convertibles. These hubcaps were also found on most '54 and '55 Oldsmobiles. Also refers to any aftermarket hubcap that mimics the Fiesta's style.

five window: A Ford coupe body style made from 1932 to 1936 that has five windows, not counting the windshield. There are other model years of Ford coupes that have five windows, but they are not referred to as such since there were no three windows produced during those years, making the additional description unnecessary.

flathead: A valve-in-block engine, usually refers to Ford V-8s made from 1932 to 1953.

flippers: A style of hubcap that features one or more bars that reflect light when the vehicle is in motion. Also known as spinners.

french: To modify by molding a separate body component, such as a headlight trim ring, antenna, or license plate, into the surrounding body panel, often recessing it in the process. The goal of frenching is to achieve a smooth, seamless appearance. The name comes from the similarity in appearance to French cuffs.

gennie: Rodder's slang for "genuine," usually used to refer to original, factory-produced parts.

gow job: An early term for a car modified for greater speed. Gow job predated the term "hot rod."

hemi: Short for hemispherical. An engine with hemispherical combustion chamber cylinder heads, in which the spark plugs are situated between the intake and exhaust valves. Hemi engines are easily identifiable because the spark plugs are located in the center of the valve covers.

highboy: A pre-1935 hot rod whose fenders have been removed and whose body sits atop its frame rails (unchanneled).

kemp: A old beatnik or jazz term used to refer to any automobile. The Kustom Kemps of America popularized the term as a synonym for custom car.

lakes pipes: On a custom car, lakes pipes are small-diameter exhaust pipes that run along the lower sides of the body and are capped at their ends. Lakes pipes are usually just aesthetic and nonfunctional. On a hot rod, lakes pipes are headers with caps (see cutouts) that can be removed for racing.

Lakester: A class designation of dry lakes/salt-flats race cars with streamlined custom-made bodywork and exposed wheels.

Lancers: A four-bar hubcap so-named because it came as original factory equipment on 1957 Dodge Lancers. Also refers to any aftermarket hubcap that mimics the Lancer's style.

leadsled: Originally a derogatory term used by hot rodders to describe any custom. The term was especially reserved for any overly modified, poorly customized car that was heavy and slow due to the customizer's overuse of lead body filler. The negatve connotations have fallen away and now the term is proudly used to describe any heavily modified late-'40s to mid-'50s custom, built in the '50s style.

louvers: Small, evenly spaced vents punched into the body panels of a car with a special metal press. Louvers were originally a strictly functional modification for improved engine cooling and

louvers

ventilation, but soon were added for aesthetic appeal as well. A body panel with louvers is said to be "louvered."

lowboy: A pre-1935 hot rod whose fenders have been removed and whose body has been channeled over the frame rails.

lowrider: A specific style of custom car developed by the Hispanic/Chicano culture. Lowriders are usually distinguished by wire wheels, hydraulically adjustable suspensions, and custom paint that often includes murals. The term can also refer to the owner or driver of a lowrider car.

mag wheels: Aftermarket racing or race-inspired wheels. Aftermarket wheels are sometimes generically referred to as "mags" because early racing wheels were made from magnesium.

mag wheel

Model A: A Ford made between 1928 and 1931.

Model T: A Ford made between 1909 and 1927.

Modified: Dry-lakes class designation for a car with a single-seat sprint car-type body that was usually cut off behind the driver. Also a type of circle-track race car.

Moons or Moon discs: Smooth, slightly domed spun aluminum wheel covers frequently used on dry-lakes/salt-flats race cars. They are named for their inventor, the late Dean Moon.

nailhead: A Buick V-8 engine from 1953 to 1966, named for its vertically mounted, relatively small valves.

nerf bar: A handmade grille guard or front/rear/side bumperette, typically chromed and usually bent from tubing or cut from flat sheet stock.

nose: To modify a hood by removing any stock trim and ornaments. The resulting holes are filled in.

pancake: To modify an opening panel by molding it in and recutting the opening so the panel is flat. Usually performed on the rounded and/or wraparound hoods and trunks of '40s, '50s, and '60s cars.

panel paint: A custom painting style introduced by Larry Watson that features large panels of contrasting or complementary color that follow and highlight a car's body lines.

peak: To modify a body panel or other part by adding or introducing a raised rib or bead along its surface. Usually applies to hoods, fenders, or Deuce grille shells.

pearl: A type of paint with finely ground reflective particles that have the soft luminescent glow of a real pearl. Pearl particles can be mixed in with the color itself or a clear topcoat.

phantom: A one-off hot rod or custom that is modified to look like a factory-stock body style that one of the major automakers could have produced but never did. A 1950 Ford three-window coupe is one example of a phantom body style.

pinstripes, pinstriping: Thin, hand-painted accent lines applied to a car as decoration. Hot rodders and customizers began adapting the age-old art of pinstriping to their cars after artist Von Dutch created a new, free-form style of striping that went beyond merely accenting existing body lines to making intricate, abstract designs.

pro street: Drag racing-inspired building style in which the car's rear axle is substantially narrowed and the stock rear inner-fender structure is modified to accept wide, treaded rear tires. Pro street cars usually have powerful engines, roll cages, and mufflers.

quick-change: A sprint car-inspired rear end with a unique center section that allows the rear-end gears to be quickly pulled and swapped for a different gear ratio. It is popular with hot rodders for its racy looks.

rat rod: A retro-styled, traditional, low-budget hot rod that eschews high-dollar paint, modern components, or billet aluminum parts in favor of primer, junkyard/swap meet-scrounged vintage parts, and raw or unfinished bodywork. Rat rods are so named for their "ratty," unrefined appearance. The term was likely inspired by the slang term "rat bike," which is used in the custom motorcycle world to describe a bike intentionally built to look grungy and dilapidated as a subversive protest of expensive, overly finished "trailer queen" bikes.

resto rod: A hot rod that features updated suspension and running gear but maintains a totally stock-appearing body, usually with many factory accessories like spare tires, luggage racks, fog lights, and hood ornaments. Resto rodding became popular in the late 1960s and early '70s as the prewar cars traditionally used for hot rods were gaining recognition as antique cars.

roadster: In hot rodding terms, a two-door, prewar, open car with a nonfixed, removable windshield and no roll-up side windows. Roadsters have only one interior bench seat (or front buckets), and some have rumble seats.

roll pan: (also rolled pan) A curved body-color panel that replaces a bumper or finishes off an abrupt, square transition at the front or rear of a hot rod or custom body.

scallops: A custom paint design that utilizes either ribbonlike shapes that accent body panels or tapered, evenly spaced spears trailing rearward from the front of a vehicle.

section: To lower the body of a car by cutting a horizontal section out of the body and welding it back together.

shave: To remove stock body trim, handles, or other protrusions to achieve a clean, uncluttered appearance. The resulting holes are filled in.

skirts: Exterior body panels on a hot rod or custom that fit into the wheel cutouts to cover the tires. They are usually removable to allow access to the tires, and almost always cover the rear tires.

small block: The smaller of a manufacturer's V-8 engines, with a block that is physically less massive (as opposed to having less displacement) than the manufacturer's larger V-8. Small blocks usually have a displacement that is less than 370 cubic inches.

smoothie rod: A hot rod with an exceptionally clean, unadorned appearance, resulting from the removal of stock trim, as well as handles, hinges, body seams, and contours.

sombrero: A style of Cadillac hubcap produced from 1947 to '52, nicknamed for its resemblance to a Mexican sombrero hat. Sombreros are popular with customizers for their smooth, attractive design, and luxury car origin.

sombrero

spotlights: The chrome-plated adjustable accessory lamps that were frequently mounted to the windshield pillars of late '40s to early '60s customs. These were used primarily for aesthetic appeal. Appleton spotlights were the most popular brand.

steelies: Solid, stamped-steel wheels. Usually refers to 1940s-era Ford wheels, or replicas thereof.

Streamliner: A dry-lakes/salt-flats racing class designation for a car with custom made, streamlined bodywork that envelops the wheels.

suicide axle: A front axle that is mounted in front of the frame instead of underneath it. Always seen on T-buckets, occasionally seen on Model As and Deuces.

suicide doors: Vehicle side doors hinged at the rear. The name comes from the potential danger of the doors unlatching and being blown open when the vehicle is in motion.

supercharger: (also, blower, huffer) An engine-driven device used to force intake air into the engine to increase its power. An engine with a supercharger is called a "blown" engine.

street rod: Any hot rod built primarily for street use. With the formation of the National Street Rod Association, the term is usually used to refer to street-driven pre-1949 hot rods.

T-bucket: A fenderless hot rod usually based on a pre-1926 Model T roadster or shortened T touring body with a radically shortened Model A or Model T pickup bed, Model T turtle deck, or exposed gas tank mounted behind the body, and a suicide front axle.

teardrops: 1939 Ford taillights. Very popular on hot rods and named for their teardrop shape.

three window: A Ford coupe body style made from 1932 to 1936 that has three windows, not counting the windshield.

tracknose: A sleek, hand-formed nose, typically with a grille opening and fabricated grille bars, usually seen on dry-lakes and circle-track racers.

tracknose

track roadster: An early fenderless roadster, usually a Ford Model T, that is modified to compete in small oval dirt-track races or at least look like it does. Track-roadster characteristics include tracknoses and nerf bars.

trailer queen: A derisive term for an overly finished hot rod that is not driven, but hauled, to events on a trailer.

tub: A touring or phaeton body style, usually used to describe 1934 and earlier model-year cars.

tuck and roll: (also roll and pleat) Custom upholstery with the interior fabric (usually Naugahyde) stitched in narrow vertical and/or horizontal pleats.

tunneled: Refers to any component that has been deeply recessed into a body panel; most often used to describe head- and taillights.

turnkey: A completely finished hot rod built by a professional shop that requires no additional work. All the owner needs to do is get in and turn the key.

V'd: A vehicle component, such as a windshield or frame-horn spreader bar, that came with or has been modified to have a V shape.

wide whites: Tires with wide white sidewalls.

woodie: Any car with a wood body. Woody wagons were popular among surfers in the 1960s because of the surfboard-carrying utility they offered.

Z'ing: Cutting the frame of a car at an angle over the front or rear axle and rewelding the cut-off portion above the center frame section to lower the ride height. Z'ing the front of a hot rod gives it a raked stance, while Z'ing both ends drops the whole car "down in the weeds."

INDEX